Dragon on Centre Street

New York vs. Donald Trump

Jonah Bromwich

ISBN: 9798893310382
Specs: Hardcover, 6 ⅛″ × 9 ¼″
Price: $30.00 US / $39.99 CAN
Publication Date: 5/27/2025

DRAGON
ON
CENTRE
STREET

DRAGON
ON
CENTRE STREET

NEW YORK VS. DONALD TRUMP

Jonah Bromwich

 AUTHORS EQUITY

Authors Equity
1123 Broadway, Suite 1008
New York, New York 10010

Cover design by Chris Sergio.
Cover art by Shutterstock.
Book design by Scribe Inc.

Most Authors Equity books are available at a discount when purchased
in quantity for sales promotions or corporate use. Special editions, which
include personalized covers, excerpts, and corporate imprints, can be created
when purchased in large quantities. For more information, please email
info@authorsequity.com.

Library of Congress Control Number: {to come}

Print ISBN 9798893310382
Ebook ISBN 9798893310450

Printed in the United States of America
First printing

www.authorsequity.com

CONTENTS

Midway through Donald Trump's first term in office, the rapper Kanye West announced to his Twitter followers that he and the president had something in common.

"The mob can't make me not love him," West said. "We are both dragon energy. He is my brother."

Six years later, the first criminal trial of Trump began, a showdown between the rule of law and dragon energy in the midst of the 2024 presidential election.

This is the story of that trial: how it happened, why it happened and why it matters.

CHAPTER ONE

CODE NAMES

INDICTMENT

Manhattan's criminal justice system operates from a series of hulking buildings clustered along Centre Street, a downtown strip squeezed between Tribeca and Chinatown. Courthouses dot the street, and the U.S. attorney, the police commissioner and the Manhattan D.A. all work nearby, attended by infantries of cops, court officers and other uniformed creatures of the law. Occasionally, tourists will stop to take a picture of the regal Roman facade of 60 Centre Street, famous from its cameos in "Law and Order." But more often, unless some excitement arises—a sudden outburst of chaos, a notorious defendant mugging for news cameras—outsiders are pulled toward the most recognizable nearby landmark, the Brooklyn Bridge, leaving the neighborhood natives, uniformed and not, to their daily routines.

No excitement was apparent on a cold Thursday morning in March 2023 as two New York Times stringers descended on Centre Street for a stakeout. But they believed something extraordinary was taking place within one of the anonymous buildings: Prosecutors working for the district attorney, Alvin L. Bragg, were on the verge of persuading a grand jury to indict an American president. By law, grand jury presentations are secret and, in the normal course of events, reporter-proof. To confirm their suspicions, the stringers, Nate Schweber and Sean Piccoli, would have to spot a pattern meant to be invisible in the neighborhood's post-pandemic bustle.

They keyed in on Hogan Place, the narrow one-way corridor that ran between two of the block-long court buildings on Centre Street. On the north side of Hogan, court officers stood idly under scaffolding that shadowed the entrance to the D.A.'s office, embedded within the borough's main criminal courthouse on 100 Centre Street. Across Hogan was 80 Centre, the building reserved for special grand juries, dedicated to specific, long-term investigations. Special grand jurors show up three days a week, like students in a college seminar, watching prosecutors question witnesses. When prosecutors are satisfied, they explain the charges, then leave the grand jurors to vote on whether to indict. Usually, they do.

Nate and Sean were aware that the grand jury in which they were interested met Mondays, Wednesdays and Thursdays. But the jurors themselves would be difficult to identify, and there were few clues as to when prosecutors would ask them to vote. Nate, lanky and long-haired with a zen demeanor, told us shortly after noon that he'd spotted a "wonderful red-tailed hawk" flying over a park behind the D.A.'s office. "Nothing else of note . . . yet," he said.

The stringers knew that, whatever it was they were going to see, they needed to see it first. In 2018, a *Times* investigative reporter named Willy Rashbaum had broken the story that the district attorney's office was scrutinizing the president's company. In the five years that followed, Rashbaum and his colleagues broke every major story about the office's investigation. By 2023, Willy was working closely with two other *Times* staffers—Ben Protess, a driven investigative reporter in his late 30s and me, a relative newcomer to the courts beat. Earlier that month, we broke the news that Bragg was on the verge of bringing an indictment. We expected the president to be charged with a criminal cover-up: falsifying documents to disguise a hush money payment to a porn star.

Our competitors—reporters from CNN, CBS, NBC—were sniffing around the D.A. headquarters at Hogan Place, too. The *Times* stringers were under heavy pressure to keep our streak going. Each of them had a digital dossier listing dozens of people that Willy, Ben and I associated with the case. The dossier included numerous witnesses whose names were fused in the public imagination with that of the president. There was diminutive, mustachioed David Pecker, the former publisher of The National Enquirer, whose alliance with the president peaked during his first White House run. Hope Hicks, the child model turned 20-something White House spokeswoman who channeled her boss's words to the public. And Michael Cohen, a disbarred lawyer with a seemingly permanent hangdog expression who in 2016 had paid off the porn star Stormy Daniels, just weeks before his idol, the man after whom he'd modeled his entire persona, won the presidential election.

All three witnesses had come and gone. Nate, Sean and a third stringer, Kate Christobek, clocked them when they made their way into 80 Centre to testify before the grand jury. Just the day before, the D.A.'s office had conducted a virtual meeting with Stormy Daniels. So on that Thursday morning, March 16, we suspected there was little left for the prosecutors to do, other than indict.

Kate was our chief advantage. She had been a Manhattan prosecutor until her interest in broadcast news became impossible to ignore and she'd left the halls of justice for the back alley of journalism. She knew the courthouse personnel and the rhythms of Centre Street. She advised us that, when the grand jurors were on the verge of a vote, one of the prosecutors might carry a copy of the penal law, a phonebook-sized tome used to guide the jury through the charges. "Size of a bible," Kate explained. "Typically bright blue."

Thanks to Kate, the stringers had eyes on a key player our competitors didn't seem to be tracking: the grand jury warden overseeing the testimony. When the indictment was filed, he would likely be the one to file it. We didn't know his name, but we had a blurry picture of him, masked and carrying a tote bag from Target. So we dubbed him "Target Bag Guy." T.B.G. for short.

In the early afternoon, Sean spotted him under the scaffolding on the north side of Hogan and sent a series of iPhone pictures to the team. They showed a solidly-built man with close-cropped brown hair walking toward Collect Pond Park, the green space across from the criminal courthouse that functioned as a makeshift halfway home for a handful of struggling people the pandemic had driven onto the streets.

Willy and I were at The *Times* Midtown headquarters when the pictures of T.B.G. showed up in our text group. Willy peered closely at his phone, investigating.

"Who's this guy?" he asked after a few moments.

"Willy! It's T.B.G.!" Ben said, from his house in New Jersey. "You may not recognize him without his mask and Target bag, but that's him for sure."

We had our man, a walking indication that the grand jury was active. T.B.G. was the Where's Waldo of our daily drama. If we could keep an eye on him, we might just be able to confirm when the indictment was filed.

Soon after that, the stringers spotted a trio of high-ranking prosecutors as they emerged from the D.A.'s office and crossed Hogan. There was Susan Hoffinger, the office's new head of investigations, with her short, curly hair and perennially grim expression. Chris Conroy, the thin D.A. veteran who'd been working the case longer than anyone. And calm, unassuming Matthew Colangelo, known in government circles as one of the brightest young lawyers in the country.

Once we saw the prosecutors march into 80 Centre, Ben made sure the whole team was in position. Kate may have been our secret weapon and Willy, a one-man scoop machine, but Ben was our leader—writing, reporting, and organizing six unruly reporters into a single, coherent unit. He assigned Nate to the clerk's office in 100 Centre. Along with the district attorney's executive offices, the art deco courthouse housed the borough's criminal courtrooms, many lesser grand juries and the clerk's office, where all official criminal paperwork was sent. With any luck, Nate would be able to clock the indictment as it was filed.

The other reporters hanging around Hogan Place noticed our stringers were onto something.

"There's definitely a lot of 'What is the *Times* doing?'" Sean said. "I'm being unhelpful but friendly with everyone."

"Unhelpful but friendly also describes the clerks," Nate said, messaging from the 10th floor. The clerk's office was alternately buzzing and slow, he said, "but no sign of The Thing." He asked one of the clerks if a certain high-profile indictment would get special treatment.

"Nothing gets special treatment," she said. "That's how things work best."

The office closed for the day at 5 p.m., as it always did. Friday was quieter; no grand jury that day.

But over the weekend, Donald J. Trump got directly involved. He gave us a small taste of how it would feel when his command of the American gaze intruded on the justice-blind institutions of Centre Street.

❖   ❖   ❖

Trump was holed up in Florida, a plane ride from the center of a universe that had once revolved around him. But he retained his talent for making news on his own terms, sending reporters scrambling no matter the time. At 7:30 am on Saturday, March 18, he made an all-caps announcement on his personal social media platform.

> "THE FAR & AWAY LEADING REPUBLICAN
> CANDIDATE AND FORMER PRESIDENT OF
> THE UNITED STATES OF AMERICA, WILL BE
> ARRESTED ON TUESDAY OF NEXT WEEK.
> PROTEST, TAKE OUR NATION BACK!"

He had no idea what he was talking about. The date appeared, in retrospect, to have been his best guess. It didn't matter. He was impossible to ignore. The call for protest was a none-too-subtle echo of the exhortations that, two years earlier, brought a mob to the U.S. Capitol. The attention returned, on Trump's terms.

His prediction summoned a new energy to Centre Street. An ecosystem of partisan sentiment and free-floating intrigue attached itself to every investigation into the former president and Trump's post alerted the world to the secretive proceedings downtown. No longer did our stringers have the freedom to surveil Hogan Place without distraction. When they returned to the court buildings two days later, on a beautiful, sunny Monday, they found the territory transformed by that chaotic energy, rising like vapor from the downtown sidewalks.

Our private, professional endeavor was now a public spectacle. Newscasters deployed their cameras and anchors in a line outside Collect Pond Park, across the street from the main criminal courthouse. The scaffolding outside the grand jury building at 80 Centre shaded a horde of reporters and photographers piled atop each other, jabbering, fighting and carrying on. They were accompanied by a collection of sign-carrying pro-Trump protesters. Some of the signs lobbed insults at the district attorney: "Alvin Bragg," one said. "Releasing the violent, prosecuting political enemies."

"There's just more of everything," Nate reported. "Officers. Cars. French barriers like it's New Year's Eve in Times Square."

The surge of competition rattled us. Previously the reporters had been spread out. Now they were densely packed and rumormongering. One rumor quickly hardened into conventional wisdom: If Trump was to be arrested Tuesday, he would have to be indicted Monday.

"This is so gossipy now," Kate said. "Like a bad game of telephone."

Word was that a former federal prosecutor named Robert Costello—a sworn enemy of Michael Cohen—was already in the building, seeking to convince the grand jury not to indict Trump on Cohen's word. Trump's lawyers requested that the grand jurors hear Costello out; apparently, the jurors had agreed. We learned later that Costello sought to persuade the jurors that prosecutors were hiding information from them and insisted that Cohen wouldn't tell the truth, even with a gun to his head.

Sean entered 80 Centre to try to spot Costello, following the lead of the other reporters gathered there, while Kate posted up at the back of the building, doing the same. Neither was watching for T.B.G.

Out in New Jersey, Ben got annoyed. The indictment could be coming at any moment. We couldn't let a witness distract us.

"The focus is on T.B.G.," he said. "Please plan as if indictment is happening today. T.B.G. is priority."

Kate bristled. "I think it would be helpful for Sean and me to get some instruction on how to play the next few hours."

"Just watch for T.B.G.," Ben said.

At 4:55 p.m., Kate spotted our Waldo, keys jangling on his belt, a manila folder under his arm. He was trailed by the prosecutor trio, Hoffinger, Conroy and Colangelo. Willy asked Kate to follow them. But they entered the D.A.'s office on 1 Hogan Place through a private door.

Nate reported from the 10th floor of 100 Centre that the clerk's office was officially closed for the day. No indictment. But we thought the prosecutors might appear after hours, taking advantage of the privacy to file. We asked him to stay and keep watch.

There was no sign of them. The office remained dark. Shortly after 5 p.m., two court officers swept in, confirmed the room was empty and politely ushered Nate out. One assured Nate that nothing was ever filed after business hours. We believed him. It was typical of 100 Centre to hew to routine and for many, that meant a prompt end to the work day.

Trump hadn't been indicted that day. He wasn't going to be arrested the next day. We began to wonder if the district attorney was getting cold feet.

"Should I have tackled T.B.G. to see what these papers are?" Kate asked.

"Wait, you didn't?" Willy asked. He promised to get her a tackling dummy so she could practice.

❖　❖　❖

By the time we were on indictment watch in March 2023, Alvin L. Bragg, the first Black Manhattan district attorney, had been responsible for prosecuting crime in the borough for 15 months. A big, friendly man who affected an impassive look in public, Bragg had an easy smile in private. Most people who met him, liked him. But he struggled with the press.

Bragg seemed uncomfortable whenever there was a microphone or a camera pointed his way. Allergic to sound bites, he spoke instead in a measured lawyer-ese, frequently interrupting himself as if trying to edit sentences he was already in the midst of speaking. Early in his tenure, the New York Post installed photographers outside 1 Hogan Place, the D.A.'s side entrance to 100 Centre Street. Their readership was rewarded with frequent pictures of Bragg slouching into work, weighed down by a messenger bag like some second-year associate.

The images distracted from Bragg's polished resumé. He attended Harvard and Harvard Law School. He clerked at the Southern District for Judge Robert P. Patterson Jr., the son of President Truman's War Secretary. Later, Bragg became an assistant U.S. attorney in the Southern District. A trove of talented trial lawyers, Southern has long been the most prestigious prosecutor's office in the country, led by a succession of famous men including Robert Morgenthau, Rudy Giuliani and

James Comey.

But Bragg didn't stay at Southern, or climb to the next rung of achievement. Instead, he decamped to work at the New York Attorney General's office, where he led a unit that investigated the police killings of unarmed people, many of whom were Black. Most prosecutors considered Southern an elite posting; the state attorney general's office, a downgrade. For Bragg, it was a broadening of horizons. It was also an early sign that he didn't make a religion of the hierarchies that had surrounded him for much of his professional life. His reluctance to think top-down was clear when he ran for D.A. in 2021. He routinely kept Important People waiting because he was absorbed in conversation with a stranger he hadn't known an hour earlier.

The D.A. campaign was one of my first assignments as a Manhattan courts reporter for *The Times's* Metro desk. Previously, I'd been on the Styles desk, where I often wrote trend stories about the way social media was changing our daily lives. The only Trump-related news I covered for Styles was a November 2020 press conference during which Rudy Giuliani insisted his boss had won the presidential election until his sweat began to drip in color and black streaks streamed down his cheeks.

I found Bragg's vision during the 2021 D.A. campaign straightforward and easy to understand: Treat powerless people who committed petty crimes mercifully, and hold powerful people who committed serious crimes accountable. He won a hard-fought Democratic primary in June 2021 and after dominating the general election in November, was sworn in at midnight on New Year's Day.

Bragg's early tenure was a disaster. His nemeses at the New York Post proclaimed that his policies were a plot to aid criminals and destroy New York City. The traditional news media, when it considered Bragg at all, did so because of the Trump investigation. Bragg's other intentions for the office were often engulfed by the attention vortex that shared the former president's name. When, two months after he was sworn in, it became public knowledge that Bragg had halted a potential indictment of Trump, pundits and talk show hosts turned on him. He became a laughingstock and soon enough, an afterthought.

But if Bragg suffered under the bright lights, he benefitted when attention was elsewhere. And he was insistent on taking the time he needed. Though his Trump investigation was thought dead, Bragg and his team kept working. The press was in the dark until November 2022, when Willy, Ben and I broke the news of a rejuvenated criminal inquiry into Trump.

❖   ❖   ❖

Thus, for all our Monday evening disappointment over the lack of news, we knew it was unlikely that the delay was meaningful. The following day, the chances of a filing were slim to none—Trump's prediction notwithstanding—because the grand jury didn't meet on Tuesdays. But when Wednesday passed without incident, our colleagues in the press grew visibly antsy, primed to leap on any tidbit of information, no matter how small or questionable.

On Thursday morning, Business Insider published a story saying the grand jurors wouldn't be hearing the Trump case that day. The byline belonged to Laura Italiano, a hard-working reporter who made her bones at a trio of New York tabloids. Though we couldn't know Laura's source, we suspected her information had come from the court officers, the system's own police force. There was a natural divide between court officers and reporters: differences in class, temperament, and daily quotient of time-spent-on-feet. The two groups tended toward trivial feuds, as officers asserted their authority and reporters, their skepticism of authority. But for veteran journalists like Laura, the officers could serve as sources.

At the *Times*, the higher-ups urged us to match Business Insider's reporting and write our own story saying the grand jury wasn't expected to hear the Trump case that day.

We were irritated. Though we had sources who agreed with Laura's reporting, we didn't think it was news. And frankly, we weren't all that good at taking orders on a subject we felt we knew better than anyone. But Nestor Ramos, our editor, was usually able to find a synthesis between what top editors were asking for and what we wanted to do. He persuaded us.

About 15 minutes after we published a story asserting that an indictment was unlikely that day, Kate spied a problem. Or rather, three problems.

"Conroy, Hoffinger, Colangelo, all walking over with a purpose from 1 Hogan Place to 80," she reported. "Definitely them. Very grand jury energy."

"Huh," Ben said.

There was no world in which the three prosecutors seeking an indictment of the former president were working a little gang case on the side. We'd been wrong to think we could trust anyone purporting secondhand knowledge of the grand jury's docket. We shouldn't have published anything.

It was only a minor relief when Thursday ended with no indictment filed. We vowed not to make the same mistake again.

Though the grand jury wasn't in session, Friday didn't offer much respite from the circus. Trump, in a post on Truth Social, hinted at "death & destruction" if he were charged. Someone sent an envelope filled with white powder to the D.A.'s office, attached to a note that said "ALVIN: I AM GOING TO KILL YOU" with 13 exclamation points.

"Filming in Progress" signs had appeared behind the D.A.'s office, identified by the project name "Juliet." Nate learned from a friend at a nearby bookstore that it was the "Joker" sequel, starring Joaquin Phoenix and Lady Gaga. Kate heard a rumor that 700 extras were being summoned to appear that weekend for a "Joker" action sequence. We expected that the movie shoot would only increase the feeling of mass psychosis that surrounded 100 Centre.

"If Lady Gaga is here and we're joined by paparazzi," Kate said. "We may all lose our minds."

On Monday, March 27, we repeated the routine, rising early to report on the biggest news of our lives, only to slowly deflate as the hours crept by. By 5 p.m., the clerk's office was closed. No indictment. On Tuesday, reporters started spreading a new rumor—that the grand jury wouldn't be meeting for a week, or maybe two, or maybe the entire month. By Wednesday, Politico, the Washington Post and CNN had all published some version of that story, suggesting that the Trump indictment could be delayed indefinitely. But Kate and Sean once again suspected the court officers were behind the rumor. So our watch continued.

Thursday morning was frigid. The sidewalks outside 100 Centre Street were emptier than they'd been in weeks. A lot of our competitors were at the federal courthouse a block south on Pearl Street, mobbing the crypto mogul Sam Bankman-Fried, who was charged with stealing billions.

Shortly after 10:30, Kate and Sean listened in on two court officers having a private conversation. One told the other there was a rumor going around. Today would be the day. "They said it to each other, not us," Kate said. "We just overheard. They may have been fucking with us."

Over at the clerk's office, Nate was joined by Frank Runyeon of *Law360*. Frank said he thought the month-hiatus thing was a "bunch of hooey." Frank was one of the leaders of the courthouse press corps, an agent of order in a sea of chaos. He often spoke as if he'd just taken a time machine in from the 1950s.

The grand jury began hearing cases around 2 p.m. We filled the time until then with paranoia: about how the prosecutors might try to hide the handoff or use a back staircase, making it impossible for us to see anything. Or maybe they wouldn't need to disguise it. Maybe Thursday was yet another dud and we'd be back to the routine on Monday. Maybe we'd be doing it forever.

Shortly after 1 pm, Kate spotted a bulky figure with close-cropped hair and a solid build.

"T.B.G.!" she said.

"What's that man up to?" I asked.

"Wearing purple shirt today," she said.

"What's the importance of the shirt?" I asked. Drunk on secret symbols, I figured purple was the official color of an indictment vote.

"So everyone can spot him?" Kate said.

But there was still no sign of the prosecutors, just a half hour before the grand jury was meant to be in session. I sunk low in my chair in the small conference room where Willy and I had spent weeks diagnosing ourselves with various nerve-related diseases. Willy, never short on aphoristic wisdom, gave me a pep talk about emotional resilience. I informed him my generation had determined that stoicism was a dangerous form of repression. Moping was far healthier.

At 1:45, we got another text from Kate: "Susan escorted with security to 80 Centre."

Susan Hoffinger. Never before had she been accompanied by an escort: two security officers, one blonde, one bald. (We quickly nick-named them Blondie and Baldy.) She was soon followed by the other prosecutors, Chris Conroy and Matthew Colangelo. The veteran, Con-roy, was holding a phonebook sized tome in his arm, bright blue and bookmarked with Post Its. Willy and I jolted up in our seats. This was it. We alerted Nestor, who advised us to move to a bigger conference room. The top editors at the paper would want to be there if we con-firmed our suspicions.

I wouldn't dare to even estimate how many outgoing calls we made from that conference-room-turned-war-room. Willy was on the phone continuously, mining a constant stream of rumor and innuendo. *Have you heard . . . ? What about . . . ?* Ben beamed in from New Jersey, but spent half the time on mute, speaking to his sources. I made calls too, and eventually began to leave the room to do so, given the presence of all those top editors.

Back on 100 Centre Street, the media presence, which had been so scarce earlier in the day, was growing. As our anticipation built, so did our fears of getting beaten. Kate overheard a Fox News reporter saying the words "this could be a false alarm, but . . ." She didn't hear the rest.

The afternoon crawled along. Our paranoia grew. There was no glimpse of the prosecutors, no further signal from 80 Centre that sug-gested today was the day. Hoffinger with the security escort, Conroy with the penal law—they'd seemed like such obvious signs. But maybe we'd misread them. At 4:15, with only 45 minutes to go before the clerk's office closed, Nate gave us a depressing update from the scene: "For now it is very chill. Notably low-energy."

Ben, Willy and I tried our sources, but no one knew anything. At The *Times* building, Nestor, our editor, started raising other contingen-cies. He asked what we should do if there was no indictment, whether it was worth pursuing another story. He was right to bring it up. But I couldn't engage with that line of thinking yet. There were 40 minutes to go.

"This is so painful waiting," Kate texted.

"Yeah, this is very tough today," I said.

"I'm going to look very dumb if this is not the vote," she said. Kate always blamed herself.

"No, you won't," I said.

It was 4:40—20 minutes to go. Nate said some of the clerks were preparing to leave for the day.

Then, Kate saw them. Colangelo and Hoffinger had emerged from 80 Centre and were crossing Hogan. Hoffinger still had Blondie and Baldy in tow. They entered via the D.A.'s office. Kate hurried into 100 Centre to see if she could spot them inside the building as they headed toward the clerk's office. But there was no sign of them.

Two clerks left the office. They were replaced by journalists from The New York Post and CNN. We could tell Nate was tense because he was texting in sentence fragments. "Watching door and back of office," he reported.

Only five minutes left.

Ben asked a reasonable question. "Is it possible they started deliberating and didn't finish?"

"Ugh, I really hope not," Kate said.

We knew so little about how the grand jury procedure might work in a case like this, a case unlike any other. The jurors might deliberate quickly, or for hours. It was all a matter of circumstance, unknowable from outside the room.

Our phones buzzed. A text from Sean. "Tbg," he wrote. "Conroy."

He sent pictures of the grand jury warden crossing the street in his purple dress shirt accompanied by the prosecutor. They too used the D.A.'s entrance into 100 Centre Street. They had ten floors to go in four minutes. It was Nate's turn.

"Watching, watching," he said. At 4:57, another clerk left, headed to hot yoga. She told Nate on her way out that nothing had been filed.

Two minutes to go. Three dots from Nate. Then a text: "They're all here."

Then another: "ALL HERE. NOT DRILL."

"Thanks Nate," I said, trying to keep calm.

"INTO INDICTMENT ROOM," he responded.

I asked if any of the other reporters had seen them. Everyone had, Nate said. But, he added, it didn't seem as if the competition realized who they were. "Only that something weird happened."

We knew what had happened. This was what we had been preparing for. This is what we had learned, during those endless March days, that it was going to look like. And we had little doubt. In our midtown war room, we made some final calls as we queued up the story. Breathing quickly, I repeatedly scanned the competition to check whether anyone else had published. Nestor pulled up our draft. Our first sentence, a lede written weeks earlier, began, "A Manhattan grand jury indicted Donald J. Trump on TKday." We replaced the TK.

And then, we broke the news. An American president was charged with crimes for the first time in the country's history.

Ben and Willy didn't use Twitter. I was beginning to avoid doing so, too. But this was one to memorialize, one of the biggest news stories with which I'd ever be involved. And though I felt sheepish about it, I craved recognition for our scoop. I took some all-caps inspiration from Nate as I retyped the headline, and posted it: "MANHATTAN GRAND JURY VOTES TO INDICT TRUMP."

Our print headline, in classic *Times* fashion, paid tribute to the gravity of the moment through understatement: ***TRUMP INDICTED***.

As usual, The New York Post went for something more colorful. Their headline was splashed in caps below a picture of Trump and the porn star at the Nevada golf course from the day that they'd purportedly had sex: ***THE GATHERING STORMY***.

⚜   ⚜   ⚜

Half an hour after we published, helicopters whipsawed the sky above Centre Street. Outside the district attorney's office at 1 Hogan Place, photographers gathered in tight formation to capture an image of the first prosecutor to secure charges against Trump. Anti-Trump protesters materialized, holding small signs that said, "Trump is over," then, working in lockstep, unfurled a large black and white banner: "THE TIME IS NOW."

Some of Trump's notable adversaries celebrated the indictment in the media-generated version of Manhattan that was their natural habitat, the facsimile of the city that overlays and occasionally intersects with the real thing. "I have so many messages coming in that I can't respond," Stormy Daniels tweeted. "Also don't want to spill my champagne." Michael Cohen, the disloyal fixer who turned on Trump in 2018, spontaneously released an episode of his podcast "Mea Culpa," where, in a schadenfreude-deranged voice he said the prospect of Trump being booked, fingerprinted and mug-shotted "fills me with delight!"

Cohen was not alone. Far more dignified enemies of Donald J. Trump considered him a disease on the body politic, and for years, their ideal cure was clear: a strong dose of the law. Though Trump had been sued many times, he had never before faced prosecution and had never been charged with a crime.

Reasoning that the rule of law was a force with which even he would have trouble contending, many of the president's critics awaited a champion who could vanquish him from the political scene entirely. A prosecutor—heroically nonpartisan, preferably Republican—fit the bill. There had already been a cycle of would-be dragonslayers to whom Trump's haters pinned their hopes: Robert Mueller, Jack Smith, Cyrus R. Vance Jr. and Liz Cheney. Now, to the great surprise of many, it was Alvin Bragg's turn.

Bragg emerged from his office on 1 Hogan shortly after 7 p.m. The cameras flashed eagerly—and in vain as the district attorney stumbled into a black S.U.V., surrounded by a human shield of hard-faced security personnel. The vehicle disappeared into the evening, leaving behind questions that would remain unanswered for days.

A year earlier, Bragg's refusal to go forward with a Trump case was slammed as "shameful" and "cowardly." Now he had reversed what his liberal critics believed was an unforgiveable failure of justice. He stayed the course, found a case he believed in and indicted Trump. But much of the commentariat was unmoved. They wanted Trump removed from the political map. It was unclear whether Bragg's case would suffice.

"When you strike at a king, you must kill him, the saying goes," Ruth Marcus wrote in the Washington Post. "Bragg is dealing with a wounded, but still dangerous, king. I hope he knows what he's doing."

No one outside of the D.A.'s office knew what Bragg was doing. Inundated with requests to confirm the news reports, his team was granted special permission by a judge to acknowledge the indictment. But the charges wouldn't be revealed until the arraignment on Tuesday. The district attorney was not in the habit of offering surplus information, not when silence was such an attractive alternative. Trump would travel to New York to hear the accusations and, presumably, to plead not guilty. The protesters' banner was premature: The time was not now, but four days from now: April 4, 2023, at 2:15 pm on the 15th floor of 100 Centre Street.

ARRAIGNMENT

On Monday, April 3, at 2:00 p.m., the line to get into the courtroom at 100 Centre began to form outside the north border of Collect Pond Park, across the street from the courthouse. Television reporters sipped coffee and applied makeup for the occasional on-camera appearance—batting practice for the next day's big show. A small group of MAGA-heads conferenced beneath a giant flag that said FUCK BIDEN. A man held up an oil painting of a ghoulish Trump in prisoners' stripes, flanked by police officers. Another, wearing an N95 mask, held a violent, unintelligible sign: "GOD, STRIKE TRUMP DEAD. JUDGE, FREE HIM." A block south, on the corner of Centre and Worth, a man in a newsboy hat stood outside the wedding bureau with his own sign in red block letters: "WORK TOGETHER with RESPECT and UNDERSTANDING."

Reporters, irritated by the prospect of an overnight campout, began to snipe at each other. Victoria Biekempis, a mainstay of the Centre Street press room, accused a newcomer, Max Rivlin-Nadler of Hell Gate, of having started an "unsanctioned arms race" by lining up so early. Others sought to create order: Frank Runyeon, the Law360 reporter with the penchant for old-timey slang, made a list to preserve peoples' places, ostensibly freeing them to leave the line and grab hot dogs from the Sabrett truck outside of 100 Centre. Professional line sitters, from a company called Same Ole Line Dudes, showed up wearing merch advertising the name of their company and toting colorful tents. Usually, they held places for concertgoers and television audiences, but this didn't feel all that different: The first clash between Trump and the criminal court system was shaping up to be the entertainment event of the season. "Hotter ticket than Springsteen," Nate remarked. By 3 pm, there were 25 people on Frank's list.

Nate and the rest of *The Times's* team quickly arranged a schedule of shifts to hold our place in line. As the beat reporter assigned to the D.A.'s office, I would cover the arraignment in person, where we'd finally learn the charges Trump was facing.

For months, we'd expected him to be charged with falsifying business records to conceal Michael Cohen's $130,000 hush money payment to Stormy Daniels. It was a well-established public fact that Cohen was reimbursed throughout 2017, and that every time a check was sent, Trump's company indicated that the remittance was for legal services. Given that the hush money payment was not a legal service, we were certain the prosecutors considered every document related to the reimbursement a false business record. Falsifying business records is a common crime in New York's white collar prosecutions. We referred to it as FBR for short.

But there was a wrinkle. We expected felony charges—grand juries don't get involved in misdemeanors. But falsifying business records was a misdemeanor unless the records were faked to conceal a second crime, known as a predicate. Falsifying business records in the first degree, or FBR1, section 175.10 of the penal code, necessarily came packaged with a predicate. Bragg's prosecutors must have believed that the Cohen reimbursements covered up a second crime. But what was it?

PEN 175.05—Falsifying Business Records in the second degree, a misdemeanor: "A person is guilty of falsifying business records in the second degree when, with intent to defraud, he makes or causes a false entry in the business records of an enterprise.

PEN 175.10—Falsifying Business Records in the first degree, a felony: A person is guilty of falsifying business records in the first degree when he commits the crime of falsifying business records in the second degree, *and when his intent to defraud includes an intent to commit another crime or to aid or conceal the commission thereof.*

As I was bent over my desk in Midtown, thinking through the predicate possibilities for the umpteenth time, a novice courtroom sketch artist named Isabelle Brourman was sitting in Central Park with a book by Hunter S. Thompson, her muse and spiritual forebear. She heard helicopters buzzing and made her way to Trump Tower, where she asked a journalist with a news van how she could get into the arraignment downtown. He told her anyone getting in was already in line.

By 5 pm, there were 40 people on Frank's list. The line now stretched back beyond Collect Pond Park, all the way to Lafayette. Overnight, it continued to grow, like a living creature within the heart of Manhattan's civic center.

Twelve hours later, I arrived downtown, emerging from the A train to a soundtrack of helicopter blades. As I walked toward 100 Centre, the noise increased. Television trucks were stacked bumper to bumper on Lafayette Street, bordering Collect Pond Park. Reporters, stationed along a fence on the north side of the park, were snoozing in their tents. The line now stretched several blocks past the park and around Lafayette. I walked to the front of the line and relieved our stringer, Brittany Kriegstein, who'd taken over Sean's spot at 2 am. In a gesture of solidarity, she offered me her beach chair.

The regular courthouse press corps was bleary-eyed but the international reporters dotting the line were already up and working. An accented journalist attempted to interview Jane Rosenberg, a veteran courtroom artist with long red curly hair and sketch materials hoisted on her back like she was about to take the Oregon trail. Jane was curt and no-nonsense, obsessed with her job. I felt a flash of sympathy for anyone inadvertently distracting her from the day ahead.

Or maybe I was just projecting. Like everyone else on line, I was desperate to get into the courtroom. It wasn't only that our jobs depended on it. It was the most New York of feelings: A chance to be at the center of things.

The young artist, Isabelle Brourman, felt it too. She woke up early in Brooklyn and turned on NPR, which noted that cameras wouldn't be allowed into the courtroom: the only people who would capture visuals of the historic day were sketch artists. It was a clarion call. She planned her outfit out carefully, trying to look bedraggled and New York-y, like she belonged, then headed to Centre Street.

We figured the D.A.'s office would send the charges out in a press release as soon as the arraignment began. Ben, working remotely, was tasked with writing them up. I would be in the courtroom, where phones were off limits and the Secret Service had decided to bar laptops. The Service's requirements were stringent; the 15th floor of 100 Centre was off limits to anyone who didn't have official business there. After the hearing was over, I'd call Ben to fill him in on the details.

Shortly before 8 am, a wooden podium appeared at the head of the line, across the street from 100 Centre. Behind it was Lucian Chalfen, the official courts spokesman, who had a nasal outer borough accent and the colorful dress sense of a Hogwarts professor. Lucian handed out colored slips of paper—green, yellow and white. Green might as well have been gold: It was the ticket given to those of us scheduled to see the arraignment in person. Yellow and white went to reporters bound for the overflow room, a spare courtroom down the 15th floor hall that was outfitted with televisions so the excess press could monitor the proceedings remotely.

I folded my green ticket carefully and headed into the press room at 100 Centre Street, a dingy old dungeon on the ground floor of the courthouse. Its walls were papered over with yellowed tabloid covers: "300 POUND GIANT SEIZED IN SEX ATTACK," "PREPPY IN CUFFS AGAIN," and "GODFATHER RUBBED OUT; SLAIN OUTSIDE MIDTOWN STEAKHOUSE." The regular press corps joined me, as we waited for 2 pm.

Other reporters felt more comfortable outside. A New York Post journalist happily showed Isabelle Brourman her green ticket when the artist asked to take a picture of it. With an hour to go, Brourman beelined for a paper store, looking for the right shade of green. She found it, then sprinted to UPS, and with the help of an angel employee, created her own Golden Ticket.

In Collect Pond Park, police officers set up barriers to allay skirmishes between different factions of protesters. Then, around 10:30, Representative Marjorie Taylor Green appeared—MAGA duchess in Gotham. She struggled to be heard through a bullhorn as a portion of the crowd heckled her. Then she retreated to an SUV where she conducted a private interview. "President Trump is joining some of the most incredible people in history today," she said. "Nelson Mandela . . . Jesus! Jesus was arrested." George Santos, the Congressman recently exposed as a pathological liar, was on the scene. So, according to a rumors in the press room, was Kanye West. (This turned out to be untrue.)

Some star anchors stayed out of the fray; instead, Lester Holt, Jake Tapper, and other bold-name journalists anchored hours-long television specials, in which they filled the time talking about Trump. Michael Steele, the former head of the Republican party, warned MSNBC viewers that Trump was "loving every minute of it, because at the end of the day, we're talking about him. It's still all about him." Finally, in the afternoon, the man himself headed downtown to survey the chaos that had rallied to greet him.

When Trump arrived at 100 Centre Street, a cheer went up. He stepped out of his S.U.V. and made a fist for the cameras before waving at the crowds. Photographers screamed at everyone who wasn't Trump to get out of the shot. After posing for several minutes, the former president turned and slowly made his way into the courthouse.

✤   ✤   ✤

In the New York system, courtrooms are referred to as parts. The 15th floor courtroom where Trump was arraigned, and eventually tried, is Part 59. It's the last courtroom at the end of a long, dimly lit hallway in which the floor is tinted emerald. The courtroom itself is large and drafty, with enormous art deco fixtures hanging from the high ceiling which bathe the room in weak yellow light. Spectators sit on hard-backed wooden benches, in a gallery bisected by a central aisle. On arraignment day, the aisle was lined with armed court officers. I imagined they would take great pleasure in shooting any journalist who made an unexpected move.

In the front of the room, the well, the defense is assigned to a table on the left side of the room. The prosecution is on the right, and to the prosecution's immediate right is the jury box. The judge sits above all others, backed by a wood-paneled wall burnished with the words "In God We Trust."

Trump entered the courtroom and every reporter turned cautiously to look at him. On first sight, the former president emanates a kind of shockwave of recognition, the most photographed man in the world, out from behind the lens. His color, created for the camera, looks strange at close range. So does his hair, coiffed in the front but threadbare in the back, such that someone sitting behind him for weeks at a time sees a different patch of his scalp each day. His eyes are small, sharklike, constantly roving, searching the crowd.

He glanced over at the jury box where the courtroom artists were seated, including the veteran Jane Rosenberg and the newcomer, Isabelle Brourman, whose gambit had worked: The authorities had accepted her DIY ticket. Brourman drew mistrustful looks from the other court artists, but she only had eyes for Trump; in person, it was easier to see the fundamentals—how tall he was, how imposing—and to sense the way his charisma exerted pressure on those around him. As she prepared to sketch, she catalogued his physical features: his arms, his hands, his ears.

When Trump sat down at the defense table, the jolt of his presence eased. Watching him in person for the first time, I was astonished by the way he seemed to shrink within himself. This man, who for years had been the center of attention in any room he was in, was almost extraneous here. His arraignment was the biggest story in the world. But in Part 59, it wasn't his show. In the criminal courtroom, the judge commands the room and the lawyers occupy the stage. The defendant is passive. He sits quietly, unless he wants to get thrown out of court.

To Trump's right were the three prosecutors our stringers had tracked: Conroy, Hoffinger, Colangelo. They were smiling and relaxed. Behind them, in the gallery, sat Alvin Bragg. He was not relaxed; he held his neck stiffly and stared straight toward the front of the courtroom.

Shortly after 2:15, the judge, Juan Merchan, a slim, grey-haired former prosecutor with steel behind his calm tone, entered the courtroom. He briefly ceded the floor to a lawyer for media organizations, Robert Balin, who protested at length the bar on laptops. Trump, still one of the most powerful men in the world, was forced to listen to Balin's grievances for ten minutes; he scoffed when the lawyer insisted that professional journalists were trustworthy.

Merchan seemed skeptical of Balin, too, and relieved when the speech concluded. The bar on devices remained in place.

"Let's arraign Mr. Trump," the judge said.

The clerk of the court boomed out the charges: 34 counts of falsifying business records in the first degree, in violation of penal law 175.10. It was the felony charge we'd expected, but our question stood. What predicate crime were prosecutors claiming Trump had concealed?

The former president, in his inimitable croak, said: "Not guilty."

"People?" Merchan said, an invitation for the prosecutors to speak.

Chris Conroy, the veteran state prosecutor, stood up. He spoke in the formal tone of the courtroom. "The defendant, Donald J. Trump, falsified New York business records in order to conceal an illegal conspiracy to undermine the integrity of the 2016 presidential election and other violations of election laws."

It was a phrase we hadn't anticipated hearing. An *illegal conspiracy*. Trump, who was so obsessed with election integrity, was accused of cheating in the only election he'd ever won. Conspiracy was a crime the commentariat could get excited about, even though it seemed that the prosecutors were still hedging their bets. Those cryptic "other violations" didn't sound nearly as sexy.

Some reporters had apparently sneaked in electronic devices because, unbeknownst to me, the word "conspiracy" began to float on social media. At the New York *Times* headquarters, editors urged Ben to match the reporting. But he insisted on waiting until he could speak to me.

Conroy then described the hush money payment Cohen made to Stormy Daniels in October 2016, and Trump's repayment of Cohen beginning in February 2017. At the mention of Cohen and Daniels, Trump hugged himself tightly, crossing his arms and ankles so that his entire body was arranged in a grimace.

"Next, I would briefly like to address this defendant's recent public statements threatening our city," Conroy said. He handed the judge a printout of incendiary posts, including Trump's March rant predicting "death & destruction."

Conroy warned that Trump's statements were contorting the system, putting the fairness of the judicial process at risk. He said prosecutors weren't seeking a gag order on Trump, yet. But if the former president kept it up, he said, that might change. Trump glared, silent, as if a gag order were already in effect.

Up stood one of Trump's lawyers, Todd Blanche, a broad-shouldered former Southern District prosecutor. Blanche, who joined the defense team just two months earlier, was popular among the Southern alumni, and many were shocked that he was representing the former president. But Blanche believed that everyone deserved a defense lawyer—and he was sympathetic to the idea that his client was being singled out for harsh treatment.

"I didn't realize we were going to give opening statements today," he said, opening his counterattack. Trump, he declared, was frustrated and upset. It was a grave injustice his client was in the courtroom at all. "He has rights," Blanche added. "He's allowed to speak publicly." He looked imploringly at the judge.

"Certainly, of course Mr. Trump does have rights," Merchan said soothingly. He said that he wouldn't have imposed a gag order, even if the prosecution had asked for it.

But the judge asked the defense lawyers to speak to their client—and, perhaps aiming for evenhandedness, the prosecutors to speak to their witnesses. Really, his warning seemed directed at only one man. "Remind them to please refrain from making statements that are likely to incite violence or civil unrest."

❖   ❖   ❖

The Secret Service held us in the courtroom until Trump was out of the building. The moment we were sprung, I called Ben and started dictating an elaborate lede I'd written in my head.

"Jonah! Jonah!" he said, interrupting me. "What are the charges?"

"What?" I said.

The D.A.'s office hadn't announced the charges against Trump to the world outside the courtroom. Reporters in the room had misunderstood Conroy, and several outlets were reporting that Trump was charged with conspiracy. But I told Ben that while the prosecutor had mentioned a conspiracy, it wasn't one of the charges. Just 34 counts of falsifying business records.

Soon afterward, the D.A.'s office sent out a press release, along with a copy of the indictment and a statement of facts. The word conspiracy didn't appear in any of the three documents, nor was there any clarification of what predicate crime Conroy had been talking about. In the late afternoon, Bragg took a modest stage on the 8th floor of 80 Centre Street, framed by the American and New York flags. The grey in his goatee looked more pronounced than usual. He began to give the most important public statement of his life. Maybe it would have gone better had there been no cameras, no microphones and no reporters there to ask questions.

Legally, there was some logic to prosecutors' decision not to commit to a single predicate crime. It gave Bragg's prosecutors multiple ways to frame Trump's conduct, in case a judge took issue with one of them in the lead-up to a trial.

But it was a disaster for public relations. A former president was criminally charged with a felony on the basis of a mystery crime. Leaving the predicate crime unsettled, Bragg instead emphasized the importance of accurate business records. On this historic day, he sacrificed his first, best opportunity to frame his case for the public.

When it was time for questions, a reporter asked the obvious one: the indictment didn't name the predicate, the reason Trump was charged with felonies rather than misdemeanors. "I'm wondering if you can specify what laws were also broken?" a reporter asked.

The D.A. gave a small smile. "The indictment doesn't specify it because the law does not so require," he said. But, he noted a couple of possible crimes.

The first predicate option was a violation of a New York state election law—statute 17–152—which made it a misdemeanor to conspire to promote a candidacy by unlawful means. That was why Conroy mentioned a conspiracy.

The second was a violation of a federal election law prohibiting campaign donations beyond a certain limit. In 2018, Michael Cohen had pleaded guilty to that crime in federal court, the theory being that the hush money payment to Daniels, having aided Trump's election, was effectively a campaign donation.

The reporter asked, reasonably, why Trump hadn't been charged with those crimes along with falsifying business records.

"I'm not going to go into our deliberative process," Bragg said. "The charges that were brought were the ones that were brought. The evidence and the law is the basis for those decisions."

The next morning, April 5, the New York Post was gleeful.

"TRUMPED UP," it read. *"Is that it? Bragg's historic case vs. Don falls flat."*

Trump immediately began to profit from the arraignment and the widespread perception that the case was bullshit seemed to help. His campaign brought in $8 million in fundraising in the first four days after the charges, as the former president called Bragg a "criminal," and Merchan a Trump-hating judge with a Trump-hating family.

As the days and weeks went by, the opinion pages of the Acela Corridor fretted over Bragg's charges. In the Washington Post, Ruth Marcus called the indictment "disturbingly unilluminating" and the case's legal theory "debatable at best, unnervingly flimsy at worst." Bragg's case, she concluded, was "a dangerous leap on the highest of wires." Trump's defense lawyers were certain to call on the judge to dismiss the case, and if it was as weak as the naysayers feared, their chances were good.

Perhaps there was something stronger on the horizon beyond New York County. In The *Times*, Nicholas Kristof welcomed other possibilities, noting that the Manhattan indictment would not necessarily be the first criminal case against Trump to reach trial. "I hope that the first case to be tried will be the strongest," he offered, as if in prayer. "For it is the first criminal trial that will be seared into history."

❖   ❖   ❖

Marcus, Kristof, and their colleagues in the commentariat had a specific alternative in mind: Jack Smith, a wild-eyed prosecutor appointed to head up two federal investigations into Donald Trump's behavior as he departed the presidency. In the first, Trump was suspected of hoarding state secrets at Mar-a-Lago; in the second, of seeking to overturn the results of the previous election, an effort that culminated in the violent attack on the U.S. Capitol on January 6, 2021.

Smith, who'd worked at the Manhattan district attorney's office at the start of his career, looked the traditional part of the sage federal prosecutor. He was thin, bearded and white. When it became clear, in the summer of 2023, that he was on the precipice of indicting Trump over Jan. 6, a collective sigh of relief arose from the nation's liberal opinion-makers.

"Finally," wrote Susan Glasser in *The New Yorker*. "This, in the end, is the heart of the matter, a long-delayed reckoning with an offense against the constitutional system so great that it is without historic precedent."

On August 1, Smith spoke crisply at his own post-indictment press conference, accusing Trump of conspiring to defraud the United States itself. The circles under his eyes were so heavy that they looked like scars. He promised to seek a speedy trial for a federal case of national import. By the end of the month, a trial date was set for March 2024. Jack Smith was poised to be the first prosecutor to take on a former president at trial, for the high crime of seeking to overturn a U.S. election.

Alvin Bragg's case was also scheduled for March 2024, albeit three weeks after Smith's. But there was no world in which the two trials could take place simultaneously. The D.A. debuted a new talking point in the sporadic interviews he gave to local media. "Broader justice may warrant another case going first," he said in an interview on New York City's beloved cable channel NY1. "But we stand at the ready." Bragg seemed perfectly happy to cede the spotlight to another case—if not downright enthusiastic.

But Jack Smith and his admirers underestimated Trump's knack for tying the federal system in knots. Trump and his lawyers understood that the law's instinct is to address any novel argument; the unprecedented nature of everything about Trump made him a singular source of legal novelty. In the fall of 2023, the former president's lawyers argued that, because Jack Smith had charged Trump for actions he took as president, he was "absolutely immune from prosecution."

Pundits scoffed. Smith responded furiously. The federal courts, however took the argument seriously and processed it in the slow, deliberate fashion characteristic of the judicial branch. The trial in which Smith would accuse Trump of seeking to overturn an election was stalled indefinitely.

But while the defense tactics stymied Smith's criminal cases, they had less traction in the New York courts. The writer E. Jean Carroll and the New York State Attorney General, Letitia James, trounced Trump in a quick succession of civil trials that spanned from the spring of 2023 to the early months of 2024. The former president did himself no favors. In two of the three trials, he stormed out of the courtroom in a temper, and throughout them all, he muttered and fidgeted in court, drawing negative attention from judges and jurors alike. By February 2024, he'd been found liable by two separate juries of having sexually abused and defamed Carroll, and by a New York judge of conspiring to exaggerate his net worth. He faced hundreds of millions of dollars in fines.

Even so, he did not yet face the stigma of criminality, nor the threat of jail time. For his most dedicated critics, those were the results that mattered. A criminal conviction would confirm their long-held view of Trump's fundamental illegitimacy as a presidential candidate and public figure. Jail time, by their calculus, would nullify the threat he posed politically.

Throughout it all, Trump posted on social media, attacking his enemies and casting doubt on the legitimacy of the trials. He blurred their details together, characterizing them—as he had all legal opposition—as one big witch hunt, led by "Deranged Jack Smith, Letitia 'Peekaboo' James' and Alvin Bragg, who apparently didn't merit a nickname. "It's Biden Investigations for purposes of ELECTION INTERFERENCE," Trump posted on February 3, 2024.

Later that month, Justice Merchan declined to dismiss Bragg's case against Trump, clearing the way for a March trial. Soon afterward, in response to Trump's nonstop posting on social media, the judge placed a narrowly tailored gag order on the former president, restricting him from making public statements about jurors, witnesses or prosecutors. Merchan declared in his ruling that Trump's statements were not only threatening, inflammatory and denigrating, but also resulted in real-life consequences for those targeted. But Merchan ruled that Trump was free to post about Bragg—or the judge himself.

Todd Blanche and the rest of the defense team persisted in their efforts to delay the trial. They appealed the gag order. They called for the judge to recuse himself. They called for a change of venue, arguing Manhattan was so liberal that Trump couldn't possibly get a fair trial there. They argued that the trial should be delayed until the Supreme Court reached a ruling as to the extent of Trump's immunity from prosecution.

None of it worked. The best they could do was to push the start date back two weeks, to April 15, 2024. To the horror of those who wanted to see Trump destroyed, Alvin Bragg's trial would be going first.

CHAPTER TWO

CAMERA SHY

Alvin L. Bragg announced his intention to become Manhattan's district attorney in June 2019. He was early to enter the race, in part because his advisers wanted some runway to teach a first-time candidate how to be a politician. He introduced himself in a short video, speaking in professorial tones over lilting piano as he asserted that Manhattan had two separate justice systems: one for the rich and powerful, and another for everyone else. "I'm Alvin Bragg," he said, facing the viewer with a hesitant half-smile. "And I'm running to change that." Then, he strode in slow-motion toward a Centre Street courthouse, his back to the camera.

It was an exciting time to be a progressive prosecutor. In Philadelphia and Los Angeles, San Francisco and Chicago, Orlando and Corpus Christi, young lawyers were winning elections by promising to reform the system. "Not all prosecutors have worked in the interest of justice," said Larry Krasner, Philly's new head prosecutor. "They are *retributive*. They are political." Krasner and his peers billed themselves as more than just an alternative. They were revolutionaries in a mass movement for justice.

Over the next two years, even people who loathed prosecutors decided it was worth competing to be the Manhattan D.A. One candidate, Eliza Orlins, had parlayed multiple appearances on "Survivor" into social media stardom. She insisted that the borough's top prosecutor shouldn't be a prosecutor at all: only a public defender like herself could be trusted.

Ultimately, eight Democrats entered the race, six of them women. Whoever won, it seemed obvious that the next D.A. would bring a fundamentally different vision to the office than the two scions of American aristocracy who'd led it for the previous fifty years.

In March 2021, three months before the Democratic primary, the incumbent Manhattan D.A., Cyrus R. Vance Jr., finally announced what had long been obvious: He was not running for reelection. The news broke in a *New Yorker* profile, written by Jane Mayer, which demonstrated that Vance was gambling his legacy on something else. The article's headline was "Can Cyrus Vance Jr. Nail Trump?" Were Trump to be charged and convicted, Mayer wrote, "he could end up serving a prison term instead of a second White House term." It was a neat illustration of the connection often drawn between Trump's legal travails and his political future.

The D.A. candidates grappled with Manhattan's most dire issues: people were dying in the city's jails. Sex crimes were being ignored or mishandled. Shootings were on the rise. But as the Democratic primary crept closer, Vance's Trump investigation crowded out every other subject. There was pressure on all of the candidates to talk about their qualifications to take over the inquiry—without seeming prejudiced, of course. The former president exerted a force that compelled people to contort themselves in response. None of the candidates could ignore a much-loathed investigative target in the thick of a competitive race.

Even in the absence of a pandemic, mass social upheaval, and a criminal investigation into a former president, the Manhattan D.A. occupies strange territory in the life of the city. He runs for office on a political platform. Then, having won office, he must assume a disinterested, upright, incorruptible posture. During the election, he courts the press; in office, he's expected to keep it at arm's length, if not shun it altogether. The contradiction breeds an inherent conflict, one which would soon test Alvin Bragg, whose fundamental good nature would be little help in the glare of the spotlight.

❖   ❖   ❖

Alvin Leonard Bragg Jr. was born on Oct. 21, 1973. His parents, Sadie and Alvin Sr., were high-school sweethearts from Petersburg, Virginia. A few years after their son was born, they bought a brownstone in the historic Harlem neighborhood of Striver's Row, which had a close-knit, community-oriented atmosphere that reminded them of the South. The family couldn't get a half-block away from their house on 139th Street without being greeted by one of Sadie's math students, or someone Alvin Sr. had helped in his work for the Urban League. The young Alvin's world was filled with surrogate parents. During his freshman year at Harvard, his roommates made fun of him because he sent more than a dozen Mother's Day cards back to Harlem.

Sadie expected big things from Alvin Jr. The joke was that she had the best-swept steps on the block because every afternoon at 3:30 she was out on the stoop, keeping her hands busy while anxiously awaiting her son's arrival from school. She was a hard-working, highly motivated woman, who wrote algebra textbooks on the side, and she demanded academic excellence from her son. Her husband was more relaxed, a fan of James Brown and the Knicks, particularly Clyde "The Glide" Frazier. He regaled Alvin Jr. with stories of his own athletic past, claiming his track buddies nicknamed him "Pretty" because his stride was so graceful. He encouraged Alvin Jr. to get outside when he could.

The younger Bragg was also a basketball fan and admired Charles Oakley, the great Knicks forward. He liked Oakley's hard hat mentality, the way he eschewed showiness for substance, showing up and doing his job every night. It was an unpopular choice in the late 1980s and 1990s, when the Knicks were outdone annually by an attention-grabbing superstar named Michael Jordan. But Bragg was never seduced by the Jordan flash and never jumped on the Chicago bandwagon. Oakley was his guy, the Knicks were his team and New York City, Harlem in particular, was his home. "Alvin is a Harlem guy, through and through," his friend Chris Michel once told me. "This is a guy who doesn't like to *eat* below 110th Street."

When Bragg was in kindergarten, his parents enrolled him at one of the city's more exclusive private schools, Trinity, on the Upper West Side a few blocks from Central Park. He was one of a handful of Black students. Sadie would take him there on the M10 bus, drilling him on arithmetic along the way. He was friendly, a bit goofy, and unusually thoughtful for his age. Unlike other kids, whose blood ran hot and who would hold grudges for weeks, he rarely seemed ruffled by a dispute. He didn't like to make a spectacle of himself and stayed above the fray during arguments among friends. He would often weigh in near the end, playing peacemaker.

Despite his parents' devotion and his tight-knit group of friends, Bragg's life in Harlem was far from idyllic. His early childhood coincided with the city's brush with bankruptcy and soaring levels of street crime. When he wasn't at school, Sadie asked him to stay within the confines of their block. But even the Braggs' block wasn't particularly safe: By the time he was 10, he'd had a knife put to his neck there in broad daylight, by some older kids. It was no accident that Bragg became watchful, keenly aware of his surroundings.

When he was a teenager, he and his friends were taking a taxi back to his house from a Central Park basketball court. 1010 WINS was playing on the radio. Suddenly, at a red light, the driver exited the car. The next thing the teens knew, there were cops at each passenger door pointing guns at them. A group of officers provided backup. The radio had reported that a group of Black teens was wanted for a crime in Central Park, and the cabbie had jumped to conclusions. The police told Bragg and his friends that they "fit the description," but ultimately let them go. When they arrived on 139th, Sadie insisted that Alvin file a report with the local precinct.

Bragg had already become publicly engaged through his church, Abyssinian Baptist, an iconic Harlem institution where religion and the fight for social justice were preached in tandem. The adolescent Bragg became the head of the church's youth council, whitewashing over advertisements that targeted poor Black people with offers of menthol cigarettes and malt liquor. He impressed a young pastor named Raphael Warnock, who would later recall that, even as a teenager, the future district attorney had the bearing and presence of a leader. Given his run-ins with the police, it follows that Bragg's ambition began to take on a lawyerly shape.

He studied his way through Harvard and Harvard Law, thinking he might become a defense attorney. But his mindset changed when he clerked for a Southern District judge, Robert P. Patterson Jr. It was Bragg's first prolonged encounter with one of the many heirs of

American aristocracy holed up in Manhattan's civic center. Day after day, prosecutors would come to Patterson to apply for court approval for investigations that, if they were successful, could eliminate guns and gangs, transforming whole neighborhoods. Bragg saw then that institutional power could be directed toward a form of pragmatic utilitarianism, attempting to do the most good for the greatest number.

He became an institutionalist looking to transform systems from inside the prestigious halls of government. He worked at the New York attorney general's office, scrutinizing police misconduct and public corruption He worked as a prosecutor in the Southern district, graduating to the public corruption unit. Then he returned to the attorney general's office, to lead the unit that investigated police killings of unarmed Black people. He rose to become one of the office's leaders.

The world of New York lawyers is small and as Bragg moved from one office to the other, he met colleagues who would later serve as trusted advisers. In his first stint at the New York attorney general's office, he was supervised by a veteran of the Manhattan D.A.'s office, Peter Pope; in his second, he collaborated with a young lawyer named Matthew Colangelo.

By the end of 2018, Bragg felt ready for something bigger. He hoped to run for attorney general but his more politically connected friends warned him against challenging a charismatic young city politician named Letitia James. Instead, they encouraged him to consider a campaign for Manhattan district attorney.

Peter Pope and other friends may have warned him that the D.A.'s office had a culture all its own, informed by the recondite rituals of the trial bureaus, traditions that had been passed for decades from prosecutor from prosecutor, all of whom shared the same title: assistant district attorney.

Still, Bragg knew he was going to run as a change candidate. Maybe he could change it.

❖   ❖   ❖

One man did more than any other to define the role of the Manhattan D.A. Robert Morgenthau ran the office for more than three decades, becoming, over those many years, the personification of the American prosecutor. He was tall and reedy, with a long, angular face and an impressive nose. He was not a comfortable public speaker. But from his headquarters on 1 Hogan Place, Morgenthau could shut out the microphones and cameras, while assiduously courting the press.

He called The *Times* Metro desk so often that when he rang, reporters would hold the phone up, asking if anyone wanted to speak with the D.A. He offered the same greeting to everyone, even Lucinda Franks, the reporter who became his second wife: "Bob Morgenthau. Got a pencil?" He gave her tips on crooked bank presidents and his own political opponents.

To an outsider looking in on New York City in the 1970s, the D.A.'s office might have seemed an ill fit for Morgenthau, an émigré from loftier heights. He first became famous in 1961 when his friend John F. Kennedy appointed him U.S. Attorney for the Southern District of New York. Operating under the direction of the U.S. attorney general, Bobby Kennedy, Morgenthau made the fight against the mafia one of the pillars of the federal office's work. But Morgenthau didn't stop with the mob. His father, Franklin Roosevelt's treasury secretary, had instilled in him an innate skepticism of bankers and he believed, he once wrote, that "society cannot operate under two sets of rules—one for the poor, and one for the high and mighty." Morgenthau brought the law to Wall Street, and introduced a new phrase into the American vernacular: white collar crime.

He indicted the chairman of the New York Stock Exchange and the Executive Vice President of one of New York's landmark banks. According to his biographer, Andrew Meier, he prosecuted more than two hundred accountants, inspectors and auditors. For years, he pursued criminal charges against Roy Cohn, a lawyer who bridged the respectability of the bar and the violence of the mob.

Then, President Nixon was elected and Morgenthau was out: U.S. attorneys serve at the pleasure of the president.

But district attorneys are chosen by the people. In 1974, Morgenthau won a special election to lead the Manhattan D.A.'s office, succeeding Frank Hogan, an eight-term district attorney who'd run the office for the previous three decades. The Manhattan D.A.'s office was seen by insiders as Southern's grubby little brother; it dealt in the island's street crimes, the ugliest murders and the pettiest robberies. By the nature of their work, its prosecutors were intimately involved in the daily churn of events, closer to the beating heart of the city. There, Morgenthau's politicking with the press would come in especially handy, helping to steer his reputation when scandal inevitably reared its head.

There was the long delay before serious prosecution of Bernie Goetz, the vigilante who shot four Black men on a subway in 1984 after they harassed him for money. Morgenthau initially praised the grand jury which, under the guidance of his prosecutors, brought only minor weapons charges against Goetz. But he changed his tune when public outrage grew, course-correcting to say he'd been "shocked" by the grand jury's flippancy.

There was the rush to prosecute the Central Park Five, a group of Black and Hispanic teenagers wrongly accused of raping a jogger in the park in 1989, just a couple years before Alvin and his friends were stopped in the taxicab. The crime ignited a city already roiling with race-based fear. Reporters called the defendants the "wolfpack." The real estate developer Donald Trump took out advertisements in four different newspapers calling for the restoration of the death penalty. Defense lawyers cried foul when statements their clients made to prosecutors showed up in the news. After winning guilty verdicts, Morgenthau insisted "this was not a racial case."

His ability to prevail in stormy weather was matched by an uncanny instinct for where the winds were blowing. It was evident in his hiring. Among the assistant district attorneys who worked for Morgenthau were Sonia Sotomayor, Eliot Spitzer, and both JFK and RFK Jr.

And it was evident in his leadership: In 2002, Willy Rashbaum at The *Times* reported that Manhattan prosecutors were investigating the claims of another man who had confessed to the jogger's rape. In December, Morgenthau moved to exonerate the Central Park Five. He was applauded for doing so.

By then, crime was dropping precipitously in cities around the country. In a later era, skeptics would cast doubt on whether any one man could have a significant influence on crime trends. Morgenthau, though, took an aristocrat's share of the credit. When he finally retired in 2009, The *Times* celebrated his reign in a glowing editorial, saying he had been "born to this job" and warning potential successors that "Mr. Morgenthau has set the bar for that office very, very high."

With crime at record lows and the media evolving in concert with the internet, prosecution came in for a reassessment on a grand scale. The year Morgenthau retired, the San Francisco District Attorney, Kamala Harris, published a book called "Smart on Crime," in which she tried to thread the needle between tough and soft (previously the only two options). Morgenthau's successor, Cyrus R. Vance Jr—whose father served as President Carter's Secretary of State—hoped to be perceived as one of the leaders of a new school of smart prosecutors.

But the *Times's* editorial warning proved prescient. In the summer of 2011, Vance was described by The *New York Post* as having overseen "a dizzying array of embarrassing losses," in an article with the headline, *"Another Debacle for Black Eye-Cy."* The "debacle" was the collapse of a sexual assault case against the head of the International Monetary Fund, Dominique Strauss-Kahn. Later that year, a prosecutor from Vance's office successfully argued for reduced sex offender status for Jeffrey Epstein. By the end of his second term, cases against Harvey Weinstein and two of Donald Trump's children were dead in the water.

No one in the know would deny, in retrospect, that Vance's accomplishments were laudable. He brought the office into the digital era, pioneering a data-driven approach to fighting crime that helped to sustain the drop in serious felonies. But his successes were often systemic, and under the hood. His failures were frequently public, and they were seized upon by critics, who used a powerful new megaphone—social media—to castigate the district attorney. A new crop of progressive prosecutors was casting aspersions on "smart on crime." They said more wholesale reform was required for justice.

In his third and final term, Vance seemed bent on rescuing his reputation and rewriting his legacy. He brought a case against Harvey Weinstein, which resulted in a conviction. And in August 2018, he opened an inquiry into Michael Cohen's hush money payment to Stormy Daniels, which was immediately paused at the direction of the Southern district prosecutors who were looking at the same conduct. For a year, the D.A.'s investigation went nowhere. It was inactive when Bragg announced his campaign in June 2019.

But the following month, the Southern district prosecutors

disclosed that their investigation had "effectively concluded." Vance's inquiry was back on. Soon, he subpoenaed Trump's company, demanding nearly a decade's worth of tax returns. Trump fought back, dragging the investigation out for years and taking it up to the Supreme Court twice. In an oral argument, in May 2020, the district attorney's general counsel, Carey Dunne, did the New York bar proud. Courtly, soft-spoken and savvy, Dunne was one of the brightest stars of the Vance era. He told the Supreme Court justices that while a president might be shielded from the law in his official capacity, he was the same as any other citizen in private.

In early 2021, shortly before the Supreme Court issued a final decision in his office's favor, Vance recruited Mark Pomerantz, the former head of the criminal division at Southern, to team up with Dunne in leading the Trump investigation. Pomerantz, who would soon turn 70, understood white-collar crime as well as any prosecutor in the country. As a category, it was often less clear-cut than street crime. A murder results in a dead body. A shooting results in a bullet wound. But the word *fraud* encompasses all manner of sins. Fraud, in its most basic form, is a lie. The gifted white-collar prosecutor takes a series of facts that demonstrate a lie and fits those facts like individual puzzle pieces into a preexisting statute. The facts and the law merge into a criminal case.

Pomerantz thought that Michael Cohen's hush money payment was fertile ground for a case. After paying Stormy Daniels $130,000 in 2016, Cohen was reimbursed by the Trump Organization over the course of the following year. These 2017 transactions were corroborated by a paper trail. Nine of the reimbursement checks were signed by Trump himself; all were classified by The Trump Organization as "legal expenses." There was no world in which a hush money payment was a legal expense. To Pomerantz, the series of payment records indisputably demonstrated the misdemeanor crime outlined in New York penal law 175.05: falsifying business records in the second degree, or FBR2 for short. It would have seemed laughable, desperate, to charge a former president with a misdemeanor.

So Pomerantz sought a second crime—the predicate—that would enable the office to charge Trump with the felony version of falsifying business records, penal law 175.10. He knew that in 2018, Michael

Cohen pleaded guilty in federal court to violating campaign finance laws as he paid for Stormy Daniels's silence. Trump might plausibly be charged in Manhattan with falsifying business documents to cover up the predicate crime of that illegal donation. But Vance's broader team concluded it was too risky to include a federal charge in a state case: Federal law belongs in federal court, and a judge might dismiss an indictment that made use of mismatched statutes.

Pomerantz flirted with other, more outlandish conceptions of the hush money case. But he couldn't join the facts and the law in a way the office's investigative team found satisfying. He felt his creativity was being stymied by the conservative culture of the D.A.'s office. He also worried the other prosecutors would think he was too aggressive, looking for a "quick kill." And indeed, some of the younger members of the Trump investigative team were growing concerned, cognizant of pressure from above to push the investigation forward while Vance was still in charge.

Pomerantz moved on to some of the other lies in the Trump compendium. Soon, he came across Trump's annual financial statements. After some useful discussion with the New York attorney general's office, he determined that Trump had overvalued his properties, in some cases by many millions of dollars, in an effort to pump up lenders' impression of his overall net worth. Poring over the financial records in solitude for months, Pomerantz came to believe that Trump's exaggerations were violations of criminal law. And Michael Cohen was willing—perhaps even eager—to testify that Trump had directed him to help manipulate the valuations.

❖   ❖   ❖

Manhattan D.A. candidate Alvin Bragg, meanwhile, was being molded into a new shape, the shape of a local politician. Campaigning was new to him. He had no social media accounts, had never raised money or visited a political club. He relied on Richie Fife, a politico who spoke in a guttural drawl, to guide him through the race. When it came to gladhanding with members of this or that political club, Bragg was a natural. But communicating his message through a screen was more complicated.

Not that he had any choice in the matter. It was a year of Zoom elections, the still-raging pandemic preventing a full-fledged campaign. Those few following the primary as it progressed through January 2021—campaign staffers, policy wonks, and reporters—got used to seeing Alvin Bragg on their laptops, confined to a little digital square, giving a stump speech that was thunderingly repetitive. It was as if he didn't trust himself to speak extemporaneously to a camera. Always, *always*, he'd mention that he had been held at gunpoint by both the cops and criminals. If you watched closely, you could see certain of his competitors roll their eyes at the repetition.

That month, I became Metro's Manhattan courts reporter. As an outsider, it was clear to me that the dynamics of social media had inspired criticism of Vance's tenure, and were shaping the race to succeed him. But it took me longer to realize that the politics of the race were in rapid flux. The fervor for criminal justice reform, which peaked in 2020 after the murder of George Floyd, lost traction as violent crime stats rose in cities around the country. Then, on his way out of office, Trump summoned the Capitol rioters to Washington. The world felt as if it were tilting out of control. Manhattan Democrats craved stability—and the tantalizing promise of Trump's permanent excommunication from the political sphere. The momentum of the progressive prosecutors on the rise when Bragg announced his candidacy in 2019 was stymied.

In February 2021, Vance finally obtained Trump's tax returns and it began to seem feasible that his investigation could result in criminal charges. The possibility permanently transformed the press coverage of the D.A. campaign. The first article about the race I worked on was headlined, *"One Question for Manhattan D.A. Candidates: Will You Prosecute Trump?"*

Some of the candidates had been incautious. One of Eliza Orlins's most notable old tweets was simply, "I DETEST TRUMP!!!!!!!!" Still, she said if she were to be elected she could evaluate evidence against the former president without prejudice. Bragg, for his part, began to say that he'd sued Trump more than 100 times. The talking point leaned on 100 "legal or administrative actions" that the New York attorney general, Eric Schneiderman, had taken against the Trump administration, per a 2017 *Times* article. But many of the actions weren't lawsuits, and Bragg's degree of involvement in them was never entirely clear. It seemed, in retrospect, as if the Trump-related talking point was just too good to pass up. There was no point at which Bragg pledged to *go after* Trump as he was later accused of doing—he always said that, informed by his experience, he would follow the facts and the law.

By March, Bragg's chief rival was Tali Farhadian Weinstein. She matched him accomplishment for accomplishment. A child of refugees, she had grown up in New York, gone to Yale undergrad and Yale Law, clerked at the Supreme Court, and been a federal prosecutor in New York's Eastern district. She was a Rhodes scholar. She was polished and smooth on camera. And she had an enormous war chest, thanks to donations from Wall Street, where her husband was a prominent hedge fund manager. She was also a credible Trump adversary; while working for the Brooklyn district attorney's office, she too had sued his administration. In the early spring of 2021, Farhadian Weinstein was thought to be in the lead, with Bragg a close second. Whichever of them won the June primary would be a shoo-in for the general election in the fall, and would succeed Vance at the end of the year.

The rise in violent crime continued to trouble the city. Knowing it was an issue with teeth for New Yorkers who still remembered the bad old days, Farhadian Weinstein positioned herself as the public safety candidate. Bragg didn't change anything he was saying. Public safety was baked into his campaign's foundation: He'd had a gun held to his head by cops and criminals alike. But in April 2021, as the more progressive candidates floundered, he shored up support from the left by memorializing his pledge to handle low-level crimes leniently in a campaign document known as the Day One memo. The premise was that the policies would be implemented on his first day in office—a classic campaign promise.

Between late May and early June, with Bragg consolidating support from the left, Farhadian Weinstein donated herself an extra $8.2 million. Then, she made a misstep: a campaign mailer accusing Bragg and another candidate of putting women and families at risk of domestic abuse. On the flyer, Bragg seemed oversized and his race was impossible to ignore. The other candidates accused Farhadian Weinstein of trying to buy the election and also, racism. Bragg, projecting levelheaded stability, cast the mailer as a response to his campaign's momentum.

The primary was held on June 22. Bragg won by about 9,000 votes—a narrow margin. I called him right afterward and asked him how he felt about the possibility of taking over the Trump investigation. He said it was just one of the many tasks on which he was focused.

"It's all a profound responsibility," he said.

◆   ◆   ◆

The next month, Vance and his team announced the indictment of Donald Trump's company and his chief financial officer, Allen Weisselberg, a bookkeeper who'd been responsible for the company's finances for decades. The district attorney's office accused Weisselberg and other executives of profiting from a tax scheme, receiving part of their compensation in special perks that went unreported to the government. Trump was not charged, but the indictment further emphasized the scope of the Vance investigation. Weisselberg, whose large eyes and bushy brows gave him the appearance of an aging Muppet, was now in the hot seat; if he cooperated, Trump might be in trouble.

Bragg was in an unusual position. He was overwhelmingly likely to become the next district attorney, but Vance was still in charge, and Bragg could not act as if he were D.A.-elect, not with the general election still months away. Mark Pomerantz continued to push the case against Trump himself forward. After a tense September meeting with Carey Dunne, two line prosecutors decided to step back from the investigation. They remained in the D.A.'s office, focused on other assignments.

In the early November election, Bragg handily beat his Republican opponent. Two days later, on November 4, the Washington Post reported that Vance had convened a special grand jury to hear evidence about Trump's company. The panel would be seated for six months before expiring in April.

Bragg was proceeding without knowledge of the investigation's progress. Guided by Peter Pope, who was serving the D.A.-elect as an adviser, Bragg decided to offer Susan Hoffinger the job of head of investigations, one of the most important positions he had to fill. A tough-minded lawyer who started her career with the district attorney's office under Robert Morgenthau, Hoffinger had long ago pivoted to criminal defense. She spent two decades in practice with her sister Fran and her well-known father, Jack Hoffinger. (He too began his career in the Manhattan D.A.'s office, under eight-term legend Frank Hogan.) Jack had died at the age of 95 just two months earlier, and Susan was hesitant to break up the family firm. But Fran advised her to take the job, telling her she'd be a gift to the people of the city of New York.

With Bragg's team waiting in the wings, Pomerantz wanted to heighten the special grand jury's purpose beyond simply issuing subpoenas. He lobbied Vance to greenlight the presentation of evidence that could ultimately lead to a Trump indictment.

On Dec. 9, 2021, the lame duck D.A. convened a meeting of outside advisers to weigh in on the potential net worth case. It was an impressive group. Some had worked on Mueller's federal investigation into Trump; others were well-known former federal prosecutors. They joined the D.A.'s investigative team: Pomerantz, of course; Carey Dunne; Chris Conroy, whom Hoffinger would soon replace as the head of the investigations division; and two line prosecutors, Solomon Shinerock and James Graham. Though he explicitly weighed the possibility, Vance decided not to invite Bragg or his team.

None of the outsiders thought the case was a sure thing. But neither did they caution against moving forward. The meeting satisfied Vance. Three days later, on Sunday, December 12, Dunne sent an email to the investigative team, telling them a decision had been made to proceed with a grand jury presentation with the intention, subject to "caveats and contingencies," of asking the jurors to vote on an indictment. James Graham, the line prosecutor, stepped back from the team after the decision was made. Bragg would come into office in January 2022 with the prosecution of the former president racing ahead, even as the Trump investigative team was shrinking.

One of Dunne's caveats and/or contingencies would likely have been that the decision was subject to the approval of the D.A.-elect. But Bragg still hadn't been briefed. His transition team began to report to 1 Hogan Place, and the new D.A. was engaged in endless meetings. His calendar filled up quickly. The pandemic continued to wreak havoc; in mid-December, a D.A. office holiday party became a superspreader event, requiring the quarantine of an entire trial bureau.

Finally, on Dec. 27, Bragg and Peter Pope had a Zoom meeting with Pomerantz and Dunne. It was Bragg's first briefing on the case. He listened thoughtfully, didn't speak too much and left after an hour. His style was not what Pomerantz expected. Still the veteran felt the call had gone well.

That month, Willy Rashbaum, Ben Protess and I asked a stringer, Nate Schweber, to monitor traffic between 100 and 80 Centre Street. We expected a Trump indictment to be handed up in short order.

⬧   ⬧   ⬧

Alvin Bragg's transition into the district attorney's office marked the first shift in power in a decade, and the second in a half century. It was a messy changing of the guard. On Jan. 3, the first Monday of his tenure, Bragg announced a whopping 18-person leadership team that included Richie Fife, Peter Pope and Carey Dunne. The new D.A. was not given to setting up hierarchies and eighteen new leaders made for a lot of leadership. It was unclear, initially, how things would work in the new regime or who, exactly, was in charge of what. Despite Dunne's ostensible presence on the leadership team, he was ejected from his 8th floor office, a sign of incipient tension between the old regime and the new guard.

Bragg felt there was one thing he had to do immediately: formalize the memo he'd pledged would become law on his first day in office. Many politicians might not have been quite so literal about the timing. But Bragg wanted to keep his promise. So that same Monday, he sent the memo to the entirety of his staff. It directed prosecutors to avoid jail time for defendants who were arrested on suspicion of robberies, assaults and gun possession. Within a week, even as Dunne and Pomerantz were growing nervous that their new boss had yet to fully engage with the Trump investigation, Bragg had himself a press scandal.

With gun crime on the rise, and the New York Post running stories about bodega shoplifting, the memo was politically untenable. Bragg faced a furious backlash, which grew when the police commissioner, Keechant Sewell, sent *her* staff—every police officer in New York City—an email saying that the D.A.'s new policies made her afraid for the safety of the public. Bragg quickly reverted to a core lesson he had learned as a prosecutor: say as little as possible to the press. It was a more comfortable posture for him anyway. He believed in letting his work speak for itself.

On Saturday, January 8, Bragg had his first formal meeting as D.A. with Mark Pomerantz—via videoconference. The two men were on different pages. Bragg wanted to find prosecutors within the office who could work on the investigation; it would have been a way to put his own imprint on the case. Pomerantz told Bragg that the case was a rocket ready to be launched, too far along to waste time on a personnel search. Pomerantz had a deadline in his head. Complex grand jury presentations can take weeks. He was worried that, if April arrived and the grand jury that Vance had convened were to expire without an indictment, the office could be accused of shopping for a favorable outcome with a new grand jury.

Three days later, Bragg and his top aides, including Peter Pope and Susan Hoffinger, met with Pomerantz, Dunne, Conroy and the rest of the investigative team in the main conference room on the 8th floor of 1 Hogan Place. The room is within the elevator shaft of 100 Centre Street, and the meeting's participants could hear the courthouse elevators clanking up and down the conference room wall as Pomerantz presented the case about Trump's exaggerations.

The presentation was compelling. It seemed clear that the Trump Organization's annual statements, which the company submitted to lenders, contained outrageous exaggerations. But Bragg was still unclear on how exactly Trump would be linked to the financial statements—the former president hadn't personally compiled them. Another meeting was scheduled. Bragg recruited veterans, including Joshua Steinglass, one of the office's most respected trial lawyers, to cast fresh eyes on the case. It was a good opportunity to get to know his staff.

Steinglass had spent most of his career focused on street crime and was known within the office as a trial savant, a familiar personality type among New York City litigators. Some become addicted to the adrenaline and the stakes, the mix of dramatic action, strategic decision-making and real-world consequences. Steinglass was particularly obsessed with juries; he would tell younger prosecutors that connecting with the jury was among the most important things they could do. It was unusual for him to be brought in to assess a white-collar case, a sign that a new path was opening up before him in the Bragg era.

Pomerantz's net worth case didn't yet meet Bragg's standards. It wasn't clear to the D.A. how exactly prosecutors would prove that Trump had knowledge of the fraud on his company's annual financial statements and the intent to lie about it: elements necessary to win a conviction. But Bragg didn't put a halt to the grand jury presentation. In mid-January, Kate Christobek and Nate Schweber clocked witnesses associated with the case heading into 80 Centre Street accompanied by the investigative team. We began drafting a story. From outside, it looked like the investigation was moving ahead.

Over the next few days, Bragg's apprehensions about the case grew, especially when Chris Conroy sent around a memo to the new leadership team highlighting some of its weaknesses—deficiencies that accorded with Bragg's own worries, and undermined the hard sell he was receiving from Pomerantz and Dunne. More memos followed, including one from a lawyer in the New York attorney general's office that further triggered Bragg's skepticism.

Perhaps the D.A. wanted to shield dissenters from the pressure they felt from the investigation's leaders. Perhaps it was his old habit of keeping discussions within a small circle of confidantes. And it may have just been practical: Pomerantz was not often in the office. But whatever the reason, Bragg began to discuss the Trump case behind closed doors, excluding Pomerantz and Dunne. It was a slight, one that led increasingly to bad blood with the men his predecessor had trusted to lead the investigation. While Bragg, like Pomerantz, was a former federal prosecutor, he was less willing to defer to the older man's reputation than Vance had been.

Meanwhile, Bragg was still dealing with the fallout from the Day One memo. The 2022 Republican candidate for governor, Lee Zeldin, called for him to be removed from office. The widow of a police officer killed on duty in Harlem criticized the D.A. as she eulogized her husband. Faced with the full mercilessness of New York's tabloid press, Bragg retained the services of a crisis communications firm in hopes of addressing his woes. But he did not fundamentally refine his message, or deliver it at scale to a mainstream audience that could help rescue his reputation. Instead, he responded with small gestures that felt comfortable. He attended a virtual event at New York University Law School. He admitted to congregants at Abyssinian Baptist Church that he'd had a challenging couple of weeks.

On Monday, January 24, Pomerantz and Dunne met with Bragg's team in person in the 8th floor conference room. Everyone wore masks, which may have added to the air of mistrust in the room. Whatever the cause, this meeting was far worse than the January 11 presentation of Pomerantz's case against Trump. Susan Hoffinger was highly dubious of Michael Cohen's usefulness as a witness in the case about Trump's financial statements. Peter Pope said that the legal theory needed work. Bragg was not talkative and Pomerantz and Dunne worried he was distracted. By the end of the meeting, Dunne was flabbergasted. "What I'm hearing is, you have great concerns," he said.

After the meeting, Pomerantz and Dunne decided to test their new boss's commitment to the case. If Bragg's team was not prepared to give them a green light, they would pause the grand jury presentation entirely. Dunne sent an email to that effect. Hoffinger responded quickly. She agreed that the presentation should be paused.

Shivering outside 80 Centre Street in the late January cold, Nate saw no sign of grand jury activity. Willy heard from a source that a witness's scheduled appearance had been postponed. Something was up. As we frantically tried to figure out what was happening, the story we'd begun drafting forked into two alternative versions: One for the investigation moving ahead under Bragg's watch, and another for an inexplicable grand jury pause.

On the morning of January 27, Pomerantz sent Bragg an aggressively-worded email telling him the case needed more of his attention. "You need to respect our judgment, our decades of experience as prosecutors and defense lawyers, and the work that we have put into the case, more than you have to this point," he wrote before conceding: "Of course, you are the elected DA, and you must make your own judgment."

Bragg agreed to give Pomerantz as much time as he needed to make his pitch. They decided on three presentations, to be made remotely; Pomerantz was recovering from minor surgery. He would not be in person as he strove to convince the new administration of the strength of his case. He and the D.A. would never have a one-on-one meeting in the same room.

Had Pomerantz been closer to the action, he might have noticed that Bragg was not prone to moving quickly, even in the face of immense outside pressure. It took over a month for the new D.A. to finally walk back a portion of the Day One memo. On February 4, he admitted in an email to his staff that it had been a source of confusion rather than clarity.

Pomerantz's three presentations went poorly and he and Dunne smarted as Bragg continued to discuss their case with his aides, not with them. In a private email, Pomerantz compared the new regime to the Politburo. "I fear that my comments amounted to the only summation that will ever be given in this jurisdiction with respect to the crimes of Donald Trump," he wrote. On February 20, Bragg told Pomerantz he was not ready to move forward with the case. Pomerantz responded that he would leave the office if charges were not authorized. He warned Bragg that the press coverage of his decision was unlikely to be friendly.

Three days later, on February 23, Pomerantz made good on his promise, submitting his resignation letter. "I and others believe that your decision not to authorize prosecution now will doom any future prospects that Mr. Trump will be prosecuted for the criminal conduct we have been investigating," he wrote, calling the choice "a grave failure of justice."

That day, Ben Willy and I were putting the finishing touches on our story about the unexplained pause in grand jury proceedings. We'd been working on it for more than a month and I was ready to be done with it. But every time we were poised to publish, one of us got another phone call. And as morning turned to afternoon, we learned that Dunne and Pomerantz had resigned. It was a shocking development. We broke the news of their departures, writing that the future of the investigation was in serious doubt.

Coincidentally, I had an interview scheduled with Bragg that day and to my surprise, he kept the appointment. I headed downtown to 1 Hogan, and took the elevator to the 8th floor. The D.A.'s office was grand and spacious, with heavy wooden furniture that looked better suited to an embassy or the Harvard club than a courthouse. We sat at an enormous conference table in the center of the room. Bragg looked uncomfortable; it was the most awkward I'd ever found him during the dozen or so encounters we'd had to that point. I asked him about the resignations, and the most recent details we'd heard about the case.

"There's a part of me, the non-lawyer part, that wants to have a conversation with you," he told me. "But the part that's been a career prosecutor tells me I can't." He gave a small laugh. "As an office we can't say anything more than the investigation is ongoing. You've reported on *a lot* that I can't comment on at all."

Clearly, Bragg hoped that would be the end of it. But in March, we got ahold of Pomerantz's volcanic resignation letter, and published that, too. This time, Bragg declined an interview request. His communications director, Danielle Filson, said that nothing more could or should be said about an ongoing investigation.

The uproar Pomerantz had predicted swiftly followed. Alvin Bragg was a punching bag. The talk show host Jimmy Kimmel predicted Bragg would be "reviled all around the world" for backing off the case. On Twitter, anonymous users accused him of accepting a payoff from Trump. A *Washington Post* opinion piece refused to take the D.A. at his word that the investigation was continuing. The *Daily News* asked him to explain himself. And for three weeks, the world waited for that explanation.

＊　＊　＊

Prosecutors are sworn to be nonpartisan, objective in their pursuit of justice. It was something Pomerantz grappled with when it came to Donald Trump. The former president caused in him stronger emotion than any defendant he'd dealt with in his career as a trial lawyer. "I saw him as a malignant narcissist, and perhaps even a megalomaniac who posed a real danger to the country and to the ideals that mattered to me," Pomerantz wrote in a book detailing his experience in the office. "But," he added, "on a professional level, I could not allow my emotional reaction to Trump to affect my activities."

He was not the first to undergo such a struggle. There's an innate tension between prosecutors motivated to pursue high-profile cases against the villains of the day and colleagues who insist on trusting to a slower process, even if it ends without any charges. The tension has an especially rich history in New York. One of the best examples played out in Bragg and Pomerantz's old stomping grounds a couple blocks away: the Southern district.

In 1983, thirteen years after Nixon fired Morgenthau as U.S. attorney for the Southern district, Ronald Reagan appointed Rudolph W. Giuliani to the post. The fight against the mob remained the federal office's priority, and Giuliani's appointment landed him a mention in a *New York Times* magazine article headlined *"Italian Americans Coming Into Their Own."* Giuliani told journalists the mob had victimized his own family and cast a pall on his people. He wanted to end its reign for good, and burnish his reputation in the process. The magazine article noted that there was "hopeful" chatter about the possibility, someday soon, of an Italian-American president.

Giuliani billed himself as the quintessential New York crime-fighter and provided quotes to any reporter who needed them. He was, *Time* declared, "a modern haiku master who can distill a complicated answer into a crisp, 15-second sound bite." When the F.B.I. announced in August 1983 that it was dedicating individual squads to each of the five mafia families in New York, he praised it as "an excellent approach."

The prosecutor in charge of organized crime at Southern was named Walter S. Mack Jr. Unlike Giuliani, Mack ignored reporters. He thought prosecutors who talked to the press were courting disaster, potentially angering judges and making themselves vulnerable to defense lawyers. He believed speaking to reporters was inherently political. He told any journalists who dared to bother him that if they were interested in a case, they should come to the courtroom and see it for themselves.

Mack was a Vietnam veteran, who'd seen combat while stationed at Da Nang Air Force base. He thought of trial lawyering as the closest thing the civilian world had to a gun battle, an adrenaline-fueled performance where split-second decisions were the difference between victory and defeat. He was highly respected in the office, a fearsome litigator and an honorable man.

Mack followed the F.B.I.'s lead, hoping to make comprehensive criminal cases against each mafia family. But Giuliani wanted to go faster, hit harder, strike a death blow against the mob. He knew the families coordinated their dealings through a supervisory body, a guild of dons known as the commission. Giuliani assigned aides to cherry-pick the best material that had been gathered by the agents and prosecutors working on each family case, with the goal of bringing a super-case, charging the commission, the mafia bosses, in a single indictment.

Giuliani believed that cutting off the heads of so many snakes would leave the mob wriggling in disarray. But Mack disagreed. The bosses on the commission were old, on their way out. Mack told Giuliani he was sacrificing the stronger cases, and that the most violent mobsters would be unaffected by a commission trial. He believed, he told me years later, that Giuliani had been "skimming off the top for publicity reasons." Eventually, Giuliani demoted him.

The Southern district indicted nine members of the Commission in February 1985. Giuliani was gleeful. He told *Time* that the Commission prosecution was the "case of cases." "Our approach," he said then, "is to wipe out the five families."

The defendants, including three dons, were convicted. It was a media relations coup that would fuel Giuliani's political career. But there was truth to what Mack had told his boss. The most violent mobsters continued the five families' work with little interruption.

Between the February 1985 indictment and the November 1986 conviction, the head of the Gambino family, Paul Castellano, was assassinated in broad daylight outside a Midtown Manhattan steakhouse called Sparks. The killing was coordinated by a 45-year-old mob solider named John Gotti, who worked with mafiosos his age from multiple families to engineer the killing. Even as Giuliani basked in tabloids and on TV news, Gotti was minted as a star, nicknamed the Teflon Don. He played the part to the hilt, wearing double breasted silk suits, mugging for the cameras and waving his finger at detectives stalking him on stakeout, mouthing "naughty, naughty." Giuliani became New York's mayor. Gotti became the most famous criminal in America.

In the long run, Walter Mack's view prevailed. It took many more trials, many cooperators, and many years for the mafia to be as diminished as Giuliani had predicted. There are some forces that a single criminal case is ill-equipped to destroy.

Channeling Walter Mack's approach, Bragg's office initially kept to its single-line comment: That the investigation into Donald Trump was ongoing. But it was clear that the press furor would not cease without a more substantive response. On an overcast day in early April, Willy and I were invited for an interview at 1 Hogan Place.

Until I began working with Willy and Ben, I had done almost all of my reporting spontaneously, without much of an agenda. That's not how it was with those guys. We talked for hours about how we would proceed—with a story, with a meeting, even with a single conversation. As we passed under the green scaffolding that hedged Centre Street, Willy and I discussed our game plan. Willy would introduce himself and explain how we worked and why we were skeptical that the investigation was ongoing. I would lead the charge on specific questions.

On the elevator ride up to the 8th floor of 1 Hogan Place, we reviewed a statement the office issued that day. It was about 500 words. It offered a bit of Bragg's professional biography, asserted that the Trump team was interviewing new witnesses and exploring new evidence, and again insisted that the investigation was ongoing. It read like the result of an internal struggle, between someone insistent that it was necessary to say *something* and a D.A. who was highly reluctant to do so. In any case, the statement wasn't going to move the needle on the public's understanding of the investigation's status, or its trust in Bragg.

The D.A., flanked by Danielle Filson and another press aide, Emily Tuttle, greeted us warmly inside his private office. After some brief, awkward small talk, Willy began the interview we'd planned, explaining our methodology with one of his patented analogies.

"You start out the day with rumor or with a little crumb," he explained as Bragg sat across from him, affecting a look of intense interest. "And generally—not at the end of that day, but at the end of another day—you have a cookie." He paused for a response from the D.A. None was forthcoming.

"You've built a cookie out of lots of little crumbs," Willy said again, concerned that Bragg hadn't gotten it. He made to continue, but I cut him off.

"We thought it was worth saying this partly just to say this is the world in which we're operating," I explained. "We're looking for concrete signs of investigative activity and thus far we haven't been able to see them."

The pipes in the old building creaked. The district attorney was quiet.

"We don't purport to be able to see everything, but we do see a fair bit," Willy said.

We both looked at Bragg. He glanced at Danielle, asking her to kick him if he should go off the record. Then he leaned forward, and smiled.

"One," he said. "Happy you're here." His tone was extra friendly.

"Thank you," Willy said.

"What you're saying is both the conundrum I'm in but also something I'm proud of," Bragg said. "I pride myself—and perhaps in some ways it's hurting us here—on how discreet we are. What you've just told me, unless y'all are great poker players, is that you don't know what we're doing."

"That gives me some pride," he added. "Because you're not *supposed* to know."

I peppered Bragg with questions about the specifics of the ongoing investigation. Who were the new witnesses? What industry did they work in? But the district attorney refused to say anything that went beyond the office's official statement.

"We spent a lot of time on the statement," he said, almost apologetic.

Willy told him it didn't seem like enough to merely assure our readers that something was happening. "There's an expression," he told Bragg. "Show don't tell."

Bragg looked as if he were up against a physical barrier. He said that he wanted the public to have faith in the D.A. when he said that something was happening. "I understand 'show your work,'" he said. But at the same time, "I have a limitation that I can't cross."

"You're essentially—and I'm not taking issue with it at all," Willy said. "Because you're not answering any questions, you're in effect asking us and our readers to take it on faith that this is ongoing. Can you speak directly to our readers and tell them why they should take it on faith? That you're still pursuing this investigation actively?"

Finally, Bragg seemed annoyed. His eyes narrowed and his voice rose.

"This is not new to me," he said. "I've been doing this. I think it important that the public know that. And know that I—as a career prosecutor—say we are taking steps. But, consistent with my obligation, not telling you what those are. As the district attorney of Manhattan, building on the fine tradition of this office, that's what we're doing. So it's up to you how to report it."

"It is *painful*," he said. "And I think *injurious to broader justice principles* to have the institution not believed."

That was it. We thanked him politely and walked out. On the street, under the scaffolding, Willy fumed. The fine tradition of the office? What had he been talking about? "Morgenthau leaked like a sieve!" he said.

❖   ❖   ❖

What we might have heard, had we been able to read perfectly between the lines, was that, in the spring of 2022, Bragg was starting over. Susan Hoffinger was named the investigation's leader. Peter Pope was heavily involved. Chris Conroy remained in the mix. And after the last of the old line assistants, Solomon Shinerock, stepped back from the inquiry, Bragg recruited new prosecutors from within the office. Rebecca Mangold, who went by Becky, and Katherine Ellis, who went by KC. The new team had a big advantage: Vance had spent almost five years collecting evidence. There was a lot to review. At first, their progress was erratic. No one quite knew where to start.

But both Bragg and Pope were intrigued by the issue that Vance's team had considered and set aside several different times: Michael Cohen's hush money payment to Stormy Daniels, who, incidentally, was about to make her pseudonym legal. In May 2022 she filed for a name change from Stephanie Gregory Clifford to Stormy Daniels Barratt. The alter ego originally chosen for adult entertainment—one she'd always preferred to Stephanie—would become her legal name.

At 1 Hogan Place, the hush money case had been considered, dispensed with, and brought back to life so many times that the line assistants had dubbed it the "zombie case." There were differing opinions on Bragg's team about how to make the conduct work as a criminal charge in New York state. Some thought it was acceptable to charge Trump with falsifying business records to cover up a violation of federal law. But others thought they needed a predicate crime that couldn't be easily thrown out by a state judge.

Susan Hoffinger broke off to prepare with Joshua Steinglass for the trial against Trump's company and the Muppet-like bookkeeper Allen Weisselberg.

But Conroy, Mangold and Ellis began to meet weekly, studying the timeline of the hush money payment and all of the people involved. There were a lot of them. Not just Michael Cohen and Stormy Daniels, but David Pecker, the formidable former publisher of the National Enquirer, and his top editor, Dylan Howard. Karen McDougal, who also received a Trump payoff, and Keith Davidson, the Los Angeles lawyer who represented Daniels and McDougal in 2016.

Allen Weisselberg—who in August pleaded guilty to the tax fraud scheme for which he was indicted, leaving Trump's company as the only defendant—was included in the roster of hush money actors, too. He was the architect of the method used to reimburse Cohen and supervised various Trump Organization subordinates who helped send Cohen his checks. And finally, there was Robert Costello, a lawyer with close ties to Rudy Giuliani who provided eyebrow-raising counsel to Michael Cohen in the spring of 2018, as Cohen began to question his loyalty to Trump. Cohen and Costello quickly fell out and ever since, Costello was like a vengeful ghost following the former fixer wherever he went to warn anyone predisposed to listen that Cohen was a liar, a schemer and a son of a bitch.

Given the expansive cast of characters and the intricate chronology that led to the final reimbursement to Cohen in December 2017, there was a lot for the prosecutors to take in. Though many discrete parts of the story were known to the public, piecing it all together took no shortage of work. In this sense, the fact pattern—the conduct assessed in any evaluation of potential criminal charges—were highly characteristic of the Trump era, so abstruse that only someone wholly dedicated to the story would be able to understand it.

Peter Pope often joined Conroy, Ellis and Mangold in their 2022 meetings, though he would also pursue his own hunches and ideas on the side. Initially, as the team worked, they proceeded under the assumption that if no better option came to light, Trump *could* be charged with having falsified documents to cover up the federal crime to which Cohen had pleaded guilty.

But one afternoon that summer, Bragg held a discussion with

some of the team's members. Federal statutes tended to have equivalents in state law. Perhaps there was a state election law that would work, allowing the prosecutors to avoid the risks of importing a federal crime into state court.

The line assistants were gearing up to look for a state law that fit, when they received an email from the D.A. He had found something: a little-known election statute known as §17–152:

> **ELN 17–152—Conspiracy to promote or prevent election:** "Any two or more persons *who conspire to promote or prevent the election of any person to a public office by unlawful means* and which conspiracy is acted upon by one or more of the parties thereto, shall be guilty of a misdemeanor."

If Trump could be shown to have *criminally* conspired to promote his own election in 2016, the calculus of white-collar law might allow the office to charge him with FBR1—felony falsifying business records—without having to rely on a federal predicate crime. Bragg began to believe it could work.

He wanted to wait until completion of the tax fraud trial of Trump's company to ramp up the investigation into the former president himself. Privately, he began to analogize the trial of the company and the investigation into the former president as chapters in a book—the trial against Trump's company would precede any legal action against Trump the individual.

While preparing for the tax fraud trial, Steinglass and Hoffinger developed a sibling-like chemistry, complete with occasional bickering. In December 2022, Steinglass delivered the case's closing in bombastic fashion. The jurors' verdict—guilty on all counts—proved that Steinglass could be as formidable an opponent to a disembodied corporation as he'd been to murderers and crooked cops. The conviction he and Hoffinger won against Trump's company was the first major victory of Bragg's tenure. Perhaps, after the bumpy start, he could begin to recover his reputation in his second year in office.

After the sentencing in January 2023, Bragg took his pet analogy public. The sentencing, he said, "closes this important chapter of our ongoing investigation into the former president and his businesses. We now move on to the next chapter."

That month, Bragg announced the hiring of Matthew Colangelo, who'd worked for him at the New York attorney general's office. Colangelo had been working at the U.S. Justice Department for two years, commuting down to Washington from New York and he was tired of the travel taking him away from his family. He began to cast about for a job in the city, and soon connected with his old boss. Bragg was thrilled at the chance to hire Colangelo. The official announcement indicated that the new senior counsel would have a broad remit—and that he would work on the office's "most sensitive and high-profile white-collar investigations."

Though the Trump investigative team was already on the road to an indictment, Colangelo plugged in nicely as an even-keeled lawyer with Bragg's trust, and his ear. He helped remedy some of the chaos and infighting that marred the team's initial months working together, and helped steer the case as, early in 2023, the prosecutors began to present evidence to a newly empaneled grand jury.

❧   ❧   ❧

To envision the full scope of the crime as Bragg's team saw it, it's best to start chronologically. In the summer of 2015, National Enquirer publisher David Pecker was summoned to Trump Tower for a meeting with the new presidential candidate. Pecker and Trump had been scratching each other's backs for years: Pecker would feature Trump in his magazines. In return, Trump would clue him in on celebrity gossip.

In his office on the 26th floor, with attorney-fixer Michael Cohen on hand, Trump asked Pecker what his magazines could do for the campaign. Pecker said he would promote Trump's candidacy and denigrate his opponents. He also pledged to keep an eye out for stories damaging to the campaign. He would notify Michael Cohen, who would bear some responsibility for squashing the stories.

To Bragg's thinking, that 2015 agreement was a conspiracy to promote Trump's election—the beginning of the violation of state election law 17–152, the predicate crime needed to indict Trump with a felony. Trump was a silent partner, guiding Pecker and Cohen's actions while keeping his own hands clean.

The election law statute required that the conspiracy be pursued by unlawful means. The way prosecutors saw it, the unlawful means of promoting Trump to public office were taken along the way: Pecker and Cohen falsified a number of documents as they bought silence from those who possessed damaging information about Trump, while simultaneously masking their actions.

Pecker ultimately fulfilled his promise, suppressing two stories, one of a doorman who falsely claimed the candidate had a baby out of wedlock, and one of the former Playboy model, Karen McDougal, who had an affair with Trump the same year he slept with Daniels.

But Pecker was never reimbursed for the first two deals and refused to pay for Stormy Daniels's story. On October 7, David Fahrenthold, a *Washington Post* reporter, alerted the world to the existence of the "Access Hollywood" tape. On the tape, recorded years earlier, Trump talked with gusto about grabbing, kissing and groping women. "When you're a star, they let you do it," he'd said. "You can do anything. Grab 'em by the pussy."

After the "Access Hollywood" tape was released in October 2016, Cohen felt he had no choice but to buy the story himself. He did so with Trump's permission, making an illegal campaign donation in the form of a hush money payment. That was another of the potential unlawful means that allowed the legal theory to function.

One of the oddities of the Bragg theory was the way that the crime was spread through time: The conspiracy was formed in 2015, and Pecker and Cohen played their assigned roles throughout 2016. But it was only in 2017 that the final piece slipped into place: The cover-up, in the form of falsified business records.

It was agreed that Michael Cohen would be reimbursed for his troubles, not in a lump sum of $130,000—bound to invite questions—but over a period of 12 months. The D.A.'s office possessed records of every document relating to that reimbursement—11 invoices sent by Cohen, 11 checks received by Cohen and 12 entries in the general ledger of the Trump Organization. (The reimbursements preceded the prosecution's final example of "unlawful means" used to advance the conspiracy: Trump Organization tax forms which inaccurately classified the payments to Cohen as compensation.)

Prosecutors believed that Trump approved the repayment scheme in January 2017, at a second Trump Tower meeting just before his presidential inauguration. There were three participants in that meeting: Trump, Allen Weisselberg and Cohen. But only Cohen would testify about it for the prosecutors, who did not trust Weisselberg, let alone Trump himself, to tell the truth.

Cohen would be an utterly crucial witness. Others could provide evidence of Trump's involvement in the payoffs. But only Michael Cohen would say that Trump himself had given the order to falsify the documents, which put him squarely in violation of the law. Cohen's story about the hush money payment and the falsified reimbursements had remained consistent since he turned on Trump in 2018.

But unfortunately for the prosecutors, Cohen's credibility was questionable at best. He'd pleaded guilty to nine criminal counts in the Southern District in 2018, some related to the hush money payments to Daniels and McDougal and others for making false statements to a bank and to Congress. Though he said he'd made the payments on Trump's behalf, his attitude toward his former patron was so poisonous that defense lawyers would inevitably accuse him of having a vendetta against the president.

Ultimately, each of the 34 counts of falsifying business records with which Trump was charged included an accusation of at least two other criminal acts: the election conspiracy and one or more of the "unlawful means" that Pecker and Cohen used to carry out the conspiracy. To the horror of my editors, I began to compare each of the charges in the indictment to a Russian Nesting Doll. Falsifying Business Records in the First Degree was the outermost doll. The second doll was the election law violation, 17–152. And the third doll was any one in a varied set of unlawful means: false records related to the catch-and-kill transactions, the illegal campaign donations that prosecutors believed the transactions represented and the tax law violations represented by the Trump Organization tax documents.

It was complicated. Explaining it reminded me of trying to walk a friend through the fundamentals of the blockchain, or the applicability of quantum mechanics. You could understand it one day and forget it the next.

Ultimately, it was a criminal case whose legitimacy was in the eye of the beholder. Once understood in all their complexity, the charges could be considered elegant—or hopelessly jerry-rigged.

Come April 2023, many in the commentariat would opt for the latter. The charge of falsifying business records was often said to have been "elevated" by the state election crime, as if a misdemeanor was being hoisted onto the shaky stool of another misdemeanor in order to qualify as a felony. That was the hierarchical way of looking at it. Falsifying business records was the top charge, after all.

But Bragg was not a hierarchical thinker, and there was another way to understand the charges. They could be viewed horizontally, with the conspiracy, the violation of the election law, in the center as the most important piece. Bragg's prosecutors accused Trump, Cohen and Pecker of conspiring to hide information from the American public during the 2016 election campaign. That was the original crime, that, in combination with the cover-up, merited felony charges.

A Morgenthau or a Giuliani might have worked harder to figure out the perfect sound bite. But sound bites weren't part of Bragg's skill set. Besides, he'd been burned by the press. He and his office would heed Willy's show-don't-tell adage. They were not going to expend a lot of effort explaining to people why their case was significant. Instead, they would show their work—at trial. And like Walter Mack used to say, if journalists wanted to understand it, they would have to come to the courtroom and see for themselves.

CHAPTER THREE

ATTENTION SEEKING

On April 7, 2024, twelve days before he killed himself outside a Manhattan courthouse, Max Azzarello ambled downstairs to his neighbors' apartment in St. Augustine, Florida, holding a fistful of glowsticks.

Max, short and wiry, with brown, shoulder-length hair, would often go "cat fishing" with his neighbor, Mandy McAlmont. Together they would drag a small toy alligator across her carpet for the neighborhood strays, Skittles and Midnight. Max had a similar idea for the glowsticks. He, Mandy and Mandy's boyfriend, Steve Satterfield, went outside to their sprawling, shared backyard, where high above the camphor trees in the cobalt North Florida sky, a family of bats circled.

Max and Steve hurled the glowsticks toward the trees to draw the bats' attention. It didn't work. Mandy suggested Max wave his glowstick around. That didn't work either. Then, as if he'd been touched by some cosmic force, Max made a particularly elegant toss. As the neon glowstick arced perfectly through the air, a bat swooped down to kiss it.

"Hey hey hey hey!" Max said, delighted. "I got him!"

It was a rare win for Max. Lately, he'd been struggling to be noticed. Growing up in Sea Cliff, Long Island, Max had relied on his mother Libby's loving attention. When Max was a precocious four-year-old,

Libby drilled him on triple-digit multiplication problems on family road trips. When Max was a teenager, curious about the way the country was organized, Libby spoke to him at the dinner table about politics and policy. The conversations stoked Max's lifelong interest in civics and his growing concerns as a young adult about failures and fault-lines in American society.

He was intrigued by alternatives to the mainstream. Socialism maybe, or anarchism. Given his interest in widespread change, he was not notably upset when Trump was elected in 2016, certainly no more so than any of his friends. Like many New Yorkers, he had a third-degree connection to the new president. One of his sisters had worked as a wardrobe assistant on "Celebrity: Apprentice."

For years, his mother had been fighting obstructive pulmonary disease, and as COVID hit, Libby's chronic illness worsened. In 2022, Max moved from Philadelphia to St. Augustine, determined to take care of her. But nothing worked. She died in April, the month after he arrived.

Then, in the spring of 2023, Max was captured by an obsession he could not stop talking about. He came to believe that almost everyone in American public life was a secret fascist. Donald Trump, Joe Biden and the Clintons were secret fascists. So were Elon Musk, Sean Hannity, Whoopi Goldberg and the creators of "The Simpsons." Max's downstairs neighbor, Steve, was a big music fan, but Max warned him that most of the famous musicians were also fascists: The Doors and Pink Floyd and at least some of the Rolling Stones. Max had already written off Skittles, the cat, as a secret fascist, and he was growing concerned about Midnight, too. Three days after he went bat fishing, the day before his 37th birthday, Max caught the black cat giving him an odd look. "Not you too, Midnight," he groaned.

Max posted constantly on Instagram about secret fascists, eager for allies to help spread the word. On the back of his white Toyota 4Runner, he wrote: "TRUMP IS WITH HILLARY AND THEY'RE ABOUT TO FASCIST COUP US." He struggled to convince anyone. When he started explaining his theory, people just shut down. Even his family—his father, Richard, and two sisters, Pasqualina and Katy—seemed at times to have run out of patience.

In August 2023, four months after Trump was indicted, Max was arrested several times for disorderly conduct. His probation ended in early April 2024. Having never before mentioned any plan to do so, he told his neighbor Mandy that he was now free to go to New York. He packed a suitcase full of homemade pamphlets and flew up on Sunday, pulled to his home state by an unseen force. He told Richard that he planned to stay in an Airbnb on 140th Street

He was one of many people who that week found themselves compelled to attend the Manhattan trial of Donald J. Trump. The place where all the cameras were going to be. The place where, finally, Max could get his message out.

❖   ❖   ❖

On Monday, April 15, the hubbub manifested outside 100 Centre Street before dawn, settling in for a long spring run. In the early morning darkness, sirens flashed on police cars stationed outside metal barricades that formed a blocks-long perimeter around the courthouse. Outside the border, city life continued, oblivious to the commotion. But when the sun rose over the municipal buildings, it illuminated a legion of reporters and ranks of television cameras packed so densely around Collect Pond Park that a falcon watching from a nearby rooftop would be hard-pressed to see any sidewalk.

Ben Protess, Willy Rashbaum, Kate Christobek and I had been preparing for months, and now the day was here. The first criminal trial of Donald J. Trump. The scene resembled the arraignment a year earlier, but the feeling was different: This time, the fanfare was planned in advance and the circus was expected to last at least six weeks. It was not a one-off news event—more like the first day of school.

The trial would not be broadcast in any form—New York law forbade video and audio recording without express permission from on high. Court officers were trained to treat cell phones like grenades. It would be up to the press to tell the world, through the increasingly anachronistic medium of text, what was happening inside 100 Centre Street each day. The *Times* was planning to run a daily live-blog, commenting on the proceedings moment by moment as if we were sportscasters. The journalist Jeffrey Toobin, who'd become famous covering O.J. Simpson's trial in the 1990s, predicted that, given the absence of television cameras, the trial would fail to become a public obsession. But we were determined to make up for the lack as best we could.

Sean Piccoli showed up that first day on assignment for Deadline, the Hollywood trade site for which he sometimes freelanced. But the rest of our team was intact, and our ranks were expanding: Kate Christobek would be in the courthouse each day, while Nate Schweber patrolled the outskirts of Collect Pond Park for news. Maggie Haberman, the *Times*'s foremost Trump reporter, would be joining us for the trial, as would Jesse McKinley, a longtime political reporter and graceful writer, and Sue Craig, an investigative reporter who'd obtained Trump the tax returns Trump had refused to share. Michael Rothfeld, a former Wall Street Journal reporter who'd helped to break the first stories about the hush money payments, was on standby.

While jury selection was ongoing, only six journalists at a time would be permitted entry to Justice Juan Merchan's domain. That meant many of the reporters who'd packed the gallery for the arraignment in April 2024 would now be shunted to the overflow room. There they'd watch the proceedings on the closed-circuit TVs that transmitted with a tape delay, crowded together in a sweaty smelly stew, missing out on the small moments that would give the coverage life, the shame and grandeur of a president on trial.

The seating was so limited because the vast majority of the gallery was reserved for prospective jurors. Hundreds of Manhattan residents had been summoned to 100 Centre Street for jury duty on April 15, 2024. Twelve would determine whether the former president was guilty. They were ordinary people, thrust temporarily into the most consequential seats in the republic. Commentators were predicting that the jury selection process would take two weeks or more, given how difficult it would be to find New Yorkers who could be fair to Donald Trump.

In official accounts of newsworthy trials, jury selection is often overlooked. Yet it's among the most crucial elements of the entire process. For the dedicated trial lawyer, the jury is by far the most important audience, and jury selection is the only period during which the lawyers get to scrutinize that audience. All of the attention in the well of the courtroom is fixed on the jury box. Once the jury is seated, the roles are permanently reversed. The jurors' attention flows toward the lawyers, until it is time for a verdict. In the weeks before Trump's trial, Justice Merchan determined the jurors' identities would be permanently withheld from the public. The threat to those deciding the former president's fate was too great for their anonymity to be violated.

Justice Merchan was a standout among state court judges. Having been on the bench for nearly twenty years, he was known as a bastion of sanity in the Wild West of the New York court system. Born in Colombia and raised in New York, he was the first in his family to go to college. Like many homegrown lawyers who occupy seats of judicial prominence in New York, he started his legal career as a prosecutor at the Manhattan district attorney's office under Morgenthau. He became a judge in 2005 and quickly displayed a knack for keeping the courtroom under control.

His ability to get a jury seated and the trial proper underway would be his first real test. Merchan had every intention of confirming his reputation. He would do all he could to halt Trumpian chaos at the double doors of Part 59.

By 9 am, the reporters were shoulder to shoulder in the back row on the right, clattering on the laptops that Robert Balin, the media lawyer, had helped win us the right to use. By 9:30, Trump was seated at the defense table, his eyes bleary, accompanied by his triumvirate of lawyers, while reporters traded around a Truth Social post he'd sent minutes earlier calling Michael Cohen a serial perjurer. By 9:50, Alvin Bragg was seated in the second row, leaning forward intently as if the proceedings had already started. And at 9:59, Merchan took his seat on the bench. The trial was set to begin.

But it didn't.

Defense lawyers Todd Blanche, Emil Bove and Susan Necheles had made multiple last-ditch efforts to force a delay—a standard defense tactic that Trump's representatives ratcheted up to an extreme. A large part of their strategy involved burying the judge in aggressively worded motions, some of them repetitive, requesting everything from a change in venue to overturning the gag order that kept Trump from attacking witnesses and jurors. Merchan still hadn't dug himself free of the pile of papers that they had heaped atop him. The motion now holding up the trial called on him to recuse himself from the case. It was not the first time the defense had made the request.

Among the numerous reasons Trump's lawyers listed for recusal were the affiliations of the judge's daughter, Loren Merchan, the president of a political marketing firm who'd worked with Democratic candidates, including Kamala Harris and Adam Schiff. Years earlier, Loren Merchan had mentioned on a podcast that her father disliked when politicians used Twitter.

Merchan declined to recuse himself on the basis of those comments, or his daughter's work. He said Trump's lawyers made use of "inferences, innuendos and unsupported speculation" to build a case against him.

He asked Joshua Steinglass and Todd Blanche if there were any issues to address before the trial could start.

There were. The prosecutor and the defense lawyer were equally concerned with the evidence that Merchan would allow. A judge has broad authority over the facts jurors are permitted to hear and the lawyers fought each point of contention to the hilt. Merchan ruled that the prosecution could *not* tell the jury that Melania Trump had been pregnant during Trump's affair with Karen McDougal, but that they *could* show jurors negative headlines about Trump's opponents that had appeared in the National Enquirer in 2016.

Trump fell asleep, his head creeping toward his chest, before snapping back upright. Shortly before noon, Merchan lost his patience. He told Blanche and Steinglass to act like professionals and work out the remaining issues on their own time.

"We have about 500 jurors waiting," he said. "I'll be honest with you, I'm really not interested in getting involved in this minutiae."

❖   ❖   ❖

One of the 500 was a greying bookseller and devoted Democrat named Michael Zorek, who in that moment was seated in a downstairs assembly hall.

Zorek was fully aware that Trump's trial was kicking off that morning—he had passed through the hordes of onlookers to get in the building and carry out his civic duty. But neither the frenetic energy outside 100 Centre Street nor the caged frenzy on the 15th floor had spread to the lower echelons of the courthouse. Zorek felt like he was at the DMV. He spent the morning drinking Diet Coke, his favorite, and busying himself with his volunteer get out the vote efforts. At one point, a court staffer called on him to present his official jury summons and slashed through his name with black Sharpie, leaving only his number, B113, as identification.

Zorek believed the likelihood of actually being chosen for the Trump jury was akin to winning the lottery, and he was not sure that he or any of the dozens in the same room with him were even in the selection pool. He figured they would all be piped into different courtrooms throughout the enormous building, distributed like the balls in a Plinko game.

Soon, it was time for lunch. Zorek asked a small group in the elevator whether anyone knew of a spot to eat nearby. Timi Lee, a veterinarian, volunteered a Chinese restaurant, Uncle Lou's, one of the best in the city. Over a plate of beef and string beans, Lee told Zorek she was absolutely confident they were in the pool for the Trump trial.

By the time he got back to 100 Centre Street, Zorek was contemplating life as a Trump juror. Avoiding the news would be onerous. He would have to stop reading *The Times*, to fix his alarm so it stopped blaring NPR every morning. But he was confident he could do a good job. Around 2 pm, his musings were interrupted as the first panel of prospective jurors, 96 of them in all, was finally summoned upstairs.

The group got off the elevator to a dark, green-tinted 15th floor hallway flooded with security personnel, and formed lines to pass through ancient body scanners. They were shepherded by aggravated court officers in navy uniforms. Tense men in suits and earpieces watched closely. After making it through security, the prospective jurors were marched past a pen filled with photographers, their cameras studiously pointed toward the ground. Zorek and the others proceeded toward the opposite end of the hallway and walked through the double doors of a dimly lit courtroom. *Wow*, Zorek thought to himself. *I guess this is where it's happening.*

Light streamed in from enormous windows behind the jury box, illuminating a once-grand room fallen into disrepair. Zorek passed a row of reporters in the back, Maggie Haberman and five others, staring up from their laptops at the new arrivals. He sat down two rows behind Alvin Bragg. He picked out Justice Merchan and some of the other lawyers, who he'd seen in the news. He looked over to his left. There, at the defense table, was Donald Trump.

Like many New Yorkers, Zorek, had encountered Trump before. After all, the former president was at one point a Manhattan main character, a colossus within the media-generated version of New York. There was Trump in "Home Alone 2," giving Macaulay Culkin directions in the lobby of the Plaza hotel. There was Trump in "Sex and the City," flirting absentmindedly with Samantha. Trump had even appeared the blog that Zorek ran as a stay-at-home dad in the early 2000s. The blog featured photos of celebrities with his infant son. Its tagline was "where the elite meet the petite." The celebrities included Bill Clinton, Sean "Puffy" Combs, Anderson Cooper—and Trump, scowling from the signing table at a downtown Borders, where he was promoting his new book, "How to Get Rich." Zorek's son, sitting pink-faced on the table next to the future president, scowled too.

That was ages ago, back when Trump was just a celebrity, as opposed to THE celebrity. From the defense table, his stare carried a more heightened charge. Zorek felt a little stunned. But he reminded himself that he was there for a reason. This was a court of law. And Trump was the defendant.

The prospective jurors rose as one in the gallery, raised their right hands and swore to tell the truth. Then, from his perch on high, Merchan addressed them for the first time, speaking the trial into reality.

"The name of this case is The People of the State of New York versus Donald Trump," he said. Trump, his arms folded in resignation, closed his eyes. Merchan continued for 30 minutes, giving no indication to the group that anything about the case was out of the ordinary. In the solemn unfamiliarity of the courtroom, many jurors look to their judge as a surrogate parent. Merchan's insistence on the normality of the proceedings was not lost on them.

Once he was finished, Merchan asked those who felt they couldn't be fair and impartial to raise their hands. Fifty-three people did, and were dismissed one-by-one. Soon, the courtroom was more than halfway empty. In the back row on the right, the reporters continued their typing. Zorek kept his place.

The sergeant at arms stood and began to yell out juror numbers, assigning each to a seat in the jury box. Seat number six belonged to

Juror B113. Michael Zorek walked past Trump and filed into the box, where he could see the lay of the whole courtroom. A court officer handed him a piece of paper with more than three dozen questions, the first phase of the selection process. *In what neighborhood do you live? What do you like to do in your spare time? Have you ever considered yourself a supporter of the QAnon movement? Do you have strong opinions about whether a former president may be criminally charged in state court?*

The lawyers silently took notes as, one at a time, the eighteen citizens in the jury box answered the questionnaire aloud, occasionally appealing to Merchan for guidance. Zorek was surprised how curt others were when asked if they had strong opinions about a former president being charged in state court. "No," said the brunette oncology nurse in seat number two. "No," said the salesman with the subtle Irish accent in seat number four. To Zorek, it seemed the appropriate answer required a little elaboration.

"I feel that nobody is above the law," he said when it was his turn. "Whether it be a former president, or sitting president, or a janitor."

Several more jurors answered their questionnaires, none with Zorek's performative flair. A few minutes before 4:30, they were dismissed for the day. Not a single juror had been seated.

Once the prospective jurors were gone, Justice Merchan made to excuse the lawyers. But Todd Blanche stopped him. There was an issue he wanted to discuss. Oral arguments in Trump's appeal before the Supreme Court—that his status as a former president granted him broad immunity from prosecution—were set for the following Thursday, April 25.

"President Trump very much wants to attend," Blanche said. At the defense table, the former president offered the judge a small smile.

"Look, arguments before the Supreme Court are a big deal. I could certainly appreciate why your client wants to be there," Merchan said. "But having a trial in New York County Supreme Court with a jury of twelve and perhaps six alternates, that's also a big deal. It's important that your client be here in person."

"Judge, I very much agree," Blanche said, disagreeing. "We don't think we should be here at all right now. Certainly, an accommodation for something like a Supreme Court argument—"

Merchan cut him off. "You don't think you should be here at all?"

"Correct," Blanche said. He reminded Merchan that the defense objected to holding the trial, given the ongoing presidential campaign.

Merchan sighed. "Let's move along from that, ok? I've already ruled on that. Your client is a defendant in New York County Supreme Court. He's required to be here."

Blanche's comments would shadow my understanding of the defense's role in the weeks to come. Trump and his team were in a posture of permanent refusal when it came to the trial. They objected to the idea that it was progressing, that it was lawful, and that it represented a threat to the former president's freedom. That was why they fought to delay the proceedings at every turn. Though they were grudgingly participating, their real goal was to halt the trial and, if possible, end it altogether.

⚜   ⚜   ⚜

That afternoon, Alex Bronzini-Vender, a high school senior, strolled to Washington Square Park to enjoy the sun during his lunch break. Near the Bobst Library, he encountered Max Azzarello, holding a sign that said "N.Y.U. Is a Mob Front."

Bronzini-Vender enjoyed a good conspiracy theory, and he approached to ask about the sign. Max launched into an elaborate monologue that the high schooler could barely follow. All the same, Bronzini-Vender took a liking to him; Max didn't come across as a grifter, a self-promoter, or someone in crisis, but rather as a loopy Samaritan, concerned about the state of the world. Max handed him a pamphlet, which repeated the claim about N.Y.U. Bronzini-Vender tweeted a picture of it to his followers. "Learning," he joked.

Max didn't mind the gag; he reposted the high-schooler's tweet on his Instagram stories. Social media was ground zero for his efforts to convince others about the threat posed by the fascist elite.

His online persona had offered a clue to his private struggles since March 2023. That month, he changed his title on LinkedIn, proclaiming himself self-employed as a "research investigator." He changed his bio, too. The new text: "We've got a secret fascism problem."

The following month, exactly a year after his mother's death and immediately following Trump's arraignment, Max went missing for about a week. When he reemerged, he began to tell anyone who would listen about the conspiracy. Cryptocurrency, he believed, was a Ponzi scheme on a global scale, designed to destroy the world economy and in the aftermath of collapse, elites would initiate a coup.

Max would stay awake for 36 hours at a time, fueled by amphetamines, obsessed with finding the root of the conspiracy so he could expose it to the world. It was a bizarro version of his long-lasting interest in civics, but there was little room for nuance, or reason. It was as if the synapses in his brain had been forced into alignment with his theory, and they never shifted back. He could appear normal in conversation, as sweet and engaged as ever. But when he began talking about his theory, his whole personality, even his voice, changed. He bombarded his Instagram followers with his ideas, but that only served to alert his social world that something was wrong.

Max was increasingly in pain. No one would listen to him. In August 2023, he threw a glass of wine at a framed autograph from President Clinton in the lobby of the Casa Monica hotel in St. Augustine. He was arrested. He was arrested again, and again. Finally, he was jailed with no bond, and placed in solitary confinement. He called it the torture box. His breakfast was brought to him at 4:30 in the morning and he told his sisters he was being beaten by jail officers. Still, when he called them, he would take the time to ask them to look up the price of Bitcoin. His theory was alive and well.

His family asked that Max receive court-mandated treatment and therapy. In October, he was sentenced to six months' probation, along with an outpatient treatment program that lasted only 12 weeks and consisted of "group therapy" in which an official would read a booklet to a group of four to eight men sitting at a table. It was worse than nothing at all.

❖   ❖   ❖

Shortly before noon on Tuesday, April 16, the prosecutor Joshua Steinglass addressed Michael Zorek and the other prospective jurors directly for the first time. Steinglass was a large man with a large head and small glasses. He stood at a wooden lectern behind the prosecution table, smiling at the jurors like he was hosting them in his home. He did not so much as steal a glance at the former president seated to his left.

Despite his success at the Trump Organization trial, Steinglass had been eager to return to the homicide cases with which he was comfortable. But after Trump was indicted, Bragg asked the prosecutor to join the trial team. Steinglass didn't say yes right away. First, he reviewed the case. Then, he said yes.

To the prospective jurors I've interviewed, Steinglass seemed honest, humble, maybe a little bumbling, but basically like a stand-up guy. In reality, any clumsiness was a façade; he was fast on his feet, aggressive and smart.

It was time for voir dire, the final hurdle before the first jurors could be seated.

Given that every prospective juror seated in the box had been given the option to leave voluntarily, it followed that all of them were willing—and perhaps, eager—to be chosen. But Steinglass didn't acknowledge that potentially unflattering fact. Instead, he appealed to any reluctance they might feel.

"I'm sure many of you are saying to yourself, *how am I being considered for this case?*" he said. "We are going to ask you not to try to get out of it. Just to kind of resist the urge to flee the courtroom." A few of the prospective jurors smiled weakly.

He asked whether their political beliefs would affect their judgment. They assured him politics were irrelevant. He asked them whether they could believe witnesses regardless of minor discrepancies in their accounts. They said they could.

He noted that many of the witnesses carried *baggage*. After all, they included a tabloid publisher, an adult film star and the notorious former Trump lawyer, Michael Cohen, who'd pled guilty to several federal crimes, including lying to Congress. Steinglass asked the group if they could keep an open mind to what those kinds of witnesses had to say. They nodded.

Then, he unfurled a more complicated question. He asked the prospective jurors to imagine a husband who hired a hit man to kill his wife. Even if the husband wasn't present at the scene of the killing, Steinglass asserted, he was every bit as responsible for the murder as the person who pulled the trigger. "Can you all follow the same kind of logic in this case?" he asked them.

The jurors said they could. By analogy, Trump was the murderous husband directing others—not to kill, but to falsify documents. The defense lawyers were surprisingly silent, watching like spectators, with no hint of an objection. Steinglass sat down, satisfied.

Todd Blanche walked to the lectern. His broad shoulders were clothed in an expensive suit. His collar was stiff, well-fitted. He introduced himself: "I represent President Trump."

Blanche was at a natural disadvantage. In a Manhattan jury pool, there were bound to be numerous prospective jurors who hated his client. Blanche was irrevocably associated with Trump. He wasn't planning on distancing himself.

Instead, the defense's hope was to smuggle onto the final panel at least one juror who might look askance at the prosecution's case. Though there was little hope for a full acquittal, one appropriately skeptical juror could result in a hung jury, a mistrial, and an irreversible delay.

Blanche told the group seated in the jury box that he didn't mean to be judgmental at all. But it was fairly easy to simply say one would be fair and impartial. He announced that he would use his first interaction with the potential jurors to "test that a little bit." He told them not to worry about offending him, or the former president. There were no wrong answers.

Justice Merchan watched quietly as Blanche went down the line of 18, asking each person for their opinion of his client.

"I don't really have one," said a first prospective juror.

"I'm not someone who's really into politics," said a second.

"There's things associated with him that I agree with and things that I don't really have an opinion on," said a third.

Blanche arrived at Zorek.

"I believe you're juror number 113," Blanche said.

"Yeah," Zorek said.

Blanche asked him to talk about his opinion of President Trump.

"My opinion of President Trump—whether as a President, former President, or candidate—has absolutely no bearing on the case that you're presenting," Zorek said.

"I appreciate that," Blanche said. "What is your view of President Trump?"

"That's what I'm saying," Zorek said. "My view doesn't matter. If you were sitting in a bar, I'd be happy to tell you, but in this room, what I feel about President Trump is not important."

It was the first conflict between a lawyer and a prospective juror, and the tension bounced off the walls. The reporters in the back row typed more rapidly.

Blanche swapped out blunt force for finesse. "Give us a little bit," he said. "We want to evaluate whether you're fair and impartial—not just me and not just President Trump, but everybody in this room."

"You're asking me to play my political views into a criminal case and to me, they're two different things," Zorek said. "I'll say I'm a Democrat. So there you go, but that's it. I walk in here, and he's a defendant. That's all he is."

Blanche moved on. He asked the other prospective jurors about their opinions of Trump.

"I find him fascinating and mysterious," said Juror B-89, an older man with curly hair down to his shoulders. "He walks into a room and he sets people off, one way or the other. I find that really interesting. *Really? This one guy could do all of this? Wow.* That's what I think."

✦   ✦   ✦

Mayor Eric Adams paid a visit to the courthouse during the lunch break, enjoying the unseasonably warm weather. He strolled along Centre Street as if on tour, his head reflecting the glare of the midday sun. The reporters stuck outside the courthouse thrust their cell phones up in the sky, recording video as he greeted them.

"Mr. Mayor, what do you say to people who say Donald Trump can't get a fair trial in New York City?" one asked him.

The mayor shook his head. "That is beyond my pay grade," he said.

Inside the building, the lawyers couldn't take much of a break. They spent the early afternoon poring over their notes as they sought to win an advantage through the dismissal of unwanted jurors. Each side had ten peremptory challenges, which meant ten chances to dismiss any juror they wanted, without explanation. In a deep blue borough, the defense would need to be careful to conserve those challenges. The best way to slow the proceedings would be to convince Merchan to dismiss jurors "for cause"—that is, for a legitimate reason—by persuading him that they could not be fair. "For cause" challenges were unlimited.

When Merchan returned to the bench at 2:15, Todd Blanche stood up and informed him that the defense was in possession of a number of social media posts that contradicted the would-be jurors' statements during voir dire.

Most of the items dated to Trump's time in the White House. The first real poster president, Trump tended to inspire mimicry. Even his critics often expressed their views in an overblown style reminiscent of the president himself.

Blanche started with "a series of extraordinarily hostile Facebook posts" made by juror number one. Asking that she be dismissed for cause, he handed a sheet of paper up to the judge.

Merchan glanced at it for a moment. "I'm not sure I was handed the right thing," he said. The sheet displayed two screengrabs from a video posted in November 2020.

Blanche explained that they were posts from the day that Trump lost the 2020 election.

"Show me the bias?" the judge asked.

Susan Necheles, who had far more experience in state court than Blanche, helped her colleague out. "This is a woman who specifically said she had never attended an anti-Trump rally or campaign," she said. "This is clearly an anti-Trump event. She is out celebrating and partying."

Merchan summoned the prospective juror, a dark-haired teacher, back to the courtroom. She marched toward the front, standing alone in the spotlight as the lawyers, the judge and the former president stared down at her. As she disavowed the political significance of the posts, and insisted she was ready for the duties of a juror, Trump mumbled something under his breath. Soon, the lawyers were satisfied. Merchan asked her politely to step outside.

After she left, he turned to Blanche.

"Your client was audibly uttering something," Merchan said, angrily. "I won't tolerate that. I will not have any jurors intimidated in this courtroom. I want to make that crystal clear." He told Blanche to speak to Trump.

Furthermore, the judge said, he would not dismiss the juror in seat one for cause. Trump glared at him. The defense had no choice but to burn its first peremptory challenge on juror number one, who was immediately dismissed. Izzy Brourman, the court artist, wrote Merchan's stern warning onto the drawing she was working on, an image of multiplying Trumps and Blanches, each duo locked so closely in conversation that the two men's bodies were melding into one.

"Who is your next one," the judge said.

Blanche asked him to dismiss the prospective juror in seat two for cause. This time, Blanche's argument was persuasive. In 2017, Juror B-38, a creative director with Land's End, posted on social media that Trump should be locked up. The judge agreed to dismiss him for cause.

Next, Blanche called for the dismissal of the juror in seat three. Her husband had posted insulting memes about Trump. One of them pictured Obama next to Trump, with the caption, "I don't think this is what they meant by 'Orange is the new Black.'" Trump, who'd been handed a sheet of paper with the meme, leaned in close to study it.

Merchan got angry. By now it was three o'clock. "We are not going to keep going through this," he said. "Honestly, if this is the worst thing that you were able to find about this juror, that her husband posted this humor—albeit not very good humor—from eight years ago, then it gives me confidence that this juror can be fair and impartial."

In a show of respect, Blanche did not object to the jurors in seats four or five. He skipped straight to seat number six. Michael Zorek.

It emerged that, in late March, Zorek had posted an AI video of the former president's voice with the words "have to share." In the video, the Trump voice asserted that "only the most hopelessly gullible morons would still support me after 91 felony indictments." The video's caption read, "Trump 2024: I am dumb as fuck."

Zorek walked back into the courtroom. He confirmed that the Facebook account was his and that he had reposted the video.

"Did you watch this before you posted it?" Blanche asked.

"I don't think I did," Zorek said.

"You just reposted it?"

"I think so."

"Why?" Blanche asked.

Steinglass stepped in. "Let me ask you this," he said. "Do you have a highly unfavorable overall impression of Donald Trump?"

"I would have to say that politically, yes, I do," Zorek said.

Merchan thanked Zorek, and he left the courtroom. He was dismissed for cause. He exited the courthouse and headed to Wegman's, where he bought more Diet Coke.

I realized, reflecting on the proceedings, that the courtroom inverts the dynamics of the online world. On social media, attention-seeking behavior is often rewarded. A person who posts incessantly and hyperbolically can attract followers, intrigue and conversation.

But inside 100 Centre Street, if you want to be a juror, you'd best avoid drawing any attention to yourself. Memorable is bad. Unobjectionable is better. Bland is best. The jurors who were seated by the end of the day on April 16 had signaled that they were *willing* to sit on the jury, but never did they give the appearance of being overly interested in doing so.

Over the next hour, the oncology nurse, the man with the subtle Irish accent and six others who had not drawn too much attention to themselves were seated as jurors. I posted on the *Time's* liveblog that a man from Ireland could help determine a former American president's fate, and the post was scooped up by Irish meme accounts celebrating their countryman's selection.

Up on the bench, Merchan looked satisfied. He was more than halfway there. He told the eight who had been selected that he expected them to return the following Monday, April 22, for opening statements. Shortly after 5:30, the courtroom was adjourned until Thursday, when jury selection would resume.

❖   ❖   ❖

That evening, Max Azzarello called his father, Richard, to report that his Substack was thriving. He never showed up at the Airbnb in Harlem; instead, he'd booked a room at the SoHo54 Hotel, a 15-minute walk from 100 Centre Street.

There is no public record of Max's movements on Wednesday and it's unclear whether he even went outside at all. It would have been a good day to stay indoors. The premature spring faded back into a more typical April gloom, and foot traffic in Washington Square Park was sparse.

On Truth Social, Trump referenced the Fox commentator Jesse

Watters as he claimed: "They are catching undercover liberal activists lying to the Judge in order to get on the Trump jury."

❖   ❖   ❖

On Thursday when we returned to the courthouse, it was still grey and cold, and the streets outside the courthouse felt grim. As I stood on line to get into 100 Centre Street, my phone began to blow up with rumors that some of the seated jurors would soon be unseated.

Proceedings started at 9:20 and it soon became clear that the rumors were correct. Juror two, the oncology nurse, walked into the frigid courtroom wearing a tan trench coat and told an irritated-looking Merchan that, thanks to the press, she'd been outed as a juror. She was scared, and concerned about whether she could be fair and unbiased given the attention.

The judge had little choice but to dismiss her. Once she was gone, Merchan turned his attention to the back row, where I sat with five other journalists.

"There's a reason this is an anonymous jury," he said, squinting in irritation. "It kind of defeats the purpose of that when so much information is put out there." He directed us to stop using physical descriptions. "There was really no need for anyone to mention that one of the jurors had an Irish accent," he said.

I made a face, but I could hardly stand up and object on my own behalf, unless I wanted to be thrown out of court. And I didn't think it was worth getting Robert Balin, the media lawyer, involved; it wasn't clear that Merchan would listen to him.

Joshua Steinglass, the prosecutor, suggested that the prospective jurors stop naming their prior and current employers, the information that made them so easy to identify. The judge agreed and we moved on. There was an issue with juror four, B-89, who found Trump fascinating and mysterious. After being called into court, he was dismissed as well. Now Merchan was less than halfway to completion of the seating of the jury. It felt like the trial was going backwards.

❖   ❖   ❖

Everyone was in a bad mood and we hadn't even reached the Thursday lunch break. In the overflow room, crowded with journalists and members of the public, experienced court reporters handed gum to their neighbors, while the novices suffered an unrelenting assault of coffee breath, cortisol, and nonstop surveillance by the court officers. Among the newcomers was Olivia Nuzzi, one of an influx of political journalists quickly becoming familiar with the strict rules of the courthouse. She took a picture of a Bottega handbag on the floor, struck by the contrast between the gaudy purse and the drab courthouse. Court officers immediately chastened her—picture-taking by a non-photographer was totally unacceptable. They warned her not to do it again.

Nuzzi may have been unfamiliar with 100 Centre Street, but she was highly familiar with Donald Trump. She was one of the best-known magazine journalists in a country that in the course of a decade had stopped caring about magazine journalists. Writing for *New York* magazine, Nuzzi had covered Trump's presidency colorfully, making great use of the access she was granted, and even access she wasn't.

One of the funniest examples came on October 11, 2018. It was a big day at the White House. Kanye West, having recently proclaimed himself to be the president's brother thanks to their shared dragon energy, was visiting. Sarah Huckabee Sanders, the White House Press Secretary, wanted to limit the number of press present and she told Nuzzi and a *Times* reporter, Katie Rogers that they wouldn't be allowed into the Oval Office for the day's events. Not to be deterred, Nuzzi and Rogers found someone else who gave them entrée. When they walked in, Trump was seated at the resolute desk, his face caked in makeup. Kanye sat across from him wearing a MAGA hat, switching topics constantly. Trump was having trouble keeping up.

"They tried to scare me to not wear this hat, my own *friends*," West said, gesturing at the hat. "But this hat, it gives me power in a way." He said the hat—and Trump himself—instilled in him a feeling of raw masculinity that had long been missing in his life, given that he was constantly surrounded by Kardashian women. "When I put this hat on it made me feel like Superman. You made a Superman cape for me!" Trump cocked his head and nodded along.

Nuzzi and Rogers wanted to keep watching, but they were discovered, dragged out of the Oval and reprimanded. Momentarily, it seemed as if they might be in real trouble. But in the end, there were no consequences. Nuzzi became used to that sort of thing, covering Trump. He created a lawless space, and those around him were free to act lawlessly, or as lawlessly as their personal ethics allowed.

By the time the former president was indicted in Manhattan, Nuzzi was suffering a certain amount of Trump fatigue, and trying to diversify her subject matter. In November 2023, she profiled the unlikely third-party presidential candidate and former assistant district attorney, Robert F. Kennedy Jr. In April 2024, just a week before trial started, she covered Arizona's senate race, rhapsodizing over the beauty of the southwest. But by the third day of jury selection, she found herself drawn to 100 Centre Street. It was the next chapter in a story she'd promised herself she would see through.

Watching the closed-circuit television in the overflow room, Nuzzi was blown away by the scene. Stripped of his power, Trump was reduced to a small, garish human trapped in the municipal monochrome of the courtroom. Trump in the courtroom was unlike Trump anywhere else—he was reduced to an actor in someone else's script, and any attempt to center himself risked the ire of the judge.

❀   ❀   ❀

In fact, around the same time Nuzzi was scolded by the court officers, the prosecution called for Trump to be chastened. Chris Conroy, the veteran prosecutor, declared with anger in his voice that the former president had violated the judge's gag order ten times. Conroy referred to multiple posts calling Michael Cohen a "serial perjurer" and Trump's false claim about "undercover liberal activists lying to the jury."

Conroy asked that Trump be held in contempt, and fined $1,000 for each infraction. Merchan scheduled a hearing on the posts for the following Tuesday, April 23.

❀   ❀   ❀

In the afternoon, there was a new group of prospective jurors in the box answering questions, trying to keep their teeth from chattering. Trump, who'd sent a message to his donors declaring that he had "JUST

STORMED INTO COURT," hugged himself to keep warm. Todd Blanche whispered furiously into his ear.

Merchan apologized to the prospective jurors for the temperature and called the court back into session. Voir dire continued with the new panel in the box and Steinglass delivered nearly the exact same speech he'd given on Tuesday, an actor hitting his lines.

Given Trump's passivity, the jury pool was becoming inured to his presence. More were staring at him outright. As everyone got accustomed to the routine, the voir dire process began to speed up.

There was one notable moment. One of the prospective jurors, a literary agent, had mentioned to a court officer that she had once spent a night at the house of Trump's lawyer, Susan Necheles. Steinglass asked the agent whether it would pose any problems for her at the trial. She said it wouldn't, and Steinglass, satisfied, sat down shortly thereafter.

Necheles walked to the lectern. She had more of a human touch than Blanche. She told one of the prospective jurors that he looked like he was cold.

"I'm freezing," the man said.

"Do you have any strong feelings about President Trump?"

"No, not really."

Necheles asked the literary agent the same question.

"Yes," the agent said.

"Can you tell us about those?" Necheles asked.

"Um, I disagree with most of his policies," the agent said.

Other prospective jurors teed off on the former president, seated just feet away. One woman called him selfish and self-serving. Another said that the way he carried himself in public left much to be desired. Trump looked unmoved. But when a prospective juror said he had read "The Art of the Deal," he nodded in approval, and winked at Emil Bove.

Soon, the prospective jurors left the room. Necheles asked the judge to dismiss the literary agent for cause, citing a review the agent's husband had written of Maggie Haberman's book about Trump. In the back of the courtroom, the other reporters on pool duty turned to look at Maggie, who ignored them. I wasn't surprised. I'd learned early on that Maggie did not enjoy public recognition, or acknowledgement of her journalistic fame. She just wanted to work.

The judge summoned the literary agent back into the room. He asked whether her husband's opinions would affect her ability to be fair. She said no.

"Well," said the judge, once she'd stepped out again.

Necheles renewed her objection. The woman had slept at her house. "It's awkward," she said.

"That's not grounds," Merchan said. "She doesn't really know you. She said she met you once about 15 years ago."

"But I knew her husband very well at the time," Necheles said.

"He's not on the jury," the judge said. He declined to dismiss the literary agent for cause. The defense was forced to burn another peremptory challenge. They were down to three.

Soon, the defense's challenges were used up and Merchan moved to seat twelve jurors and an alternate, who could rotate in if one of the original twelve had to be excused. All that remained was to pick five more alternates. The end of the week would be easy.

The twelve jurors—seven of them men, five women—possessed the following qualities:

- Three quarters were college-educated, and several had higher degrees, including two with law degrees.
- Two-thirds were New York *Times* readers. Only one was a New York Post reader.
- Only one followed Trump on social media.
- None had read "The Art of the Deal."

Trump, upset, strode out of the courtroom and approached the cameras mounted in the hallway. Flipping through a stack of press clippings, he asserted that legal experts everywhere had spoken out against the trial. "The whole world is watching this New York scam," he grumbled. "I'm sitting here for days now, from morning 'til night, in that freezing room. Freezing! Everyone was freezing in there."

※   ※   ※

That day, Nate Schweber was stationed in Collect Pond Park. He, too, was having a stressful week. All the action was inside the courtroom and Nate was stuck outside. His reporting yielded a few comic details, though. One park inhabitant chanted, "We love Trump! We love sex!" A small group of women from China alternated scorn for the lamestream media with random bouts of generosity. "Shame on you!" they told Nate. "You are fake news! Would you like some cantaloupe?"

Nate approached a wiry man in a charcoal jacket. He was holding a neatly written sign. "Trump Is With Biden and They're About To Fascist Coup Us."

"It's cold so I figured Washington Square won't be buzzing," Max told Nate. "I thought I'd check out the Trump trial."

They talked for about ten minutes. Max was polite and engaging, but when he explained his concerns about cryptocurrency, his cadence sped up, as if to outrace the speed at which people typically stopped paying attention to his spiel.

After they finished talking, Max shouted at the line of television cameras. "Biggest scoop of your life or your money back!" No one paid him any mind.

❖   ❖   ❖

For Justice Merchan, the hard part was over. But on Friday, April 19, the final day of jury selection, something felt off, both outside and inside the courtroom. Once the proceedings started, prospective alternates kept making surprising confessions, bursting into tears or both.

An insurance broker from Queens said he'd been trying to find a wife in his spare time and added "it's not working out." An Upper East Side woman expressed frustration that, after having served two years in prison in Massachusetts, she kept being summoned back to court for jury duty. She answered the questionnaire, close to tears. Trump watched her closely, then seemed to get bored once she pulled herself together. When she left the courtroom, Merchan applauded her bravery. "I just want to encourage the press, please be kind to this person," he said.

There was something odd in the air, and it was affecting everyone.

Outside, Nate was looking to interview jurors who'd been dismissed. But a police officer warned him to stop, or risk having his press badge confiscated. Nate retreated to the fence outside Collect Pond

Park, facing the courthouse door where dismissed jurors were most likely to emerge. The Centre Street entrance to the park was blocked off, to try to keep things orderly.

At noon, Trump sent a fundraising email with the subject line "42 Days of Hell!" "A Democrat Judge in New York pledges to keep me on trial for SIX WEEKS!" the email said. **"ELECTION INTERFERENCE!"**

Susan Hoffinger took Josh Steinglass's place for the Friday voir dire. She asked a juror if she could evaluate evidence against Trump with an open mind.

"I have to be honest, I feel so nervous and anxious right now," the juror said, apologizing.

"I would not want someone who feels this way to judge my case."

"Do you want to take a minute?" Hoffinger asked.

"I just thought I could do this," the juror said. "But this is so much more stressful than

I thought it would be." The judge excused her.

But a second alternate was chosen, then a third. Susan Necheles tripped up a juror with old social media posts and he was excused for cause. A fourth alternate was chosen, then a fifth. Then, at 1:30, a sixth. A full panel of twelve jurors and six alternates was seated. Merchan had triumphed, completing the process in a week. Opening arguments were set for Monday.

❖   ❖   ❖

A couple of minutes later, outside Collect Pond Park, somebody shrieked and Nate whirled around. Max Azzarello was standing near the reflecting pool, dousing himself in liquid from a cannister he held above his head. Then he brought his arms to his chest, and lit a flame. It quickly consumed his entire body.

Nate could feel the heat of the flames from where he stood. Ashes blew east. People screamed for someone to help the man. But the police were on Centre Street and the entrance to the park was blocked. It took them far too long to reach Max. By that time, he had collapsed.

Richard Azzarello was working outside in the back of his house in St. Augustine. He came in to make a little lunch. Curious to hear if the last alternates on the Trump jury had been seated, he turned on MSNBC. They cut to a reporter in front of the courthouse. She got a few words out about the jurors, then interrupted herself, describing the spectacle of the man on fire. Richard said to himself. *Oh no. Please don't be Max.* But he put it out of his head. After all, there were ten million people in New York City. It could be anyone. About 90 minutes later, one of his daughters called him, hysterical.

❖   ❖   ❖

Trump brought the eyes of the nation to 100 Centre Street and everyone who'd been compelled to attend the trial was caught up in his slipstream. That was what Zorek and the other dismissees who'd posted about Trump on social media shared in common with Max Azzarello. Max didn't care too much about Trump—just another secret fascist—but he understood that the former president had summoned to the courthouse what he needed to get his own message out. The need for attention—banal and ordinary or insistent and ultimately devastating—followed Trump wherever he went.

Ironically, in the courtroom, Trump himself could not take advantage of it. As Olivia Nuzzi told Chris Hayes on MSNBC that evening: "He needs attention, he absorbs it, he comes out more energetic. This is the opposite of that."

❖   ❖   ❖

Max's death cast a pall on the trial, but did nothing to impede the proceedings. With the prospective jurors gone for good, the courtroom gallery became the country's media epicenter. On Monday, April 22, we began a routine that would last until the end of the trial.

About five dozen of us had permanent seats in the courtroom. We lined up outside the north entrance of 100 Centre Street before the sun rose, gossiping and bickering, talking sports and guessing at who would be called to testify—the prosecutors refused to announce the witness names in advance, for fear that Trump would subject them to abuse online. Cliques formed among the reporters. Other than Maggie, with whom I consulted and gossiped every chance I got, I found myself hanging out most often with Frank Runyeon of Law360 and Emily Saul, of the New York Law Journal. Frank and Emily were smart, and remarkably idealistic about the power and necessity of journalism. They were also near the front of the line each day, and standing in the front meant sitting near the front of the courtroom, a better vantage point from which to observe the trial.

In theory, each individual outlet was promised a single courtroom seat, but it often seemed as if the television reporters dominated the mix. NBC for example, was granted seats for NBC News, MSNBC, and its local affiliate. Celebrity anchors also found their way into the courtroom each day: Though MSNBC's main spot typically went to Lisa Rubin, the network's legal correspondent, she was continually supplanted by more famous anchors, particularly Lawrence O'Donnell, who apparently could not get himself enough trial.

O'Donnell was only the most devoted. It seemed as if every star anchor was duty-bound to take a tour. When a celebrity journalist was there—a Rachel Maddow, an Anderson Cooper, a Jake Tapper—others crowded around them, seeking attention and favor and, every so often, a selfie. Even in the line, fame exerted its force.

Alongside the anchors was a set of older commentators whom I came to think of as The Pundits. They wore business casual and comfortable shoes and their ire toward the defendant was frequently obvious. George Conway, the Never-Trump Republican and ex-husband of Kellyanne, was foremost among them. He was there under the auspices of The Atlantic, but his animus against Trump was overt. Like many critics of the former president, he surfed atop the negative attention Trump attracted, promoting himself by association.

The new court spokesman, a buzz-cutted former *Times* reporter named Al Baker, diligently checked each of us in, handing us the slip of paper that would guarantee our access to the courtroom. Then around 8:00, the stress-inducing sprint to get the best seat in Part 59 began: navigating three security machines downstairs attended by ornery court officers, rickety elevators that took forever to close, then two more machines before we were held in a final line in the 15th floor hallway, just outside the pen where the photographers jockeyed for angles hours in advance of the former president's arrival.

Once inside the courtroom, we set up laptops, external chargers, hotspots and thermometers, all under the harried eyes of the court offi-cers. We draped the floor with our jackets, sweaters, gloves and scarves until the brown vinyl tiling was covered in detritus.

Activity in the well began soon afterward: a trio of young parale-gals from the district attorney's office wheeled in a small metal shop-ping cart filled with trial exhibits, positioning it to the right of the prosecution table, just in front of the jury box. Joshua Steinglass, Susan Hoffinger, Matthew Colangelo and the rest of the prosecutors fol-lowed in their wake. Trump's every move was broadcast in advance, but the final step before his entrance each day was the buzz of the walkie talkies. Trump walked in with his lawyers and sat down heavily at the defense table, awaiting the judge. Proceedings began at 9:30.

❖   ❖   ❖

That morning, nine court officers patrolled the room, and a row of U.S. Secret Service agents sat behind the defense table on the left, more conspicuous now given the absence of the jury pool. Merchan launched into a long spiel about how the trial would work, concluding with a review of the weekly schedule—no trial on Wednesdays. He said that, as Juror One, the man with the Irish accent would serve as the foreper-son and would eventually announce the verdict. Then he asked the prosecution to deliver its opening statement.

The jurors were rapt as Colangelo approached the lectern and began explaining the prosecution's case with a clarity that few out-side the courtroom had ever heard. His performance was captured on closed-circuit monitors—four 60 inch screens placed in the front of the courtroom, with smaller displays anchored to the lawyer's tables.

Colangelo was not an experienced criminal lawyer, and he'd never before delivered the opening at a criminal trial. But he was eloquent, and he'd practiced in front of his more experienced colleagues over and over again, until he got it right. His sole focus was the jury. They were his audience.

"This case is about a criminal conspiracy and a cover-up," Col-angelo said. He described the August 2015 meeting at Trump Tower between David Pecker, Michael Cohen and the future president. He outlined the three payments—two by Pecker, one by Cohen—that had buried potentially damaging stories during the presidential campaign.

After the release of the "Access Hollywood" tape, Colangelo told the jury, Trump was adamant that Stormy Daniels's damaging story be kept under wraps. So Cohen paid her, "at Donald Trump's direction and for his benefit."

Colangelo did not once use the phrase "hush money" and there was none of the original indictment's equivocation about "other crimes." The case made use of a single predicate, New York Election law 17–152, and it was that predicate that informed the most compelling part of Colangelo's opening. Because he centered the election conspiracy rather than the single payoff to Stormy Daniels, his explanation of the crime was far grander and more malevolent than the simple disguise of a hush-money payment. The 34 false business records represented the finishing touches of Trump's first attempt to criminally corrupt a presidential election.

As Todd Blanche and Donald Trump chuckled together over some private joke, I realized with a jolt that all the complexities of the charging structure were distractions from the true subject at hand: The hidden dynamics of Donald Trump's 2016 campaign. That race was often said to have in some way broken the time-space continuum, so unlikely was his eventual victory. Over the next seven weeks the prosecutors would inspect the site of the breakage. The 15th floor courtroom was the laboratory. There, time was artificially slowed, Trump's powers were suppressed and the attention of the room was focused on witnesses and evidence. The president risked imprisonment if he made a spectacle of himself. As at the arraignment, he would sit quietly in the courtroom, eventually summoning a vast team of surrogates to speak his words and send his message.

If Bragg's prosecutors were able to convince the jury that Trump was guilty, they might simultaneously convince the public that a series of criminal acts could well have made the difference between victory and defeat in the 2016 presidential campaign. If they were successful, their case could transform our general understanding of recent history, and the dominant public figure of our time.

Colangelo's preview of testimony that would spotlight Trump's role in the coverup passed quickly. He said there were two conversations in which Trump agreed to the scheme to disguise the reimbursements to

Cohen as payments for legal fees—in other words, the scheme to falsify business records, the violation of penal code 175.10. The first of the conversations was in January 2017 at Trump Tower. The second was at the White House the following month. Colangelo didn't preview what exactly Cohen would say about those all-important conversations. We'd have to wait for the former fixer's testimony to find out.

Colangelo's opening took less than an hour. He concluded by telling the jurors that, at the end of the trial, his colleague Joshua Steinglass would review the evidence, and explain that it led inescapably to a single conclusion: "Donald Trump is guilty."

❖   ❖   ❖

"President Trump is innocent," Todd Blanche announced at the lectern, just moments later. It was the defense's turn. "President Trump did not commit any crimes. The Manhattan District Attorney's Office should never have brought this case." It was an assertion that Blanche truly believed, that he'd believed since the very first moment he'd seen the indictment.

The 34 counts, Blanche said, were just "34 pieces of paper." The idea that Trump, Cohen and Pecker had conspired to influence an election? "There is nothing wrong with trying to influence an election. That's called democracy." And the fact that Cohen had paid $130,000 so that Daniels would agree not to spread what Blanche called "false claims about President Trump"—that wasn't illegal either.

Blanche paced back and forth in his fitted navy suit, often stepping briefly away from the microphone to allow himself some room to gesture, causing the sound to cut out in the overflow room to the frustration of Kate Christobek and the other journalists stationed there. Trump turned to watch Blanche from the defense table as the lawyer explained to the jurors that he would be referring to his client as President Trump, as a show of respect.

"None of this was a crime," he told the jury, echoing his client, who'd made "NO CRIME" a catchphrase. Juror One, the newly elevated foreperson, frowned to himself. Juror Seven, a balding civil litigator seated in the row behind the foreperson, stared expressionless at Blanche.

This was Blanche's refrain: the sheer absurdity of the charges. Unlike Colangelo, he was playing to multiple audiences. Along with the jurors, there were the reporters filling up the gallery, eagerly taking down his every word. And most importantly, there was the former president, his client. Blanche's argument could not be a showcase of pure persuasive rhetoric. He had too many masters to please.

His comments about the illegitimacy of the case may have been least effective with the audience that would be asked to determine the verdict. For a juror, the idea that the case before them wasn't in fact a case was the height of illogic. They were seated in a courtroom, staring at an indicted defendant. If there were no real crime alleged, why were they being instructed by a judge on the facts of the case?

Blanche did not introduce a full-fledged theory about his client's conduct to compete with those facts. Instead, he suggested multiple threads that the defense might weave together down the road: that Trump, as a family man, was seeking to protect his home life from women who said they'd slept with him; that the former president had nothing to do with the payments to Michael Cohen.

It isn't unusual for defense attorneys to put multiple underdeveloped options on the table in their opening arguments. Unlike prosecutors, who are compelled by the charges to hew to a certain script, the best defense lawyers are frequently geniuses of improvisation. Their job is to sow doubt, constructing an alternative narrative, often out of the fabric of the prosecutor's case. The gloves at O.J. Simpson's trial came from the government, recovered by the police. Johnny Cochrane transformed them into one of the most famous pieces of exculpatory evidence in American history.

There were certain details that Blanche told the jurors to scrutinize closely. For instance, why, if Cohen had paid Daniels $130,000, had he been reimbursed $420,000? "The people told you that President Trump is known as a frugal businessman, that he pinches pennies," Blanche said. "Ask yourself: Would a frugal businessman, would a man who pinches pennies, repay a $130,000 debt to the tune of $420,000?

Like his client, he seemed most comfortable attacking Michael Cohen.

The prosecution's story about Cohen was a streamlined chronology of before and after: before the summer of 2018, he consistently lied for Donald Trump; after lack of support from the White House in the midst of a federal investigation that summer prompted Cohen to question his own loyalty, he turned on the president and consistently told the truth about the payoff to Stormy Daniels and all that followed.

But Blanche had studied Cohen for months—his podcasts, his television appearances, his TikToks—and grown convinced that no right-thinking juror could believe a man so obsessed with payback had an ounce of inner integrity. Cohen had literally written a book called "Revenge." He talked openly about his desire to see Trump in prison. And he'd lied under oath multiple times, and pled guilty to perjury in federal court.

"He has a goal, an obsession with getting Trump," Blanche told the jurors. "And you're going to hear that. I submit to you that he cannot be trusted."

The defense lawyer adopted an aw-shucks tone as he concluded.

"Listen, use your common sense," he said. "We're New Yorkers. That's why we're here. You told all of us—you told the court, you told me—that you would put aside whatever ideas you have of President Trump from the past eight years, the fact that he was President, the fact that he is running again for an election this November. And we trust you to do that. We do. We trust that you're going to decide this case based upon the evidence that you hear in this courtroom and nothing else. And if you do that, there will be a very swift, a very swift not guilty verdict."

He sat down at the defense table and Justice Merchan excused the jurors for a brief, late-morning break. When they returned, he instructed the prosecution to call the first witness. Joshua Steinglass strode to the lectern and called the name David Pecker.

CHAPTER FOUR

TABLOID POLITICS

David Pecker appeared from a door on the left side of the courtroom, small, mustachioed and serene, his skin browned and tough like a walnut. He shuffled toward the witness stand, trailed by the eyes of the press corps, the lawyers and the jurors. If he felt any nerves, there was no sign of them. As he ascended to the witness stand, it was if a spotlight fell on him: David Pecker would command the first, crucial episode of the prosecution's case.

He had practiced his testimony in an empty courtroom and the rehearsal had done him good. He seemed completely unfazed. When asked to identify Trump, shortly after taking the stand, he pointed calmly at the defense table, ignoring all the iconography—the hair, the tie, the name—and instead identified the former president as a man wearing the dark blue suit.

Pecker had realized decades ago that Trump possessed a quality he valued above all else: an ability to hold people's attention. The two men were kindred spirits, outer-borough New Yorkers with a hard-earned understanding of the hierarchies that animated the elite jockeying in their hometown. Never cool, and much-mocked by those to whom cool came easy, they made names for themselves nonetheless. And toward the end of the 20th century, as Pecker's interests turned to the profitable overlap between celebrity and politics, they began trading favors.

Pecker was born in the Bronx in 1951. The youngest son of a

bricklayer, he was early to teach himself the math of making money. Before he finished college, he was already moonlighting as a professional accountant and his entry into the glossy world of magazines came through the basement door of bookkeeping. He was one of many accountants in CBS's magazine division, based in Greenwich, Connecticut, and he rose steadily. Toward the end of the 1980s, he hung on by his fingernails as the division was spun off, acquired and sold. When the roller coaster of corporate transactions came to a halt, Pecker was an editorial boss, the North American head of the French magazine publisher Hachette, with a legendary temper, a tendency to ream out his employees and an office on Broadway in the heart of midtown Manhattan.

It was the heyday of the magazine. Hundreds of new publications were founded each year. They were cultural institutions, lifestyle bibles; there were multiple magazines for every personality type and what you read was who you were. Subscriptions were cheap and circulations were enormous. Magazines ran on the advertising money that would eventually be poured into search engines and social media platforms. Even television took its cue from the glossies: A single story's juiciest details would be picked up by shows like "Entertainment: Tonight" and "Access Hollywood." Events sparked weeks of dialogue before something else big enough to change the conversation happened.

Trump's ubiquity began in this era of deep cultural processing. The real estate magnate loved magazines and they loved him right back. He was brash, entertaining, and preposterous. He understood what readers responded to, a quality he called "flair." "If a man has flair and is smart and somewhat conservative and has a taste for what people want, he's bound to be successful in New York," he told The *Times*. By the end of the 1980s, Trump's flair had earned him a *Time* cover, featuring his face and the line: "This man may turn you green with envy—or just turn you off." Trump's personality was polarizing, even then, but negative attention sold magazines, too. Trump was irresistible, even to those who only wanted to mock him, and he made himself available to be lauded or mocked, as suited the interests of the magazine editors.

Trump and Pecker were united by their passion for acquiring well-known assets and reimagining them to be more eye-catching, more garish. At the helm of Hachette, Pecker bought new titles aggressively, stuffing them full of ads. He had little regard for the church-and-state separation between editorial and sales. And when it came to actual content, there was a single element to which Pecker was devoted above all else. "I realized early in my career that the only thing that was important is the cover," he testified.

In the mid-1990s, a new idea fell in Pecker's lap, one with instantaneous advertiser-appeal and remarkable cover potential. It came from John F. Kennedy Jr., the son of President Kennedy. After passing the bar on his third attempt, John Jr. had worked as an assistant district attorney under Robert Morgenthau. But he left prosecution for journalism, and by 1995, had decided that he wanted to create a "post-partisan" political magazine, a lifestyle publication that would assert culture's supremacy over politics. Kennedy was driven by an insight, informed by his own biography: his father's legacy expanded well beyond the bounds of government, merging with the broader apparatus of pop culture. By the Clinton era, celebrity was part and parcel of political life. The politicians of the 1990s appeared on the "Late Show" with David Letterman, Imus in the Morning and all the rest of the profusion of talk radio and television shows.

Conde Nast and Hearst couldn't see John Jr.'s vision. But Pecker knew the value of the Kennedy name. He snapped up the magazine, and soon began asking JFK Jr. to accompany him on trips to court advertisers. George Magazine—named for George Washington—debuted in September 1995. The launch event was held at Federal Hall, the Wall Street memorial where Washington was sworn in as president. Journalists flocked to see JFK JR., who greeted them wryly. "I don't think I've seen as many of you in one place since they announced the results of my first bar exam," he said.

As promised, the first issue offered a prescient blend of culture and politics. Cindy Crawford was on the cover, made up as a founding father. Inside, Madonna was asked to imagine her own presidency. But the magazine also featured an essay on the demise of the two-party system, a profile of Newt Gingrich's activist sister and JFK Jr.'s interview with George Wallace. Media critics were puzzled by the mix. "This schizophrenia cannot last long," wrote Larry Williams in the Hartford Courant. "Either the serious or the frivolous will prevail."

The magazine kept chugging. The early issues sold well. Cover stars included Robert DeNiro and Arnold Schwarzenegger. In February, Pecker and Trump co-hosted a party for potential advertisers at Mar-a-Lago. Trump could not have known how close the magazine's philosophy was to predicting his rise, but he liked to be where the action was.

Pecker understood Trump's utility in much the way he understood JFK Jr.'s. In 1997, they started a magazine together. It was called Trump Style and it celebrated Trump's image with characteristic hyperbole. It was the beginning of a lucrative, symbiotic relationship.

By the late 1990s, image had become Trump's chief selling point. His near-ruin toward the end of the previous decade had transformed his business and he had begun lending his name to properties that he did not own outright. His vocation as a real estate mogul was becoming secondary to his myth.

The myth had remarkable durability in the media-generated version of New York. Writers kept finding new ways to cover Trump, to make his divisiveness seem interesting. In a 1999 story in *Vibe* magazine, Nancy Jo Sales profiled the future president as he attended Sean "Puffy" Combs's 29th birthday party. "Trump was hip hop before he himself knew," Sales declared, substantiating the assertion by acknowledging Trump's habit of splashing his names on his buildings and going to war with his haters. She wrote that if Clinton could be called the first Black president, then Trump, by a similar logic, "may be the first African-American billionaire."

Just before the turn of the century, Pecker changed jobs. He took over American Media Incorporated, A.M.I., a publishing company most closely associated with The National Enquirer. Trump was one of the first to call and congratulate him.

Around that time, Donald Trump was featured on the cover of George Magazine, for a story pegged to the presidential run he'd announced in the fall of 1999. The author, Christopher Byron, didn't think Trump was serious; he noted that it was the businessman's second flirtation with the White House since the 1980s and that the first one had just so happened to coincide with the publication of "The Art of the Deal." Byron concluded that the run was a stunt, a self-promotional con.

Trump soon discovered a less laborious means of self-promotion.

In 2004, he was reinvented as a reality television star, the main attraction of "The Apprentice" on NBC. His talents, his flair, were a perfect fit for the medium. The show ran for fifteen seasons, developing over time into "The Celebrity Apprentice," when it became even more valuable to Pecker. As the head of A.M.I., celebrity remained his bread and butter, and Trump gave him inside information about the show before anyone else.

"It was very beneficial for my magazines," Pecker told the jury.

❖   ❖   ❖

Pecker only testified for 30 minutes on Monday, April 22; an alternate juror had scheduled an emergency dental appointment to address a toothache and the president's trial broke early. As Trump and his lawyers departed the courtroom, we were told by the court officers to remain seated. The reporters in the overflow room were held as well. Ten minutes passed, then 20. . . .

Those of us familiar with the courthouse knew the rules of the place, and knew to take them seriously. The court officers ran the show. Ignoring them was risky and in that first week of testimony, they were particularly tense, coordinating with the Secret Service to maintain order. They brooked no dissent. Some of the politics reporters, particularly those who became famous in the chaotic realm of the Trump White House, were not used to dealing with such strict authority in such shabby surroundings. One of our number was about to learn that the hard way.

Delayed indefinitely in the overflow room while the Secret Service secured Trump's exit, Olivia Nuzzi chatted with Ben Wittes, the editor-in-chief of the site Lawfare. He was wearing a t-shirt with a large picture of a dog on it, a practice that had become an in-joke for his audience. Wittes asked Nuzzi to tell a mutual friend about the shirt. Nuzzi raised her phone to snap a picture. A court officer descended on her and hauled her out of the room. Brendan Mullaney, the red-haired, white-shirted lieutenant in charge strolled over. He asked Nuzzi where she worked and after she told him, he instructed her to leave the courthouse, and not to come back. She'd been permanently banned from the trial. Rules may have been suggestions in the Trump White House; on

100 Centre Street, they were absolutes.

Nuzzi was staying at the Standard Hotel in the Meatpacking District. She walked west from 100 Centre, distraught, calling everyone she knew who she thought might be able to help. Nothing worked. Nuzzi bought herself a coffee and sat alone in an outdoor dining shed, visibly distraught. She looked up and saw Chris Rock standing close by, as if was about to say something to cheer her up. Then, apparently thinking better of it, he kept walking.

⁂

The next morning, bundled up in line, I sought distraction from a trial that in the span of a week had completely taken over my life. Sports offered easy small talk. The N.B.A. playoffs were in full swing, and the Knicks were locked into a hard-fought series with the 76ers. Philadelphia was led by Joel Embiid, a titanic, shameless big man and outsized social media personality who postured online as a villain, much to the Philly fans delight. The Knicks had stars, but no one quite as dominant; their wins were characterized by a tremendous team effort.

The evening before—the first night of Passover—the Knicks had overcome a five-point lead in the last three seconds of the game, beating Embiid and the Sixers in spectacular fashion at Madison Square Garden. I stifled a yawn in line as I enthused about the game with Graham Kates from CBS and Ben Kochman from the New York Post.

Kates nodded toward George Conway, standing a ways back in the line.

"Did you see him?" he said.

I was confused. "What do you mean?"

"Conway," Graham said. "He was at the game. They showed him on the big screen."

That morning, Conway was putting on a show in line, doing a mocking Trump impression with a seder-inspired spin, in honor of the holiday. He was joined by Adam Klasfeld, an MSNBC contributor with pointy, Seussian hair who'd acquired a following by comprehensively live-tweeting court proceedings.

"And lo, with an outstretched hand, the Lord did call it a "witch hunt," Conway offered.

"And legal scholars did, like the three kings, say 'No Case,' capital N, capital O, case," Klasfeld responded.

I was ambivalent about attracting that kind of attention. But my editors had given me an assignment that made it more difficult to avoid. At the end of each trial day, after live-blogging the proceedings, then working with Ben Protess on a story that summed up the day, I had to film a short video recap, explaining it all again. It was an uncomfortable task. I was a writer, not a commentator, and I couldn't get used to seeing my face on The *Times's* home screen. But the paper was searching for new subscribers, attempting to transition to some form of mass media. Words without images weren't going to cut it anymore.

❖   ❖   ❖

Everyone snapped to attention as the court officers opened the north entrance doors and we began the march up to the 15ᵗʰ floor. It was time for the hearing Justice Merchan had scheduled on whether Trump had violated his gag order. So with the jurors absent and oblivious, instead of testimony, the reporters in Part 59 were treated to the most contentious confrontation thus far between Todd Blanche and the judge.

Initially, things went as planned. Chris Conroy, the veteran prosecutor, began the hearing by standing at the lectern, describing the ten statements prosecutors believed ran afoul of the order that barred Trump discussing witnesses and jurors.

There was Trump's repeated repost of the article calling Michael Cohen a "serial perjurer." There was his claim that "they are catching undercover Liberal Activists lying to the Judge in order to get on the Trump Jury." And then there was my personal favorite violation, the most ridiculous: In an April 10 Truth Social post, Trump claimed that a 2018 statement from Stormy Daniels "WAS JUST FOUND!"

"WILL THE FAKE NEWS REPORT IT?" he asked.

The statement, which would be an exhibit in the trial, was not "just found." Under pressure from Michael Cohen and her lawyer Keith Davidson, Daniels issued it reluctantly in early 2018, asserting that she had never had an affair with Donald Trump. But she soon recanted it and went on "60 Minutes" to tell Anderson Cooper the story of having had sex with Trump in 2006 after a celebrity golf tournament in

Nevada.

Trump's all-caps lie was a minor falsehood, banal and familiar, and were it not for the gag order, it would never have merited comment. But in Merchan's courtroom, a casual relationship with the truth was unacceptable.

Once Conroy was done with his arguments, it was Todd Blanche's turn. He argued that Trump's posts were permissible, because they were examples of political speech, necessitated by attacks from Daniels and Cohen. But when Merchan asked Blanche to identify the attacks to which each of Trump's posts was responding, the exercise broke down immediately.

Asked about Trump's "WAS JUST FOUND" post, Blanche began by saying that Stormy Daniels was a political adversary who'd talked about Trump's qualifications for office.

"This was a response to what specific attack?" Merchan asked, refocusing the conversation.

"There have been . . . again . . ." Blanche began, but Merchan interrupted him. "I am assuming that there must have been a very recent attack to cause him to pull out a document that's six-years old and was going to be used at trial."

"It's not that it was pulled out," Blanche said. "It's a public document. It's publicly available, Judge."

"It says, look what 'was just found,'" the judge said, reading from the post. "Was that just found?"

"No, absolutely not," Blanche said.

"So that's not true? That's not true?" the judge said, agitated.

"That is not true. I don't think anybody thinks that's true. Everybody has seen the document for years and years," Blanche said dismissively, as if he were not completely contradicting his client's post.

"Whether somebody thinks it is true or not, I need to clarify," Merchan said, exasperated. "I need to understand what I am dealing with."

They continued back and forth for a bit, and then again, Merchan asked which of Daniels' attacks Trump had been responding to with the post.

"I didn't get an answer to . . ."

". . . I did answer you," Blanche said. "I'll answer you again. There were repeated, repeated specific . . ."

"Give me one. That's not specific," Merchan said. "Give me one that he was responding to here."

"Yes, your honor," Blanche said. "So there was . . . I don't have a particular tweet that it was responding to."

Blanche's argument didn't get any stronger as he continued to defend each of the ten posts. There was no doubt Trump felt Cohen and Daniels were political adversaries who he had every right to attack. He'd simply ignored the fact that he was barred from doing so, leaving Todd Blanche in the impossible position of cleaning up the mess with a straight face.

Toward the end of the hearing, Blanche assured the judge, "President Trump is being very careful to comply with Your Honor's rules."

The look of utter scorn on Justice Merchan's face had to be seen to be believed.

"Mr. Blanche, you are losing all credibility," the judge said. "I have to tell you that right now. You are losing all credibility with the court."

❖   ❖   ❖

After the hearing, the jurors filed back into the courtroom and David Pecker returned to the witness stand. Alvin L. Bragg sat in the second row of the gallery, face scrunched up in concentration. He had little to be worried about. The publisher was already a sensation. There was no sign of his quick temper—he was calm, almost gracious, as the prosecutor, Joshua Steinglass, asked him about his career history. Reporters, grateful for the luridness of his testimony and impressed by his self-possession on the stand, took to calling him the "tabloid grandpa."

The witness's frankness made him seem honest and respectable, even as he described some of the ugliest practices in the media business. The National Enquirer paid for stories—Pecker called it "checkbook journalism"—and buried them if it made business sense.

Pecker's history trading favors with Trump was prelude to the main event. On Tuesday, just before noon, Steinglass began to ask questions about the 2015 meeting between Trump, Pecker and Michael Cohen.

Pecker said he'd received a call from Michael Cohen, who'd said that The Boss wanted to see him. Pecker hadn't known the purpose of the meeting. But, of course, he went.

"Can you describe for the jury what happened at that meeting, please?"

Pecker said that the novice presidential candidate had asked him what he and his magazines could do for the campaign. Pecker didn't have to think too hard.

"I said what I would do is I would run or publish positive stories about Mr. Trump and I would publish negative stories about his opponents," he testified. "And I said I would be your eyes and ears. If I hear anything negative about yourself or if I hear anything about women selling stories, I would notify Michael Cohen, as I did over the last several years. He would be able to have them killed."

Fire engines wailed outside the courthouse as if to punctuate the importance of Pecker's explicit description of the infamous catch-and-kill scheme. The reporters in the room typed furiously, the word *conspiracy* flashing in their copy. Trump whispered something to Blanche.

Steinglass reviewed the testimony, wording his follow-up questions precisely as he sought to show the jurors that Michael Cohen was merely an agent, a pass-through, for Trump himself. Steinglass needed Pecker to say something specific: that his actions were meant to aid the 2016 presidential campaign. Were the conspiracy not undertaken to help with Trump's election, it wouldn't meet the bar set by statute 17–152.

"You offered to publish positive stories about Mr. Trump?" Steinglass asked.

"Yes."

"To publish negative stories about his opponents?"

"Yes."

"And to alert him through Michael Cohen when you came across damaging information, particularly regarding women."

"Yes."

"And the idea was that so Mr. Trump and Mr. Cohen could prevent that information from being publicized?"

"Yes."

Trump glared at Pecker from the defense table. But the witness was holding the gaze of his scene partner, Steinglass, as they staged a two-person performance.

"So you mentioned women in particular," Steinglass said. "Can you explain to the jury how the topic of women in particular came up?"

"I was the person that thought that there would be a number—a lot of women who would come out to try to sell their stories," Pecker said. "Because Mr. Trump was well-known as the most eligible bachelor and dated the most beautiful women. He glanced over at the jurors, as if he was checking to see if any would roll their eyes. Then, he continued. "When someone is running for a public office like this, it is very common for these women to call up a magazine like the National Enquirer to try to sell their stories."

"Did you have or express any ideas about how you may be able to help kind of deal with those stories by women?" Steinglass asked.

"All I said was I would notify Michael Cohen," Pecker said.

The publisher believed that the arrangement would be mutually beneficial. His readers loved Trump and his magazines were already aligned with the campaign. Besides, his most successful hit pieces concerned the Clintons. "BILL CAUGHT IN TEEN SEX RING; HILLARY'S PREZ BID IN RUINS." The negative Clinton stories sold magazines, Pecker said, and he had been happy to keep repeating them.

"How, if at all, did Mr. Trump react to your suggestion that you would continue to do that?" Steinglass asked.

"He was pleased," Pecker said.

Steinglass asked him to elaborate on what he meant when he said the arrangement was mutually beneficial. Pecker clearly thought it was obvious.

"What I'm saying," he said. "Writing negative stories about his opponents is only going to increase newsstand sales of The National Enquirer and the other tabloids."

I could see Steinglass waiting for the punchline.

Then, Pecker delivered. "Publishing these types of stories was also going to benefit his campaign."

There it was. The quote Steinglass needed to establish the conspiracy to promote Trump's election.

There are witnesses whose knowledge that they have just screwed over a defendant is written on their faces. Pecker wasn't like that. He had just fired the starting gun of the prosecution's case. He was offering testimony about a very, very powerful man, the once and perhaps future president of the United States of America. But Pecker's walnut face gave nothing away. He looked innocent up there, almost loveable. The tabloid grandpa.

✦   ✦   ✦

The conspiracy soon expanded by one member: Directly after leaving Trump Tower in August 2015, Pecker relayed the arrangement with Trump to his top editor, Dylan Howard, and instructed Howard to keep it a secret.

"Did you tell him why you asked him to keep this arrangement secret?" Steinglass asked.

"I told him that we were going to try to help the campaign, and to do that, I want to keep this as quiet as possible," Pecker said.

The Enquirer began to feature positive articles about Donald Trump and negative pieces about his campaign opponents—both Hillary Clinton and Republicans. And soon came the first of the two hush-money deals.

It originated in October 2015 when Dino Sajudin, a goatee-wearing Trump Organization doorman, came to Pecker's attention as the purveyor of a damaging story about Donald J. Trump. According to Sajudin, Trump had slept with a maid in one of the Trump Organization's buildings and fathered a daughter out of wedlock. It was a baseless claim, and A.M.I. later concluded it was untrue. But baseless claims can be damaging.

Pecker described for the jury how he had purchased the story from Sajudin for $30,000. He told the jurors that, if he'd found it to be true, he would have published it—after the election. A potential set of unlawful means lurked, like easter eggs, in the testimony, and Pecker's payment to Sajudin—a campaign contribution, in the prosecutors' thinking—was easter egg number one.

In December 2015, after Pecker determined that the story was untrue, he suggested to Michael Cohen that Sajudin be released from the agreement he'd signed; his fabricated story was no more threat than any other made-up piece of nonsense about the candidate. But Cohen demanded that Sajudin be kept quiet until after the 2016 election. Pecker obliged.

For a time, no other threats surfaced, and Trump rampaged through the Republican primary. By May 2016, he was the presumptive nominee. In June, Karen McDougal's story came to the attention of David Pecker and Dylan Howard.

❖   ❖   ❖

On Thursday, April 25, as hundreds of miles away, the Supreme Court heard oral arguments about Trump's potential immunity from prosecution, the former president was trapped in a Manhattan courtroom, preparing to listen to David Pecker's third day of testimony.

Alvin Bragg was no longer present. He had other cases to supervise, meetings to attend. On a jaunt to Think Coffee, a chain on Broadway, he was briefly taken aback when a group of older anti-Trump protesters from a group called Rise and Resist stood to give him a quick standing ovation. He gave them a broad smile, then left without saying anything.

Meanwhile, on the Trump side of the gallery, there was a new arrival dressed in a three-piece suit and enormous cuff links: Boris Epshteyn, one of the former president's chief legal advisers. The day before, he and seventeen others had been indicted in Arizona Superior Court for conspiring to change the state's 2020 election results. He would occasionally consult with Blanche, the two men chatting quietly on either side of the wooden barrier that divided the well from the gallery.

I was sitting a few rows back, hunched over my laptop, insistently refreshing a web page. The previous day, a source had alerted me to the likelihood that Harvey Weinstein's conviction—reached in the very same courtroom I was now sitting in—would be overturned by New York's highest court. Around 9 am, the decision showed up on the court's website. We published our story and I watched the news sweep around the room in real time. The journalists were stunned; many of them had covered Weinstein's trial just four years earlier. Now, the landmark conviction had been erased.

But we had little time to dwell on the significance. Soon, Pecker was back on the stand, still under examination by the prosecution. He'd begun to tell the story of Karen McDougal.

Upon hearing of the McDougal threat, Pecker honored his pledge and snapped into action, calling Michael Cohen to alert him to the danger. This time, Pecker testified, Trump got involved directly. He called Pecker, who was in the midst of an investor meeting, and asked for his advice on what to do. Pecker recommended paying McDougal off. Trump said he'd consider it, and soon, Cohen called Pecker, asking him to negotiate the story's purchase.

Pecker expected that Trump would pay him back. Cohen assured him as much, saying, "The boss will take care of it."

McDougal was represented by a Hollywood lawyer named Keith Davidson, often retained by celebrity-adjacent clients. Davidson's asking price was high: $150,000, five times as much as had gone to Sajudin. But the election was just months away, and McDougal's story had the ring of truth. Pecker ordered that a contract be drawn up for her story.

In addition to the $150,000, McDougal was to receive a monthly column on aging and fitness in three of his magazines, to be penned by a ghost writer and approved by McDougal. The articles, he hoped, would justify the money, disguising the true nature of the contract. Pecker testified that he had been aware that he might be violating federal campaign finance laws. But he had committed to helping Trump's campaign.

For the case to function, the jury had to understand that Pecker and Cohen had violated the law as they scurried around cleaning up Trump's messes. It was another unorthodox campaign donation, this one to the tune of $150,000. Easter egg number two.

Pecker urgently wanted to be reimbursed. He began pestering Cohen to pay him back. In September 2016 Cohen set up a shell company for the deal, calling it Resolution Consultants LLC. An invoice was created to facilitate the transaction and disguise the true purpose of the reimbursement. The prosecution considered this invoice a false business record. Another easter egg.

Cohen was on the verge of consummating the deal. But then Pecker realized the legal jeopardy he was courting. He asked Cohen to rip up the papers. Pecker was never reimbursed. Trump remained in his debt as the election drew to a close.

In January 2017, two weeks before the presidential inauguration, David Pecker was again summoned to Trump Tower for a meeting. When he arrived at Fifth Avenue, throngs of people were camped at the base of the skyscraper. The holiday season always brings a crush of tourists to Midtown, and since Trump's election, there had been a massive increase in foot traffic to the 58-story black monolith. The marble and gold lobby swarmed with onlookers as senators, governors and would-be cabinet secretaries made their pilgrimages up to Trump's office.

Pecker had no idea how to get in. He couldn't even approach the building. As he wondered what to do, someone tapped him on the shoulder. It was Jared Kushner, Donald Trump's son-in-law. "I'll get you upstairs," Kushner said. He guided Pecker to the entrance reserved for residents, and they took the elevator to the 26th floor.

Trump was in his office, meeting with some of the most powerful people in the country. Reince Preibus, the incoming chief of staff. Mike Pompeo, who Trump planned to nominate as the director of the C.I.A. And James Comey, the former U.S. attorney of the Southern District of New York and the director of the F.B.I. The three men sat below a wall of magazines featuring Trump's image on the cover: *Variety, Fortune, GQ, Palm Beach, Playboy*. Out the window to the north, the evergreen trees of Central Park were spread out like a carpet.

Pecker waited outside the office, under the impression that Trump was concluding a meeting about a mass shooting in a Fort Lauderdale airport. The shooter, a veteran of the war in Iraq, was said by his family members to have lost his mind. "Thoughts and prayers for all. Stay safe!" Trump tweeted in response.

Unbeknownst to Pecker, Comey had a warning to deliver to Trump. After the Fort Lauderdale meeting, he took the president-elect aside and informed him of a dossier the F.B.I. had obtained that said the Russians had tapes of him with prostitutes in a Moscow hotel. "There were no prostitutes," Trump responded. "There were never prostitutes." Comey said that he wanted the president-elect to know that the F.B.I. wasn't investigating him, but that the media might publish a report on the dossier. Then, he left.

Pecker was still waiting. Finally, Trump's longtime assistant, Rhona Graff, told him the president-elect was ready for him. He went into the office and Trump introduced him to the remaining officials.

"Here is David Pecker—he probably knows more than anybody else in this room." ("It was a joke," Pecker testified. "Unfortunately, they didn't laugh.")

Trump asked the machers to leave. He had spoken with Comey in private. He wanted to speak to Pecker in private, too. He remained concerned about the stories Pecker was keeping under wraps.

"How's our girl doing?" Trump asked Pecker, referring to Karen McDougal.

"She's quiet, easy," Pecker said. "Things are going fine."

Trump thanked him. Once the two men were finished talking, he invited Rhona Graff, into the office and asked her to make sure that Pecker was invited to the inauguration, two weeks later.

Soon enough, Trump would head down to Washington and take over the country, boxing up his old life—its clandestine payoffs, brewing scandals, and general malfeasance—and unpacking it at 1600 Pennsylvania Avenue. His swearing-in kicked off a lengthy period during which pundits suggested weekly that Trump either had or would soon grow to meet the stature of the office. The sentiment was repeated so often that it grew parodic. But it reflected a true belief in the country's institutions and an underappreciation for Trump's powers. He wasn't humbled or changed by the awesome responsibilities of the presidency. Instead, he took advantage of the media attention afforded to the nation's celebrity-in-chief and transformed the office in his own image.

Pecker's testimony about his January 2017 meeting with Trump included statements of questionable accuracy, and outright errors. He said that Trump's office was on the 24th floor, rather than the 26th. His suggestion that James Comey had been in Trump's office when he walked in was uncorroborated by Comey's own memo memorializing the meeting.

Those contradictions didn't matter too much with Steinglass questioning him. But for Pecker, the easy part of the trial was drawing to a close. It was Thursday afternoon and the first cross-examination of the trial loomed.

Steinglass showed the jurors a few pictures of Pecker and Dylan Howard at the White House in the summer of 2017. "My thank you dinner," Pecker called it.

Finally, Steinglass asked him to whether he had any bad feelings or ill will toward Trump.

"Not at all," Pecker said. "To the contrary." He said though he hadn't seen or spoken to Trump since 2019, he still considered him a friend.

❖   ❖   ❖

In their opening statements, Todd Blanche had made it clear the defense was poised to attack Michael Cohen at every opportunity. But we had no sense of the defense's plans when it came to various other witnesses, particularly a witness as potentially damning as David Pecker. On Thursday afternoon, Todd Blanche ceded the floor to his co-counsel, Emil Bove, who stepped to the lectern to begin cross-examination.

Susan Necheles, the state court veteran, had been expected to handle many of the prosecution's witnesses, including Pecker. But she'd lost cachet in TrumpWorld when she refused to sign her name to an aggressive letter denouncing the district attorney in the lead-up to trial. Her responsibilities at trial had been curtailed, leaving her two colleagues—neither of whom had anywhere close to her experience as a defense lawyer, or with state court procedure—to handle the majority of the witnesses.

But Bove was a quick-learner. Tall and olive-skinned, with a smooth, even-keeled manner, he was obsessive and detail-oriented. This was his first cross-examination.

Bove began questioning Pecker about the publisher's catch-and-kill practices, with the goal, it seemed, of making Pecker's actions on Trump's behalf seem conventional, "standard operating procedure." He noted that Pecker had undertaken similar efforts for a who's who of celebrities: Arnold Schwarzenegger, Tiger Woods, Mark Wahlberg and Rahm Emmanuel.

Next, Bove tried to cast doubt on Pecker's memory, suggesting that he'd been coached by the prosecution. At that point, the end of that long first week of testimony, Pecker finally shed his calm exterior. We saw the legendary temper that kept the publisher's subordinates in fear for their livelihoods.

Bove told Pecker that there was no record in the publisher's conversation with law enforcement of Trump having thanked him at the pre-inauguration meeting in Trump Tower. Had Pecker made it up?

The courtroom held its breath to see what he would say.

"I know what the truth is," Pecker responded curtly, with no sign of embarrassment. "I know exactly what was said to me."

Bove unearthed more contradictions, but Pecker fought back, making the lawyer seem petty, pedantic. In their final exchange, Bove asked Pecker about his obligations to the prosecution, again seeking to make him look like a tool of the state.

Pecker retorted that he was obligated to testify truthfully.

"And at this trial all sides asked you a lot of questions, right?" Bove asked.

"Yes," Pecker responded, still irritated.

"Some harder than others?"

"Yes."

"And you understand that, ultimately, they will decide whether or not they think you were truthful, right?" Bove asked.

"I have been truthful," Pecker said.

It was his final response. Bove sat down.

The defense had done nothing to dislodge the strong impression of the August 2015 and January 2017 Trump Tower meetings implanted in the minds of the jurors by Pecker's testimony. Bove might have persuaded some folks to doubt the specifics of Pecker's memory of these events. But it was difficult to imagine anyone would deny the meetings had happened, or that Pecker had agreed to suppress stories on behalf of Trump's campaign. After all, as had been demonstrated by the prosecution, Pecker went on to do exactly that.

✤   ✤   ✤

The government's witnesses could be divided, roughly, into two categories. There were minor witnesses, through whom the prosecutors, most often Becky Mangold, introduced important contextual evidence to jurors: the insults Trump hurled at Michael Cohen on Twitter, or excerpts of "Trump: Think Like a Billionaire" in which Trump stressed to readers the importance of keeping a close eye on one's money. And then there were tentpole witnesses, the key figures who passed the baton of the prosecution's case from one to another until the story reached its natural conclusion, presumably, in the shaky hands of Cohen himself.

David Pecker finally left the stand on Friday. He was followed by Rhona Graff, Trump's longtime assistant, the woman who had invited Pecker to the inauguration. In her brief time on the stand, she made it clear that she still adored her old boss. She said that he'd always been good to her, always respectful. She said the Trump Organization was the most stimulating job she could imagine. She acted as a momentary hype woman for "The Apprentice," calling it *the* most popular television show. And she said the show had elevated Trump to a whole other platform, transforming his reputation from businessman to entertainer. "Rock star status," she testified.

Despite all her adoration, all her praise for Trump, Graff, like Pecker before her, did what prosecutors needed her to do: She testified that, within the Trump Organization computer system, there was contact information for two particular women: Karen McDougal and "Stormy." And she said that she recalled Stormy Daniels visiting the 26th floor of Trump Tower.

It was to become one of the trial's prevailing trends. Trump's adversaries—Daniels and Michael Cohen—would provide crucial testimony for the prosecution. But some of the most damning statements came from people like David Pecker, Rhona Graff and Hope Hicks—people who felt real loyalty to Donald Trump.

CHAPTER FIVE

SHAME

Of all the celebrities who made cameos at Donald Trump's trial, whether at the courthouse itself, or simply in the testimony, none was more surprising—or, ultimately, more fitting—than Tila Tequila.

Tequila, whose real name was Nguyễn Thị Thiên Thanh, first attracted public notice in April 2002, when she posed as Playboy Magazine's cyber girl of the week. She posted the nude pictures on her own website, Tila'sHotspot.com, and the early social media platform Friendster, which kept kicking her off its platform.

Then she joined MySpace, and soon became its most popular user, racking up follows from adolescent boys in the tens of thousands, many of whom found that if you sent a message to Tila Tequila, she might just respond. She was accessible, opinionated and she never stopped posting. Tequila began to draw puzzled, mainstream attention through the sheer might of her popularity.

Entertainment Weekly pronounced her a "tireless titan of self-promotion." Vanity Fair said she resembled a "sex-crazed kewpie doll." In 2006, she appeared on Tucker Carlson's MSNBC show, "The Situation," where Carlson introduced her as "the most famous of a new breed of Internet celebrities. Famous because she says so, and also because millions agree with her."

"I've always had this thing where I wanted attention from everyone," Tequila told Carlson.

In 2007, she rode those qualities to the next floor of fame, starring in a sloppy reality show, "A Shot at Love with Tila Tequila." The show was a hit for MTV, and it led Tequila to a book deal: a self-promoting advice guide in which she announced her philosophy to the world in chapters titled "Sluts" and "Haters."

Tequila made frequent appearances in Pecker's magazines, and occasionally, at A.M.I. events. In 2009, at a party for Star Magazine, she professed herself a fan of the glossy. "It's gossip," she said. "You know, our world. It's Hollywood. All my friends. Scandal!" But she only seemed truly enthusiastic when asked about Twitter. "I am the queen of Twitter!" she declared.

Perhaps Tequila could have succeeded in politics, had she been inclined. Instead, she wanted to be a musician. But her music career never took off and, after a swift rise, her career plateaued.

Tequila returned to reality television in 2015, as a contestant on "Celebrity Big Brother" but was quickly booted from the show when old posts she'd made in support of Adolf Hitler resurfaced online. In November 2016, shortly after Trump was elected, she was a guest speaker at an alt-right celebration in Washington. Photographs depicted her proffering a Nazi salute.

She was perfectly representative of the era in which Trump renewed his celebrity for the digital age. Perhaps it shouldn't have been any surprise that her name would appear in the celebrity roll-call that was soon to overtake Justice Merchan's courtroom.

❧   ❧   ❧

Where Tequila used the social internet to build a career from nothing, Trump simply added to the ubiquity he'd established in the era of slow cultural processing. But he posted as prolifically and as shamelessly as Tequila, and in the course of doing so, welded his already well-established persona to the staccato pace of 2010s culture.

It's easy to understate the degree to which social internet has transformed the rhythms of our daily reality, in part because the online world has persisted in our imaginations as a space separate from "real life." In 2011, a sociologist named Nathan Jurgenson coined a term to describe that fallacy: "digital dualism."

"We are not crossing in and out of separate digital and physical realities," he wrote. The social internet and the physical world were the same, single existence. And individuals were not separated across the two spheres "as some dualistic 'first' and 'second' self." There was just one self, augmented by the online world.

The foremost site of Trump's self-augmentation was Twitter, which he joined in 2009; his first post advertised an upcoming appearance on the "Late Show." By 2012, he was tweeting constantly, often about politics, as when he announced in August of that year that "an 'extremely credible source' has called my office and told me @BarackObama's birth certificate is a fraud."

On the social internet Trump retained the polarizing qualities that had won him all those magazine covers. His ongoing stream of consciousness, of self-adulation, of combativeness, caused a similarly outsized response online. The color of the reactions to Trump ranged from opprobrium to adulation to a 'can-you-believe-he's-saying-this' irony. But the register was the same. Trump's tweets about Obama alienated many people. But others were unbothered, and some were thrilled. All engaged.

In June 2015, Trump went farther than ever in the repeating bit where he ran for president. He announced an actual run, entering a historically crowded Republican primary. The reasons Trump was dominant in the primary were legion, but one of them was his online reach. By September, Dan Pfeiffer, Obama's digital mastermind, acknowledged that the reality television star was "better at the internet than anyone else in the GOP."

He was also better at debate, a natural in the format, thanks to his familiarity with the conventions of televised competition and avoidance of the stage-managed euphemisms that made politicians so distasteful to the Republican base. His raw political instincts, jovial demagoguery and line-crossing helped too. By May 2016, Trump was the presumptive Republican nominee for president.

Trump was a living rebuttal to digital dualism. His tweets begat news cycles and moved markets; he pushed the bully pulpit online.

But there was no way to replicate that force in the courtroom. Those in the well at Trump's trial were gifted something like the clean separation that Jurgenson had warned was a fallacy. The proceedings were sealed against the internet and the jurors were barred from going online to look up information about the case. Tweets and other social media posts were printed out, quoted laboriously in legal papers and entered into evidence that would have to be reviewed offline during deliberations. 100 Centre Street inoculated itself as best it could from the 21st century.

⊹   ⊹   ⊹

Unsurprisingly, the former president looked angrier and angrier with each passing day. His fundraising emails were dour. "The Biden _SCAM TRIAL OF THE CENTURY_ has me trapped in court. This is **DISGUSTING**." Less than two weeks into the trial, the energy on his side of the gallery was lackluster, and only the occasional Trump supporter could be spotted in Collect Pond Park. The powers that had summoned a mob to the Capitol had apparently weakened, though the press continued to flock to Centre Street in greater and greater numbers, enthusing over the remarkable experience of seeing Trump pacified. Critics of the former president, including those in the gallery, basked in schadenfreude at Trump's tendency to close his eyes during proceedings. It was often posited by pundits as evidence of his decline. Trump, of course, insisted that he wasn't sleeping.

The cold air began to stream away from the island of Manhattan. April was drawing to an end and despite Trump's continuing complaints, the courtroom was warming in the spring sun. The minor witnesses who'd followed David Pecker—secretary Rhona Gaff, erstwhile Cohen banker Gary Farro, and CSPAN executive Dr. Robert Browning—didn't hold a candle to the commanding performance of David Pecker.

Ben, Willy, Maggie and I were doing all we could to get intel on the coming witnesses. On Sunday, April 28, Stormy Daniels told a Twitter follower that she was busy filming an R-rated show, tame by her standards. "Next week, it's back to anal, except it won't be me bending over," she added. I penciled in her testimony for the following week.

The Tuesday after Passover, the former president brought an entourage with him to Part 59, filling the previously empty pews on the left side of the gallery. They filed in behind him: Susie Wiles, his no-nonsense campaign manager; Texas's attorney general, Ken Paxton; and Trump's son Eric, even taller than his father. Before proceedings began, Eric stood at the front of the room speaking quietly with the former president, the two men separated by the wooden railing that divided the well and the gallery. Trump leaned on the bar during their hushed conversation and Jane Rosenberg, struck by the image, began to sketch them.

It was a quiet morning overall. In the dim light of the courtroom, chatter between the journalists was at a minimum. George Conway was snoozing in his hard-backed wooden seat.

He woke up in a hurry once Merchan strode out to the bench to make a ruling. The judge had determined that Trump was in violation of the gag order. He was holding the former president in contempt. But Merchan's delivery was rushed and vague; he spoke quickly, looking down at his notes. We had no idea how much Trump had been fined. Merchan soon changed subjects.

Luckily, a written version of his order quickly appeared on the court system's website. It was harsher than Merchan's manner had conveyed. Trump was fined $9,000 for his attacks on witnesses and the jury pool. He would be sent to jail if he continued to ignore court orders. It was the strongest assertion of the judge's authority so far.

Even if it deprived us of a spectacle, a written order didn't carry any less weight than a spoken warning. The threat of jail was real, as real as the restrictions that caused Olivia Nuzzi to be thrown out of the trial. Despite his mounting rage, Trump clearly took it seriously. No longer would he flirt with the line by threatening to violate the gag order. If his own social media posts were barred, he would have to entrust others with the responsibility of attacking enemies that the gag order placed off-limits. Those allies would soon begin to show up in person, transforming the atmosphere in Part 59.

In the meantime, it was incumbent on the prosecutors to keep the momentum going. The minor witnesses emphasized the amount of evidence prosecutors had amassed and the degree to which their case matched the image-obsessed, penny-pinching philosophy that was a part of Trump's public persona. But only the tentpole witnesses could help keep the prosecution's story going. It was time to call another one.

Shortly after noon on Tuesday, April 29, Joshua Steinglass summoned Keith Davidson, the Los Angeles lawyer who negotiated deals that silenced his clients, to the witness stand. In 2016 Davidson represented both Karen McDougal and Stormy Daniels.

In the prosecution's thinking, Davidson was the counterparty. The women he represented were not admitted to the negotiating table. It was Davidson, their agent, dealing with A.M.I. and, later, Michael Cohen. Most importantly, it was Davidson who actually received the hush money payment for Daniels, a transaction that would represent the climax of his testimony.

With flecks of gray in his well-coiffed brown hair, Davidson projected a perfect picture of lawyerly respectability when he emerged from a back room into the full commotion of Part 59. He climbed the stand and swore the oath. In the two decades he'd spent practicing law in Los Angeles, he'd learned how to make a good impression on jurors. But Davidson wasn't in Manhattan to practice law, and he wasn't used to having his own private dealings exposed. He was in for a rough experience.

Davidson's entry into the case was represented by a text he sent to Pecker subordinate Dylan Howard on June 7, 2016, the day Donald J. Trump won the Republican primary in California.

"I have a blockbuster Trump story," Davidson wrote to Howard, a frequent business partner and friend.

Howard promised to call Davidson the following morning. "I will get you more than anyone for it," he said. "You know why."

Steinglass guided Davidson's testimony through his negotiations with The National Enquirer, which by July 2016 seemed to be tapering off. Davidson reinvigorated them that month, alerting Howard that ABC News was interested in McDougal's story. Howard said he would warn Pecker of the impending danger to Trump. "Better be quick," Davidson texted.

At the lectern, Steinglass paused the narrative. "What did you mean by that?" he asked. Davidson explained that he was trying to play the Enquirer and ABC off each other, to create a sense of urgency.

Steinglass stumbled over his next question. "Is there anything wrong with that?" he offered, after some false starts.

"No," Davidson said, though he looked confused. The journalists' typing ceased for a moment.

"Can you explain why not?" Steinglass said.

"I don't understand your question," Davidson said.

"Yeah, I'm not sure I do either," Steinglass said. Self-deprecation was a go-to jury-pleaser in tense moments. He wiped his brow and rephrased: "Is there anything wrong with a lawyer negotiating on behalf of their client to get the best possible deal for their client?"

"I think that's our duty," Davidson responded. His eyes flicked over to the defense table where the former president was glaring at him, and Emil Bove was calmly taking notes, occasionally pausing to lean behind the former president's back and whisper with Todd Blanche.

Davidson's testimony was beginning to undermine the impression made by his appearance. In his private texts with Dylan Howard, he spoke callously about the negotiations and insinuated that he did not have McDougal's best interests at heart. He told Howard that she was being cornered "by the estrogen mafia" (by which he meant, counseled by women who were advising her to go to ABC.) Once McDougal's hush-money deal was underway with AMI, Davidson asked jokingly for an ambassadorship.

Davidson's cheeks went from pink to red as he read the old texts from a monitor at the witness stand, while Josh Steinglass soldiered on, guiding him to the completion of the deal that resulted in Karen McDougal's silence. The texts appeared on screens around the courtroom, too, and the journalists in the gallery tweeted them out, as evidence of the conspiracy and the general scuzziness of the catch and kill deal. David Pecker had seemed utterly blasé about his role in the business of scandal, and his shamelessness had shielded him on the stand. Davidson was different. He prided himself on looking like a lawyer, speaking like a lawyer. Given his role in the case, he was realizing that the less flattering parts of his practice were bound to come to light. His awareness of the contradictions appeared to embarrass him, and it was his embarrassment that made him seem shady.

❖   ❖   ❖

Davidson grew up in Brockton, Massachusetts, an old factory town about an hour south of Boston. He was an ambitious kid, whose family didn't have much money. His father urged him to become a firefighter, but Davidson wanted something more. Another friend's father was a lawyer, and in that family's house, there was a library, a room given over entirely to books. Davidson admired the seriousness and dignity of the room. He decided to become a lawyer.

He worked his way through Boston College, then attended night classes at New England Law School. In the late 1990s, Davidson moved west to join friends in Los Angeles, finishing up his law degree in Orange County in 2000.

It was a fascinating time in entertainment. Survivor," the ur-reality show competition, premiered that year. MySpace launched three years later. Together, the two formats—reality television, and a rung below it, the social internet—would produce a Cambrian explosion of celebrity, and new orders of fame for the residents of Los Angeles to pursue.

By virtue of the rules of jurisdiction, American cities spawn plaintiff's lawyers—lawsuit-filing lawyers—who mine the particulars of the local economy for their own ends. In Miami, they sue cruise ship companies. In Houston, they feed off oil and gas. And in Los Angeles, there is a lucrative sideline in celebrity, toward which Davidson made his way, opening a practice in Beverly Hills.

Soon, he was representing clients from Hollywood's seedier corners: strippers, porn stars and people who'd had some run-in with an actor or singer, an heiress or a newly minted social media star. His clients knew about celebrities' errant sex tapes, rehab visits and cheating scandals. Davidson gained a reputation. He could throw a punch if necessary. But with willing partners, he was happy to withdraw the threat in exchange for a mutually satisfactory agreement. No one's reputation need be marred by negative publicity.

❖   ❖   ❖

In August 2016, the Karen McDougal deal was finalized, and Keith Davidson briefly left the prosecution's story. But he resurfaced in October, following David Farenthold's Washington Post article about the "Access Hollywood" tape. The election was a month away and the last thing Donald Trump needed was more bad publicity.

What for the Trump campaign was an unmitigated crisis was, for Keith Davidson, a business opportunity. He was in possession of a singular commodity: Stormy Daniels's story. After the tape was released, and reporters began pursuing story lines about Trump's bad behavior with women, the value of the story skyrocketed. The only negative issue, Davidson testified, was the necessity of dealing with a well-known "asshole:" Trump's fixer, Michael Cohen.

Both Davidson and Gina Rodriguez, the woman who billed herself as Daniels's manager, had encountered Cohen five years earlier, when the rumor of Daniels having slept with Trump appeared briefly online. Cohen had yelled and screamed at both of them over the phone, even though they were willing to cooperate to have the story taken down. Dealing with the fixer was a deeply *unpleasant* experience. In October 2016, "no one wanted to talk to Cohen," Davidson testified.

But Dylan Howard put the Beverly Hills lawyer on a text with the New York fixer, and the two men began to negotiate. Cohen had already agreed to pay Stormy Daniels $120,000. Davidson testified that he'd just needed Cohen to add $10,000, so that he too could get paid. Then he would write up a contract and all that remained would be for Cohen to wire the money.

Davidson sent over the contract on Oct. 11, in the expectation that he'd receive the hush money three days later. But with the election in sight, Cohen was a font of excuses. First, he cited the Yom Kippur holiday. Next, he said he didn't have the wiring instructions.

"He stated that the computer systems were 'all fucked up,'" Davidson testified bitterly. His annoyance with Cohen, underwater for eight years, shot to the surface. "He stated, *'You can't believe what we're going through. The Secret Service is in here. They have so many goddamn firewalls. I can't get shit. It's not my fault. You're going to have to resend the agreements again. I never got your emails.'"* Davidson paused, then added, "Even though he previously told me he received them, and the wiring instructions."

Davidson grew convinced that Cohen was trying to stall until after the election, when the value of Daniels's story would drop as quickly as it had risen. He told Dylan Howard—who was in independent contact with Cohen—that the story would likely be released some other way, and that there would be a media firestorm.

"I can't believe Cohen let this go," Davidson texted. "It's going to be a shit show."

"All because Trump is tight," Howard said.

In the courtroom, Steinglass paused Davidson's story. "What did you understand that to mean?" he asked.

"That Donald Trump is frugal," Davidson said, cautiously, not daring to look over at the defense table.

On Oct 26, he again sent Cohen the wiring instructions so that he could get paid, never believing it would happen. He was poised for Daniels to go public. But the following day, early in the morning, there was an email from Cohen in his inbox. It said that the money—$130,000 for Stormy Daniels's silence—had been wired.

Dylan Howard checked in later that day. "Money wired I am told," he texted Davidson.

Davidson confirmed. "Funds received," he wrote back.

It was the jurors' first time seeing the transfer of the money from Cohen to Davidson, the final transaction of the Trump Tower conspiracy.

That evening, as usual, I stood on a makeshift platform on Centre Street, recording a video about the day in court, dressed in whatever business casual getup I'd thrown together 12 hours earlier. My reluctance to record myself hadn't entirely dissipated, but I was growing used to the routine and liked working with the shoestring video crew that *The Times* sent downtown each day. They realized that I was typically famished when I finally left the courthouse around 5:30, and often someone would be sent to buy me a candy bar or a sandwich. Despite the modesty of the videos themselves, which appeared on the *Times* home screen, I was being treated like "the talent."

The reception of the videos was the biggest surprise. I got more feedback, more text messages, more general *interest* because of them than any piece of journalism I'd ever done. They did not, however, prompt within my friend group a greater interest in the trial, or questions about the case. Mostly, people just asked me where I was getting my outfits.

❖   ❖   ❖

On the morning of May 2, just before the prosecution's examination ended, we got one more hint of Davidson's vulnerabilities. He had a fondness for euphemism, and often used excess verbiage to elevate base transactions.

An irony of the hush money payments was that neither of them had worked for too long. The seismic interest in Trump's candidacy and presidency, and the persistence of two Wall Street Journal reporters, Michael Rothfeld and Joe Palazzolo, unearthed both women's stories.

Rothfeld and Palazzolo discovered McDougal's story before the election and working with another reporter, Lukas Alpert, published their findings on Nov. 4, 2016, before anyone went to the polls. The story noted that A.M.I. had paid for McDougal's story and hadn't published it. It also mentioned Davidson's representation of Stormy Daniels and the fact that Daniels had abruptly halted discussions with "Good Morning America" to share the story of *her* relationship with Trump.

It took Rothfeld and Palazzolo more than a year, but in January 2018, they broke the story that Stormy Daniels had been paid off too. In response, Daniels signed her name to a statement cooked up by Cohen and Davidson, to the effect that she had not received hush money.

Standing at the lectern, Steinglass asked Davidson to characterize the truthfulness of that statement. Davidson responded that, read strictly, the denial was technically true.

"Can you explain that?" Steinglass asked. "How is that technically true?"

"It wasn't hush money," Davidson insisted. "It was consideration in a civil settlement agreement."

Steinglass asked him to explain what he meant by consideration.

"A consideration is money or something of value that's exchanged in a contract," Davidson said. "I will pay you $5 if you mow my lawn. The $5 will be a consideration."

Steinglass asked him again if he would use the term "hush money" to describe the payoff to Daniels.

"I would never use that word," Davidson said.

"And what would be the word you would use to describe it?"

"Consideration."

"Okay," Steinglass said. Soon afterward, he stepped down. It was Emil Bove's turn.

✦   ✦   ✦

Davidson and Bove made for compelling adversaries. Bove didn't come from wealth either. He was raised in Seneca Falls, N.Y., whose landmark status as the birthplace of the American women's rights movement was overshadowed by the reality of a small rural town where industry had come and gone. In high school, Bove was a three-sport athlete and salutatorian, and he went to undergrad at SUNY-Albany, where he played lacrosse. Before going to law school, he worked as a paralegal at the Southern District—like his defense colleague, Todd Blanche—and decided, with single-minded focus, that he wanted to become an assistant United States attorney.

In 2012, as his future client was promoting the idea that Barack Obama wasn't born in the United States, Bove made good on his ambition. He soon fashioned an impressive early career as a federal prosecutor at Southern, overseeing major cases including the prosecutions of Venezuela's president, Nicolás Maduro and of Cesar Sayoc, a Trump supporter who in 2018 pleaded guilty to sending 16 defective bombs to Obama, Hillary Clinton, and other prominent democrats. He had a curt, bulldozing style that rubbed some of his colleagues the wrong way, but almost everyone agreed that Bove was a highly effective lawyer.

He was good when he had a strong case, and good when he didn't. He could make a compelling legal brief out of a seemingly empty argument, buffing it into something that looked respectable. By the time Cohen was setting up his shell companies, Bove had risen up the ranks of Southern to become co-chief of its National Security and International Narcotics Unit.

But in 2020, prosecutors that he supervised failed to turn over a key piece of evidence to defense lawyers—and one, upon discovering the error, sought to "bury" the offending document in a pile of exhibits sent to the defense in an email. The defense alerted the federal judge overseeing the case: failure to turn over potentially exculpatory evidence is one of the most serious misdeeds a prosecutor can commit. Eventually, the Southern district, despite winning a conviction, dropped all charges. Though Bove wasn't directly involved, supervisors are held responsible for such mistakes. In a private text, he admitted to his co-chief that the junior prosecutors had told the defense a "flat lie." In front of the judge, though, he defended them.

In 2021, after negative press about the case, Bove's time working for Southern ended. Less than two years later, Blanche recruited him to an organization that valued the kind of loyalty he'd shown his subordinates: the sovereign administration of Donald J. Trump.

Bove worked with Blanche on the various cases against their client and steadily endeared himself to the former president. He didn't seem enamored of the spotlight, but neither did he shy away from attention. And while the first cross-examination of his defense career—that of David Pecker—had been unremarkable, he was more than ready for Keith Davidson.

Bove stepped to the lectern and introduced himself politely, inviting a courteous response. He began with a series of questions establishing that Davidson had never met Trump. Davidson agreed that he hadn't, and that he had no first-hand knowledge of the business records at issue in the case.

"In fact, everything you know about President Trump came from either TV or Michael Cohen," Bove said, breezily.

"No," Davidson said. But he agreed, again, that he'd had no personal interactions with the former president.

For several minutes, Bove established Davidson's closeness with Dylan Howard, his ongoing professional relationship with Gina Rodriguez, who'd helped manage Stormy Daniels and his opinion of Michael Cohen.

"You said something this morning along the lines that Michael Cohen could be an 'aggressive' guy, right?" Bove said.

"Yes," Davidson acknowledged.

"And you can be aggressive too, can't you?" Bove said, looking directly at Davidson. His voice was raised, his tone, sharpened.

"I don't know," Davidson said uneasily.

"What does the word 'extortion' mean to you?" Bove asked, letting the question hang in the air in front of the jurors, who appeared electrified.

"It's the obtaining of property by threat of fear or force," Davidson answered after a couple of moments. He looked miserable.

Bove provided an alternative definition: "Compelling an action by force or coercion," he said. "How's that?"

Davidson shrugged. His veneer of legitimacy was under attack. Bove was calling him a criminal.

The prosecutors whispered to each other, tilting their heads down, making it impossible to catch what they were saying.

"When you were negotiating on behalf of Ms. McDougal and on behalf of Stormy Daniels, one of your concerns was on staying on the right side of the line with respect to extortion, correct?" Bove continued.

"I suppose," Davidson said.

As Bove began to familiarize the jury with Davidson's resumé, the courtroom seemed to expand in order to accommodate a roll-call of the bold-face names of the celebrity-obsessed digital environment in which Trump rose to prominence. Davidson's ties to the ecosystem ran deep. Each celebrity named caused a new wave of excitement from the press, and a corresponding crescendo of typing.

Davidson acknowledged he'd represented the employee of a rehab facility who'd leaked information about Lindsay Lohan. He denied posting stills from a sex tape involving Hulk Hogan to a gossip website, The Dirty.com—the same sex tape that would ultimately lead to the demise of the website Gawker. But agreed that he'd taken steps to deal another sex tape, this one involving Tila Tequila. And he'd represented several clients with claims against Charlie Sheen.

"And who you extracted sums of money from Charlie Sheen on behalf of, correct?" Bove asked.

"There was no extraction," Davidson said, red-faced. The questions were striking him like blows. He was taking pauses before answering questions, thinking through the best way to respond.

"You took steps to get Mr. Sheen to pay, correct?"

"We asserted that there was tortious activity committed and valid settlements were executed," Davidson said.

A few minutes later, Bove tried to get it in plain English. "You got Mr. Sheen to pay, correct?"

Davidson lapsed briefly into Latin, his final resort in a fight. "Assuming arguendo that he did pay and there was a settlement agreement, that settlement would be confidential, and I would not discuss it here."

Bove seized upon the Latin. "Look. We're both lawyers. I'm not here to play lawyer games with you," he said. "I'm just here to ask questions and get straight answers. I'm not asking you to assume anything. I'm asking what you remember. All right? Can you answer?"

"Answer to what?" Davidson said. Something in him looked to have woken up, and now he looked ready to punch Bove. The jurors were rigid in their seats.

"I'm not asking you to assume anything," Bove said. "I'm just asking for truthful answers. Okay?"

"You're getting truthful answers," Davidson said, then added, seemingly with as much scorn as he could put into his voice, "Sir."

◆   ◆   ◆

On May 2, Alvin Bragg returned to the courtroom to watch Bove conclude his grilling of Keith Davidson. The district attorney's expression was as indecipherable as ever. It was hard to imagine two lawyers with less in common then Bragg, the camera-shy civil servant, and Davidson, the celebrity-targeting mercenary. I made myself laugh, picturing the district attorney respectfully pronouncing the name "Tila Tequila."

Bove finished his cross, having sought to convince the jury that Davidson was a serial extorter who had applied his talents to Trump in the final weeks of the campaign, just as he had to Charlie Sheen and Tila Tequila and a host of others. It was the most compelling thread the defense had established thus far and I was eager to see how they might build upon it. If they could position Davidson as a villain, maybe there was a way to exonerate Trump, arguing that the McDougal and Daniels payments were necessitated by extortion attempts, not planned as part of a conspiracy.

Squint at Keith Davidson and it was possible to see an increasingly anachronistic version of the American dream. He'd pulled himself up by his bootstraps and found himself a lucrative vocation. But the circumstances of his profession had brought him into a world of where another type of savvy yielded greater success. Reality television stars and internet personalities, influencers and politicians got by on a new type of ethic, one that he did not possess. Davidson may have been a fighter. But on the stand, he was uncomfortable with negative attention. The courtroom didn't protect him from that feeling. It exposed him.

Shortly after Bove finished his cross, Trump's Truth Social account chirped up: "Contrary to the FAKE NEWS MEDIA, I don't fall asleep during the Crooked D.A.'s Witch Hunt, especially not today," it said. "I simply close my beautiful blue eyes, sometimes, listen intensely, and take it ALL in!!!"

CHAPTER SIX

TALKING POINTS

It didn't take long for the next tentpole witness to appear. Hope Hicks entered the courtroom shortly before noon on Friday, May 3, her high heels clacking on the vinyl tile. She walked past the front row of the gallery and into the well, where the former president sat staring. Behind him were rows and rows of press who gawked shamelessly. Anderson Cooper sat on the right side of the gallery, looking up from a copy of the Wall Street Journal. Lawrence O'Donnell was on the left; as would be obvious during his show later that evening, his contempt for Hicks was hard to suppress. The only people who looked nonplussed were the jurors; it struck me that perhaps Hicks, who dealt primarily with the press, was a bigger celebrity to us than to anyone else.

It was clear that Hicks was upset. Her face was clouded and misty. When she introduced herself—noting that she was testifying because she had been compelled to do so by subpoena—her voice was throaty, low and difficult to hear. Matthew Colangelo, standing at the lectern, asked that she move closer to the microphone. "I'm really nervous," she said, addressing the jurors directly. The court officers congregated near the front of the gallery, blocking many reporters' view of the witness, as if they were instinctively drawn to protect Hicks.

Where Davidson's profession placed him several degrees away from Trump, Hicks was in direct contact, one of the first campaign aides he brought on for the 2016 race. Like her new boss, Hicks had no experience in politics and her ignorance of national elections exceeded even his. But she was energetic, hard-working and profoundly loyal, insisting to the Trump skeptics of her Gold Coast Connecticut world that he was a deeply misunderstood person.

Now, as she testified about her upbringing and early work experience, the former president fixed his eyes on her. They hadn't spoken since 2022, the year cracks in Hicks's loyalty began to appear. She didn't believe he'd won the 2020 election. She was horrified by the images of the Jan. 6 attack on the Capitol. These sentiments, expressed privately to friends, were made public when Congress started digging into the melee.

But far more than any witness thus far, Hicks's professional life was forged in the kiln of Trump's magnetism. He remained the strongest tenet of her public identity. It would soon become clear that many of her memories working for him were positive.

Colangelo asked his questions gently, and Hicks appeared to settle into some comfort on the stand, describing the world within Trump Tower, where she became an adult. "It's a very big and successful company," she said of the Trump Organization. "But it's really run like a small family business in certain ways."

Colangelo took her through her time joining the Trump campaign, and Hicks's work for and travel with the candidate. He asked her about her knowledge of the trial's primary characters: David Pecker, Rhona Graff, Allen Weisselberg and Michael Cohen. She knew them all, of course, and briefly described their relationship to Trump.

Eventually, Colangelo guided Hicks to the fall of 2016, asking a question that dissolved all the composure she had gained since taking the stand.

"Are you familiar with something that came to be known as the Access Hollywood tape?"

Hicks swallowed hard. Her jaw tightened. "Yes," she said.

"When did you first find out about the Access Hollywood tape?" Colangelo asked.

"It would have been the afternoon of October 7."

Trump crossed his arms. Now, instead of looking directly at Hicks, he fixed his attention on the monitor.

On Oct. 7, 2016, Hicks was sitting in her office on Trump Tower's

14th floor when she received an email from David Fahrenthold, a Washington Post reporter, who told her that he'd obtained the tape, and provided a transcript of Trump's remarks: *"I better use some tic tacs, just in case I start kissing her. You know I'm automatically attracted to beautiful—I just start kissing them. It's like a magnet. Just kiss. I don't even wait."*

She forwarded the email to the leadership of the Trump campaign, who happened to be debate prepping the candidate on the 25th floor. "Deny, deny deny," Hicks wrote in her email.

Colangelo asked her about what she'd written.

"It's a reflex," Hicks said. "I, obviously, was a little shocked and not realizing that the entirety of the transcript was in the email."

"It's hard to deny a tape when there is a full transcript of it that you already have," Colangelo said.

Hope Hicks exemplified the conflict that existed within Trump's people, even after they appeared to have left his orbit. They were frequently forced to choose between loyalty and honesty. On the stand in Part 59, Hicks seemed to feel she had no choice but to tell the truth. So she was candid: While under Trump's sway in 2016, confronted with an unprecedentedly damning news story, her first instinct—her *reflex*—had been to lie.

❖   ❖   ❖

The Greenwich, Connecticut of Hope Hick's childhood was a bastion of old-line Republicanism from which Prescott Bush created a dynasty that spawned two American presidents. Born in 1988, Hicks was modeling for Ralph Lauren by the time she was 13. She appeared in *Vogue* and *Vanity Fair*, and was featured on a CBS soap, a children's golf special, and the covers of a paperback book series about a precocious girl who time travels with a magical hourglass. She was early to enter Trump's image-focused universe, through a door that would have been inaccessible to many of Keith Davidson's Hollywood clients.

Hicks and her older sister, Mary Grace, were the subject of an extensive story in the summer 2002 issue of *Greenwich Magazine*. The article described a whirlwind daily routine: school, drive into Manhattan, two hours of modeling, drive back to Greenwich, two hours of swim practice, dinner, homework, television and bed. The young Hicks relied on family to make it feel worthwhile, bonding with her mother and sister on the commute.

Hicks followed her father into the politics-adjacent communications industry. After graduating from Southern Methodist University with a degree in English, she took an entry level job at Hiltzik Strategies, a PR firm run by a veteran of Hillary Clinton's New York senate campaign. One of the firm's more prominent clients, Ivanka Trump, tapped her to join The Trump Organization in October 2014—the month she turned 26. Three months into her employment, Ivanka's father, her new boss, told her out of the blue that they were going to Iowa.

"After that first trip to Iowa, it was clear he was exploring a potential political run," Hicks testified.

Around the time of that first trip, the candidate told her she would be campaign press secretary. "I had no experience and worked at the company, not on the campaign, so I didn't take it very seriously," she said. "But eventually, I just started spending so much time working on the campaign that I became a member of the campaign team."

Suddenly she was within the inner circle of the traveling roadshow that was the Trump 2016 operation. As her new boss flew from state to state, she managed all things media—an enormous job for someone with no experience—dealing with hundreds of reporter requests a day and working late into the night. She relied on the people around her—including Trump himself—to get through it, and the 2016 campaign became something like a second family.

Juror 3, absorbed in the testimony, seemed to start as Colangelo interrupted Hicks' reverie.

"Are you familiar with the term talking points?" he asked. "Is that a term that is used in the campaign context?"

"Yes," said Hicks.

"What are 'talking points?'"

"They're typically just a summary of messages," she said. "For people to remember. Like, you want to make sure everyone is on the same page about something."

She resumed her recitation. By the fall, she would leave Trump Tower around 7 every morning, fly privately to campaign stops all over the country and then—unless they were so far west that returning made no sense—flying back to New York City, to start the whole routine again the next day. She spoke to Trump constantly.

"Was there also a communications team for the campaign?" Colangelo asked.

"At that point, no," she said, addressing the jury directly. "It was just me and Mr. Trump, who is better than anybody at communications and branding." Trump was still watching her on the monitor, appearing to ignore Todd Blanche whispering in his ear.

"Who on the campaign was responsible for the overall messaging strategy?" Colangelo asked.

"I would say that Mr. Trump was responsible," Hicks said. "He knew what he wanted to say and how he wanted to say it and we were all just following his lead."

In her role as campaign secretary, Hicks heard Trump interact with David Pecker, praising his coverage of the campaign's Republican rivals, including a story about Dr. Ben Carson leaving a sponge in a patient's brain. ("BEN CARSON BUTCHERED MY BRAIN.") Hicks recalled Trump telling Pecker that the story was "Pulitzer-worthy" and three journalists behind me snorted audibly.

❖   ❖   ❖

Colangelo asked Hicks to describe her first reaction to the email from Fahrenthold, the Washington Post reporter.

"I was concerned, very concerned," she said. In that moment, her face *looked* concerned, as if she were reliving the ordeal. She rubbed her forehead.

After she forwarded the email, Hicks testified, she took the elevator to the 25th floor to discuss the matter in person. Gathered in a glass conference room with Trump, Steve Bannon, Kellyanne Conway, and Jason Miller were Jared Kushner, Stephen Miller and Chris Christie.

Hicks sought to be discreet as she beckoned the recipients of her email out of the room for a chat. But the candidate could hardly have missed what was happening, given that several extras joined, too. "Obviously, the sight of the six of us gathered out there was a sign that something was afoot," she said. "And Mr. Trump asked us to come into the conference room at some point and share with him what we were discussing."

Hicks read the email to her boss, and part of the transcript to her boss. Eventually, she handed him the transcript so he could read it himself.

The Washington Post published its story in the middle of the afternoon.

"Was Mr. Trump upset?" Colangelo asked.

"Yes," Hicks said quietly. "Yes, he was."

"Fair to say he was as mad as you've ever seen him?"

"Objection," Bove said, and Merchan sustained it. Colangelo moved on, asking her about the campaign's reaction to the tape. Hicks said that she'd been stunned. "There was consensus among us all that the tape was damaging and this was a crisis," she said.

The prosecution looked pleased. Hicks's sustained loyalty to Trump didn't diminish their strategy. In fact, it was better, far better for her to signal her clear loyalty to him—it made her damning testimony all the more convincing.

"I know Mr. Trump felt like this wasn't good," Hicks continued. "But it was also just like two guys talking privately—locker room talk. It wasn't anything to get so upset over. Certainly, he didn't want to offend anybody, but I think he felt like this was like pretty standard stuff for two guys chatting with each other."

Thus, an infamous talking point was born, from Trump's lips to the world's ears, with none of the interference that a more traditional—a more experienced—campaign spokeswoman might have offered. Hicks's testimony, as elicited by Colangelo, sent a clear signal to the jury and the reporters in the gallery. Hicks, like Cohen, was a pass-through. No matter which of Trump's underlings carried his message, the candidate was always just one-degree removed. The comment Hicks offered to the *Post* came straight from Trump. Soon "locker room talk" was everywhere because the story was everywhere.

The news blotted out the rest of the world, Hicks recalled. Hurricane Matthew, the most powerful storm of the season, was anticipated to make landfall the day after the *Post* published its story. "I don't think anybody remembers where or when that hurricane made landfall," Hicks said. "It was all Trump, all the time, for the next 36 hours."

The next day, Trump released a video, which Colangelo played for the courtroom, saying that he'd said and done things he'd regretted, including the comments on the tape. He even apologized, though he looked as if he were being held hostage. Then, an immediate return to form: He attacked the Clintons in the same manner that David Pecker had in the pages of The National Enquirer, calling Bill a sexual abuser and Hillary a bully. A day later, he traveled to St. Louis to attend the second presidential debate against Hillary Clinton. Colangelo asked Hicks who moderated that debate and she responded that it had been Martha Raddatz and Anderson Cooper.

Cooper, sitting in front of me, didn't stir, even as we all stared at him. It was bound to happen, but it was no less startling for its inevitability: a member of the media, reporting on the proceeding from the gallery, manifesting in the testimony. Political history was haunting itself.

Having reminded the jury of the specter of Pecker, Colangelo proceeded to knit Hicks's testimony into Davidson's from earlier in the week. He asked her about Michael Rothfeld's November 4, 2016, *Wall Street Journal* article about A.M.I. burying Karen McDougal's story. It was the first time Hicks had heard of McDougal, she said; she'd been on her way to an Ohio rally when Rothfeld emailed her.

Hicks began to liaise with every member of the conspiracy. Knowing Michael Cohen had a relationship with Pecker, she called him first, to see if he had intel. He feigned ignorance, so she called Pecker himself, who said McDougal had been paid for magazine covers and fitness columns and that "it was all very legitimate."

Hicks drafted statements for inclusion in the *Journal* article, all of them denying any knowledge of McDougal's story, and sent them to Michael Cohen for review. Once Trump finished giving his rally speech, he got personally involved, calling Pecker and then drafting his own statement. That statement was simple: "We have no knowledge of any of this." And McDougal's affair claim? "Totally untrue."

Colangelo asked Hicks if she'd mentioned to Trump that Stormy Daniels would be mentioned in the same story. She had.

"What, if anything, did he say when you told him that Stormy Daniels would be mentioned in The Wall Street Journal story?"

"He wanted to know the context," Hicks said, adding, "And he wanted to make sure that there was a denial of any kind of relationship."

✦ ✦ ✦

Izzy Brourman leaned forward to write the words "deny deny deny" on the heavyweight watercolor paper, a work-in-progress of Hope Hicks. She tended to adorn her images with words, a synthesis that conveyed the nature of the proceedings better than either medium alone. Hicks hadn't given the other sketch artists much—Jane Rosenberg complained that her face was too flawless, without any idiosyncratic features to capture—so it was a useful tendency of Izzy's, to accessorize her portraits with interesting testimony.

Brourman, roughly the same age as Hicks, found herself particularly interested in the ex-White House spokeswoman. Both women were outsiders, newcomers whose already-challenging jobs were made more so by the skepticism of others.

Brourman's first run as a sketch artist came unexpectedly two years earlier, when she traveled down to Virginia for the trial that pitted the actor Johnny Depp against his ex-wife, Amber Heard. Brourman had long been a fan of Depp, in part thanks to his portrayal of her spiritual forebear, in the 1998 film adaptation of "Fear and Loathing in Las Vegas." But she bristled at the insinuation that any art she might make could be understood as "fan art," aligned in some way with either Depp or Heard. That wasn't her agenda.

As an artist, she wasn't initially interested in the imprimatur of an institution like the court system. But she realized embracing the role of sketch artist was the most iconoclastic thing she could do, preserving her individuality against the push of the partisan public.

A year later, at Trump's arraignment, her rivalry with the other court artists began in earnest; they glared at her, disturbed by this newcomer in their midst. Their job was difficult: long hours, harsh deadlines, sketching realistic scenes to be sent out on the wires along with articles from the Associated Press and Reuters. Like the reporters who were their colleagues-in-arms, they often took the stress out on each other, battling for the best seat. Theirs was a small club, and Brourman an unknown, without the responsibilities that weighed them down.

Izzy, however, saw an opportunity; where the other sketch artists worked with chalky pastels, she used watercolor and pen. Where they worked in a realistic, journalistic style, Brourman drew the outsized drama of the courtroom into the characters themselves. Her version of Trump was a grotesque, but so were her other players, surreal bright-hued figured that reflected the bizarre nature of the proceedings.

Before the trial began, Brourman learned the other sketch artists had gotten together without her, devising a new system for who would get the best seat in the courtroom on a given day. She didn't sweat it. She felt lucky to be there. So what if she had to sit next to a *Times* reporter, instead of the other sketch artists? She didn't belong to either group. She was sui generis, one-of-a-kind, and missing out on the ideal perspective would just help her stand out. She wanted to take risks, to be free, to distill the story of the day into a single painting without worrying what anyone else thought.

In Part 59, Hicks was testifying that, after Trump pushed her to deny any relationship with Stormy Daniels, Michael Cohen had followed by telling her he had a statement "from Storm."

"I didn't know what he was talking about, and I didn't want to know," Hicks said.

It struck Izzy as another canvas-worthy sentiment. She began to trace the letters into her drawing.

❖   ❖   ❖

Lunch time, May 3. Outside, on Centre Street, the protesters of Rise and Resist were out in full force for the Manhattan district attorney, blocking traffic, shaking signs and chanting. One of the protesters, Julie DeLaurier, wore a New York Rangers jacket and held a placard: "It's not about hush money. It's ELECTION FRAUD." "Thank you, Alvin Bragg," she shouted.

DeLaurier wanted to shift the media narrative. Despite the clear ambition of the prosecution's case, the media insisted on labeling it the "hush money trial." DeLaurier was irritated at us for missing the point.

At 67, she was a full time Trump-protester. She was disappointed—and baffled—that so few people were engaged in the same fight. She didn't want to spend her retirement opposing the former president, but she felt it necessary. Trump lived in her brain, transforming her life in ways both large and small. She believed he was seeking to destroy the country.

Soon, the police arrived and asked the group to clear out of the street. They complied. Civil disobedience was rarely part of the R&R playbook.

As they migrated to the sidewalk, Trump supporters flooded out of Collect Pond Park to engage them. This was what the MAGA faction had been waiting for: the enemy, outside the secure environment of the courthouse. The boldest pro-Trump demonstrator, Angela, wore a Burger King crown, held a bible and kept a shofar tucked under her right arm, as if to symbolize the unified might of the Judeo-Christian right. She refused to give Nate Schweber her last name. Instead, she shouted insults at the elderly protesters of Right to Resist through a bullhorn. A police officer told her to stop; protesters were barred from any means of electrical amplification. Nearby, one of his colleagues cracked wise. "You can have it your way at Burger King, but not here."

❖   ❖   ❖

After the lunch break, Colangelo resumed his questioning. Trump, apparently tired of looking at Hicks, shut his eyes, allowing them to flutter open briefly when Blanche whispered in his ear.

Hicks was calmer, too. She was composed, leaning back, reading the witness monitor, which displayed texts she'd exchanged with Michael Cohen in November 2016, after the Wall Street Journal ran its Karen McDougal story. Cohen told her the story was a dud. "I don't see it getting much play," he texted.

On the stand, Hicks laughed. "Just a little irony there," she said, gesturing with her eyes to the rows of reporters in front of her, covering the criminal trial that sprang from the story. We dutifully quoted her in our live blogs.

As he wound down, Colangelo pursued one last scrap from Hicks. After establishing that she'd followed Trump to the White House, he asked her about the public revelation of the hush money payment to Stormy Daniels. As the jurors knew, Rothfeld and Palazzolo broke the news in January 2018, in the Wall Street Journal.

In February, Michael Cohen decided to take the proverbial bullet for his boss, releasing a statement to Maggie Haberman of *The New York Times* in which he admitted to making the payment. The gallery's attention swung toward Maggie, who ignored it.

Hicks testified that she spoke to Trump the morning after Maggie's story published. The president told her something she had a hard time believing: That Michael Cohen had paid Daniels out of the kindness of his heart, to protect the boss from a false allegation.

"How long had you known Michael Cohen by that point?" Colangelo asked.

"Three and a half years."

"And did the idea that Mr. Cohen would have made a $130,00 payment to Stormy Daniels out of the kindness of his heart, was that consistent with your interactions with him up to that point?"

Bove tried to object, but Merchan overruled him.

"I would say that would be out of character for Michael," Hicks said.

"Why would it be out of character for Michael?" Colangelo asked.

Bove tried again; Merchan again overruled him.

"I didn't know Michael to be an especially charitable person or selfless person," Hicks said. "He's the kind of person who seeks credit."

At that, a number of reporters grinned maniacally as they bent over their laptops, typing out the quote.

Colangelo asked Hicks if the president then said anything about the *timing* of the Daniels payoff becoming public.

"Oh, yes," she said. "He wanted to know how it was playing, and just my thoughts and opinion about this story versus having a different kind of story before the campaign—had Michael not made that payment. And I think Mr. Trump's opinion was it was better to be dealing with it now, and that it would have been bad to have that story come out before the election."

The answer went straight to Trump's motive. Had he simply been seeking to hide affairs from his wife, there was no reason why it'd be better to have it break in 2018—no particular date would have been more or less suitable for a revelation of marital infidelity. The image of Trump, content in the White House, telling his spokeswoman that he was satisfied with the timing, reinforced for the jury the same motive that David Pecker had established on the witness stand the previous week: The cover-up was executed for the sake of the campaign.

"No further questions," Colangelo said.

When Matthew Colangelo sat down and Emil Bove stood up to cross-examine the prosecution's third major witness of the trial, the transformation in Hicks was remarkable. All composure drained from her face, replaced by trepidation. She knew better than almost anyone how Trump dealt with disloyalty. But Bove's manner, to start, was the opposite of the approach he'd taken with Davidson: courtly, and just as gentle as Matthew Colangelo.

"Ms. Hicks, I want to start by talking a little bit about your time at The Trump Organization, if that's okay," he said.

She nodded. Bove confirmed that she had started at the Trump Organization in 2014 as director of communications, a position created just for her. And as he spoke, Hicks began to cry.

The courtroom reacted strongly to the sudden show of vulnerability. Bove, conveying sympathy, asked Merchan if the courtroom should take a brief break and when the judge asked Hicks if she wanted to pause, she nodded, still in tears. Merchan excused the jury and Hicks quickly left the courtroom. The prosecutors left the room after her one by one; the look of concern on Colangelo's face was obvious as he slipped through the door to the left of the gallery.

Each of the three sketch artists began a new drawing; a witness crying was not to be missed. But Izzy Brourman wasn't looking at Hicks; she was using her binoculars to stare at the defense table, to which Bove had returned. "It's good," she saw him whisper to Trump.

Hicks returned quickly, her eyes still red, but composed enough to continue.

"If you need a minute, just let me know," Bove said. "We were talking about The Trump Organization, and I think you said this morning that it ran a little bit like a family business while you were there?"

"Yes," Hicks said.

Bove reminded her of her closeness with the Trump family, with both Melania and Trump himself. "You felt you had his trust and respect?" he said.

"His trust and respect, yes," Hicks said, as if to herself.

Hicks was clearly willing to accompany Bove wherever he wanted to go. The first stop was an attack on Michael Cohen.

"Mr. Cohen wasn't part of the campaign, right?" Bove asked.

"He would try to insert himself at certain moments, but he wasn't supposed to be on the campaign in any official capacity," Hicks said. Like Davidson, she had a years-in-the-making reservoir of irritation with Cohen. "There were some things he did in a voluntary capacity because of his interest."

"There were times where Mr. Cohen did things that you felt were not helpful to what you were trying to accomplish right?" Bove asked.

"Yes," Hicks said. "I used to say that he liked to call himself "a fixer" or "Mr. Fix It," and it was only because he first broke it that he was able to come and fix it."

Bove chuckled, as did several of the reporters in the room. Hicks offered a weak smile.

But when the defense lawyer brought the conversation back to her experience on the campaign, she teared up again, remembering the long days and long nights. Bove was playing on her nostalgia, transporting her to some of the most exciting chapters in her professional life, an outsider press secretary for an underdog candidate who kept winning when people expected him to lose.

Bove steered the conversation to the "Access Hollywood" tape. "That concept of gathering the key campaign staff and the President to talk about an issue that could impact the campaign, that was standard for the way you were all operating at the time, right?" Bove asked.

Hicks looked confused, and so did the jurors.

Evidently, Bove was trying to pursue the "no crime" argument that had been put forth in opening statements: there was nothing unusual about the tape, or the way the campaign reacted. This tactic was successful for Trump outside the courtroom; reasonable doubt was easy to create in broad sections of the public.

But the "no crime" argument made no sense within the confines of Part 59. The prosecution's story couldn't be undermined by merely pointing at the events and saying: "That's normal. That's normal." Outside of 100 Centre Street, a simple talking point was easier to absorb than a complex story. But in the courtroom, where prosecutors were in the midst of telling that story, it seemed like a non sequitur.

Just when Bove seemed to be lose momentum, he hit another rich seam, potentially the biggest payoff thus far. He asked Hicks whether the release of the "Access Hollywood" tape was a cause of concern for Trump.

"Yes," Hicks said. "He was worried about how this would be viewed at home."

"And you said a little bit ago you got a chance to meet President Trump's wife during your work at Trump Org?" Bove asked.

"Yes."

"What about your observations of that relationship caused you to think this was causing him stress about what would happen at home."

Hicks began to answer. "He really values. . . ." She started again. "*President Trump* really values Mrs. Trump's opinion, and she doesn't weigh in all the time, but when she does, it's really meaningful to him. And, you know, he really, really respects what she has to say. So I think he was just concerned about what her perception of this would be. And, yeah, I know that was weighing on him."

Trump locked eyes with Hicks and for a moment, she held his gaze. Hicks may have left the fold, but hadn't lost her affection for the former president. If she could offer loyalty from the stand, she would.

Bove recognized the opportunity. It was the strongest alternative explanation of Trump's motive: concern for his marriage. The jurors remained spellbound.

"It continued to weigh on him as more allegations were made in the media, right?"

"Yes," Hicks said.

Bove raised the November 2016 Wall Street Journal article about Karen McDougal. "President Trump asked that the newspapers not be brought to the residence that day?"

"Yes," Hicks said.

"That there were parts of this that were very, very personal to him, right?"

"Absolutely. I don't think he wanted to—I don't think he wanted anyone in his family to be hurt or embarrassed by anything that was happening on the campaign. He wanted them to be proud of him," Hicks said. She took a sip of water, still unsteady.

Bove reached his final topic: Hicks's time in the White House. She teared up again, but this time, Bove made no move to pause the testimony.

"That office that you described, the Oval Office and the area around it, that was a very hectic space in 2017, right?" he asked.

"Yes," Hicks said.

"And from where you sat, you could see that the President was frequently multitasking, right?"

"Yes."

"And people were interrupting what he was doing, right?"

"Yes."

"And in that timeframe, in 2017, while you were focused on your job at the White House, you didn't have anything to do with the business records of the Trump Org., 200 plus miles away from New York City, did you?"

"No," Hicks said.

Bove was done with his questions. Colangelo had nothing to add. Hicks descended from the witness stand and walked past Trump who, instead of ignoring her, as he had when she entered, gave her a careful, almost shy, smile.

❖ ❖ ❖

Hicks's time on the stand was a boon for both sides. The prosecution was batting three for three with its tentpole witnesses painting a convincing picture of candidate Trump as the barely-hidden hand behind the suppression of both Karen McDougal's and Stormy Daniels's stories. Hicks's scorn at the idea of Cohen paying the hush money himself was invaluable to the prosecution's case.

But she was good for the defense, too. If Blanche, Bove and Necheles continued to lean into the idea that Trump was a family man, they had a shot at picking off the single juror they needed to thwart a unanimous guilty verdict.

And yet, inevitably, there was more conversation about Hicks's tears than her testimony. It was all anyone wanted to talk about.

On MSNBC, Lawrence O'Donnell said it plainly. "She cried," he said. "That's the big news of the day out of the courtroom." O'Donnell told his audience he'd heard three different theories for the tears. Several of his evening guests would offer their own interpretations.

One of the prevalent theories held that Hicks had cried because she knew just how bad her testimony was for Trump. But Anderson Cooper, on CNN, rejected that idea. He noted instead that courtrooms are highly emotional places, and that every time Hicks said something important, she'd heard the cicada-like sound of reporters, taking down every word she'd said.

That was closer to my theory. Every time Hicks had cried—three times in all—it had been in response to Bove conjuring up some memory of having worked for Trump. He'd asked her to travel back in time, to the Trump Organization, to the campaign, and to the White House, all vestiges of a past life working for someone with whom, to the general disbelief of pundits like O'Donnell, she had a genuine relationship. She seemed to be grieving a past life that was now inaccessible to her.

Her damning testimony about Trump's involvement with—and comments about—the hush money payment were more believable because of her personal affection for him. But if anyone could convince the jurors that Trump was a misunderstood family man, it was likely someone like Hicks, who seemed to genuinely believe it. Trump inspired loyalty, not only from everyday Americans, but from those who knew him best—even when they'd been appalled by him. That devotion was unimaginable to his critics, and a hugely underrated part of his power.

*   *   *

Up to this point in early May, the prosecution had spent nearly all of its time covering 2015 and 2016. The facts of the Trump Tower conspiracy were now well-established. The state's case was dazzling, generating reams of news coverage and, from what we could tell, strong juror interest. But the most important element of the case—the evidence to support the main charge of falsifying business records—had not even begun to be introduced by the prosecution.

Meanwhile, Michael Cohen, the key witness to that falsification, was getting battered. The prosecutors were content to have other witnesses express their disregard of Cohen to the jury; that aligned with their argument that the pre-2018 Michael Cohen was a disreputable liar. But they somehow needed to keep 2024 Cohen credible in the jury's eyes, so that he would be believable when he testified that Trump approved the falsification of the business records.

Still, the prosecution had one key witness to call before the jury's attention could be more fully directed to the falsification of records in 2017. This witness would take the jurors even further back in time—back to a Nevada golf resort, a decade before Trump's run for president.

But then, on Sunday, May 5, Stormy Daniels missed her flight.

✦   ✦   ✦

She was meant to fly out of Orlando, but as she eyeballed the growing line at airport security, she realized that she would be late. Her lawyer, a congenial Oklahoman named Clark Brewster, placed a call to Susan Hoffinger, which kicked up a panic within the district attorney's office.

Hoffinger liked to be in control. As a former defense lawyer, she was known for the intensity with which she threw herself into witness preparation, government witnesses being the closest analogue to a defense lawyer's clients. Daniels hadn't even started testifying yet and already she was throwing Hoffinger off balance. The prosecution scrambled for a replacement witness on Monday's schedule.

Daniels' cancellation led the prosecutors to rerun the endless calculations about whether it was worth it to call her to the stand at all. There'd been significant internal debate over Daniels, considered to be the riskiest witness outside of Michael Cohen himself.

The law asks for binaries: an action is criminal, or it is not. Because no one was accusing Trump of assault, it was dangerous for the prosecution to invite Stormy Daniels's story, complicated as it was by shades of power and intimidation that did not amount to a crime. Either Merchan, or a higher court, could decide those details were overly prejudicial, that they biased the jury against Trump for reasons having nothing to do with the charges. If a judge reached that determination, he or she could throw the trial out entirely.

Ultimately Bragg's team determined that there would be a hole in their case without Daniels present. They wanted to show the jurors the power of the story Trump had concealed in 2016, to suggest the influence it might have had on the election if only the porn star had spoken out.

So they'd called her. Now, the question was when—or whether—she would come.

      ✦   ✦   ✦

"Mr. Trump, it's important to understand that the last thing I want to do is to put you in jail."

It was Monday, May 6. Humidity permeated the wooden wainscoting in Part 59. The jury was outside, waiting, as Justice Merchan addressed the former president. I sat behind Trump on the left side of the gallery. He froze, staring straight at Merchan as if caught in headlights, his frantic, always-moving hands finally paused, as if to absorb the shock of the warning.

Merchan had concluded his written order threatening jail had not been so effective after all. He looked down toward the former president, explaining that he had again found Trump in contempt of court for violating the gag order. This time, the prosecutors had only managed to convince the judge of one additional violation, bringing the former president's fine to $10,000. Most of the defendants Merchan dealt with would have been more cowed by the loss of the money than they would by the threat of jail. But it was a pittance for Trump.

Merchan explained that incarceration was a last resort for him. It would disrupt the trial. It could threaten the safety of the court officers and correction officials responsible for coordinating the logistics. And then, there were the broader implications, the potentially explosive political response. Merchan didn't dwell on that. He justified the warning by explaining his institutional role in terms that a child would understand.

"I have a job to do," he said. "Part of that job is to protect the dignity of the judicial system and compel respect."

He told Trump that his violations of the gag order were a direct attack on the rule of law and that he could not allow them to continue. "So as much as I do not want to impose a jail sanction—and I have done everything I can to avoid doing so—I want you to understand that I will, if necessary." He took a deep breath. "Do the attorneys have any other questions about that?"

The defense lawyers shook their heads in unison. Trump, thawed now that Merchan had stopped speaking, also shook his head. Disgust was written all over his face. He leaned back in his seat and crossed his arms.

"You can call the trial," Merchan said to the clerk.

＊　　＊　　＊

The jurors filed in, oblivious to what had just occurred. I wondered whether they could perceive the emotional residue, Merchan's nervousness, Trump's anger. "Weird vibes in there this morning," I imagined Juror Three saying to Juror Five at the lunch break.

The prosecution called Jeffrey McConney, the former controller of the Trump Organization. His presence suggested that we might finally see the false business records.

McConney was an enormous man with snow-white hair, who vaguely resembled a walrus. Izzy Brourman perked up—she'd drawn McConney before, and loved his look—but the journalists in the crowd muttered. At the Trump Organization trial in 2022, McConney had been a difficult witness, obstreperous with Steinglass, and coughing repeatedly until he was red in the face. Eventually, it'd been announced in the courtroom that he'd tested positive for Covid, infecting Justice Merchan and threatening the jurors as well. The trial had been delayed for a week.

But on Monday, under questioning from Matthew Colangelo, McConney was pleasant, almost cheerful. He announced that he was retired, "happily." He beamed when he defined the term "accounts receivable" for the jury and fondly remembered a time when Trump had momentarily threatened to fire him. He seemed no less devoted to his former boss than Hicks, but his relationship to his work at the Trump Organization was less fraught.

It was time to skip to the reimbursements. Colangelo asked McConney whether, in January 2017, he became aware that Cohen needed to be repaid. McConney recalled that Allen Weisselberg had said as much.

"Allen said we had to get some money to Michael, reimburse Michael. He tossed a pad towards me, and I started taking notes."

Weisselberg, too, had taken notes. In the courtroom, Colangelo offered both notepads into evidence. He displayed Weisselberg's notes for the entire courtroom, prompting all the reporters with binoculars to inspect the exhibit.

They were written on a printout from a First Republic Bank account belonging to an LLC in the care of Michael Cohen. Several details stood out on what might have otherwise been a perfectly pedestrian form. The amount that had been withdrawn—$130,000. And the recipient of that sum: Keith Davidson.

And there was more. At the bottom of the page, in handwriting, someone had scrawled a series of calculations. In the first, $50,000 was added to $130,000, with a note that said "paid to RedFinch for Tech Services."

The $50,000 was a separate debt to Cohen. He'd paid a company called RedFinch Solutions to skew two online polls in Trump's favor. Even in an informal exercise of digital democracy, Cohen was willing to help his patron break the rules. As of January 2017, the Trump Organization hadn't reimbursed him for that payment, either.

On the lefthand side of the document toward the bottom was an illegible scrawl showing more math. McConney testified that the scrawl belonged to Allen Weisselberg. He translated the numbers: the sum of the two debts was doubled—"grossed up" to $360,000. Then, an additional $60,000 was added, bringing the total to $420,000.

Weisselberg apportioned the $420,000 into twelve installments to be wired to Michael Cohen on a monthly basis.

"Did he explain to you what that meant?" Colangelo asked McConney.

"That was just math," McConney said, provoking laughter in the gallery.

It wasn't just math. This document challenged one of Todd Blanche's pet arguments, about the mismatched reimbursement between the $130,000 hush money payment and Trump's $420,000 repayment to Cohen. Allen Weisselberg—so loyal to Trump that he was still in jail, having been charged with perjury after refusing to cooperate with the district attorney's office—had done the math himself.

McConney explained that the money was "grossed up" for tax purposes. If his income were taxed at 50%, Cohen would receive the $130,000 he was owed. And because Cohen believed his bonus hadn't been large enough that year—extracurricular work and all—the company had thrown in an additional $60,000 as a courtesy.

The notepad on which McConney had conducted his arithmetic was embossed with the name TRUMP at the top. "Mike to invoice us," Weisselberg wrote.

That note allowed Colangelo to pivot directly to the invoices themselves, which were soon highlighted on the four monitors overlooking the courtroom. After them came a similarly dull parade of general ledger entries and checks. In all, it was the full set of 34 documents that led to the 34 charges in the indictment.

It was necessary for the jurors to see each and every document, resulting in some of the most tedious testimony so far. To pass the time, the court officers aggressively policed reporters' use of binoculars.

On cross-examination, Emil Bove did what he could. He prompted McConney to acknowledge that he'd been ignorant as to the purpose of the payments. Certainly, he did not know for a fact that the order to pay Cohen came from Trump himself.

But there wasn't much room to maneuver. The documents said what they said and no amount of doubt cast on the witness could change them.

CHAPTER SEVEN

THREE FACES OF STORMY DANIELS

By the time of Stormy Daniels's fateful 2006 encounter with Trump, she had already made a name for herself.

Born in Baton Rouge in 1979, Daniels was a small child when her parents split up. Her mother raised her in squalor and she left the home while she was still in high school. Dancing at a strip club led to pornography, an industry where soon she began writing scripts and directing films. Daniels evinced no shame about her work. She grew up poor and flirted briefly with homelessness; she learned early on that she needed to hustle with whatever she had to hand.

An immediate success in adult entertainment, she hungered for more. She saw an open-call ad for "The 40 Year Old Virgin," and after appearing in the 2005 film, became a part of the extended Judd Apatow universe, making cameos in "Knocked Up," and "Pineapple Express." For a time, it seemed as if those appearances could lead toward the crossover success all but forbidden to porn stars. But Daniels's encounter with Trump morphed from an unusual blip in a life full of strange tales and setbacks into the dominant, defining story of her public persona. Many who associated with Trump eagerly submitted to the gravity of his fame and power. But Daniels left the future president's sphere of influence, only to be sucked back in against her will.

She was a maelstrom of conflicting tendencies. She'd lived a genuinely harrowing life, enduring multiple instances of serious abuse, but it was important to her to be seen as a strong, intelligent person, unfazed by what she'd been through. In her memoir, "Full Disclosure," she briefly described a yearslong pattern of sexual assault by an adult man while she was still a child. She told readers, though, that she was tempted to delete the entire passage, because she refused to be understood as a victim. She also told a story about a plastic surgeon unilaterally deciding, while Daniels was unconscious, to give her far bigger breast implants than she'd requested; a remarkable violation that she cruised over with barely a comment.

The struggle to tell the truth while making sure she didn't come across as a victim, combined with a long-awaited confrontation with the man who'd poisoned her life, would lend the courtroom on 100 Centre Street a uniquely combustible atmosphere. But like Trump himself, Daniels had faith in her ability to tell her own story. On Monday, May 6, she caught her flight to New York with no issue. Susan Hoffinger readied herself for the most important direct examination of her life.

*   *   *

That evening, word of Daniels's testimony slipped its leash; more and more people were beginning to hear that she might appear the following day, though no one seemed able to pin it down. I was glued to my computer, expecting the news that she was the next witness to break that evening. But somehow, the Stormy story didn't break. The next morning, standing in line in front of the hulking north entrance to 100 Centre, Frank Runyeon texted me a storm cloud emoji and a question mark. I told him it was my strong expectation.

I didn't yet know just how apt the emoji was. Though it was sunny and warm outside, the faceoff between Stormy Daniels and Donald J. Trump would generate its own weather system. He'd seen her a handful of times since their 2006 sexual encounter, but never heard her accusations in person.

It was clear, soon after we entered the courtroom on Tuesday morning, that the district attorney's office was ready for a firestorm. Its head of appeals, Steven Wu, appeared in the courtroom; he'd want to be there in case the proceedings got out of hand and the defense moved for a mistrial.

Trump walked in, wearing a gold tie, radiating fury. Rather than simply sit at the defense table, as he normally did, he stayed standing, peering over the heads of Boris Epshteyn and Eric Trump, scanning the gallery for someone who wasn't there.

Susan Necheles took the seat to the right of Trump. She may have fallen in the former president's esteem, but it was clear that the Trump team had decided that she was best equipped to take on Stormy Daniels. It was to be the battle of the Susans: Hoffinger v. Necheles.

Merchan took the bench two minutes early and Necheles immediately objected to Daniels testifying, throwing the first of what would be several Hail Marys that day. Hoffinger insisted that the details of the encounter with Trump were key to jurors' understanding.

"It's not going to involve any descriptions of genitalia," Hoffinger said. "But it's important for us to elicit how she came to have sex with him and how she felt about it."

Necheles continued to argue, but Merchan said he was satisfied, given that Hoffinger had indicated that the prosecution would not explore the details of the sex.

Hoffinger corrected him. "Well, your honor, there will be some details about the sexual act, very brief. We have to elicit that they did have intercourse, your honor."

"Well, that's fine," Merchan said, though his tone said otherwise. It was clear that he was rattled: He asked the prosecution to bring out its next witness, forgetting entirely to summon the jury.

There was a witness slated to testify before Daniels, so for an hour, the entire courtroom waited with bated breath while for 45 minutes, Sally Franklin, a vice president at Penguin Random House, read telling excerpts from Trump's books. The defense looked stressed. There was no doubt that Stormy had enraged Trump, and it was an open question whether he could keep himself in check, even with the threat of jail hanging over his head. Trump kept talking, first to Necheles, then to Bove, as if he were desperately trying to distract himself.

Then, after Franklin left the stand, Merchan again summoned the lawyers to the bench, where they huddled in tightly and looked up.

"Did you refer to feelings—that you want to get into the feelings of Ms. Daniels?" Merchan asked Hoffinger. "What do you expect her to say?"

"She's going to say that she felt numb," Hoffinger said. "She didn't expect it to happen. At one point she almost felt like she was having a panic attack."

"They are essentially making this into rape," Susan Necheles said.

"She will not say that this is a sexual assault," Hoffinger said.

The lawyers sat down, only for Merchan to call them back to the bench.

"I'm going to ask you to not get into the feelings that you just described," he told Hoffinger. "You can get into the sexual act, that there was a sexual act. You can talk about how she got there; how she ended up in the room. Just the facts."

❦   ❦   ❦

Stormy Daniels walked in from the left side of the gallery, all in black, past the former president, who did not make eye contact. She climbed the stairs to the witness box, past the normally nonchalant jurors, who now looked as if they'd had several extra cups of coffee and could not help but to stare. After she was sworn in, she spelled her legal name for the record, D-A-N-I-E-L-S. She was wearing glasses and her uncalculated appearance signaled calculation, as if she were too occupied with the task at hand to worry about what she looked like.

There was a tell, though. She wore the same black jumpsuit she'd donned for the movie "Bad President," a short movie in which the devil himself orchestrates Trump's 2016 election victory. In the overflow room, some members of the public cheered, and one man raised a fist. Daniels was an avatar of the anti-Trump resistance.

Susan Hoffinger, her voice rough but her affect respectful, stood at the lectern and began asking questions about Daniels' career, to explain how she'd moved from stripping to nude modeling to adult films. Hoffinger always said "adult," never "porn" or "porn star," conferring the courtroom's stuffy dignity onto the profession.

The jurors were unembarrassed and their initial excitement over

Daniels's appearance quickly gave way to studious blank looks, note-taking and the typical ping-ponging between interrogator and witness. This was the unimpressed attitude toward celebrities I expected from New Yorkers.

The only off-note came from Daniels herself. A nervous public speaker in the best of times, she tripped ahead of Susan Hoffinger, talking so quickly that it was difficult to understand her. Her insistence on going off-script kindled a feeling of nausea in the courtroom, of a theme park ride tilting just slightly off its track. Soon, Hoffinger guided her to the July 2006 day on which she met Trump and her life changed for good.

Everyone in the courtroom braced themselves.

Wicked Pictures, the company with which Daniels had a contract, was one of the sponsors at a celebrity golf tournament at the Edgewood Resort in Lake, Tahoe Nevada. Daniels met Trump briefly and they exchanged a few words, nothing particularly memorable. There was a picture of their encounter. Trump, squinting and sunbaked in a yellow polo; Daniels staring at the camera with a sideways, professional smile. Hoffinger offered the picture into evidence.

Daniels testified that shortly after the picture was taken, Keith Schiller, Trump's bodyguard, told her that his boss was interested in having dinner with her. Initially she declined. But she saved Schiller's contact information, which Hoffinger displayed for the courtroom. In the gallery, Boris Epshteyn looked up Schiller's number in his own phone, apparently checking to see if it matched.

After speaking to her publicist, Daniels changed her mind. She caught a ride with a friend to Harrah's Hotel and Casino, where Trump was staying in a penthouse suite. She arrived at sunset, and took an elevator to suite. Schiller was standing outside. He told her to go in, that Trump was waiting.

Susan Hoffinger interceded for a moment. Daniels was speaking so quickly that it was a wonder she was able to breathe. "You have to slow down a little bit," the prosecutor said.

The air in the courtroom pulsed. The members of the gallery were like nodes in a network, absorbing the tension coming from Trump and Daniels.

The suite, as Daniels described it, was three times the size of her apartment. She recalled the black-and-white tile floor and the sheen of a heavy mahogany table. Initially, there was no sign of Trump so she called his name. He emerged wearing a two-piece pajama set and walked over to greet her.

"Does Mr. Hefner know you stole his pajamas?" Daniels recalled saying. She told Trump to change, and he obliged, returning in a dress shirt and pants. They sat down at the table, where Daniels expected dinner would be served.

Trump asked if she'd be ok just talking for a bit, to get to know each other, and then they could go downstairs, or stay in the room to eat. He interviewed her about her life and her career. He was curious how she got into adult entertainment, and she gave him a primer on the professionalism of the industry—the films were scripted, with real budgets and real aims beyond just sex. He seemed more interested in the business than he did the sex.

In the courtroom, Daniels staved off any description of sex, too. She went on short digressions, explaining to the jury how STD testing worked in the industry, that Wicked Pictures was a condom-mandatory company, which she preferred, even though she was allergic to latex. Merchan asked her to slow down; the court reporter was having trouble following her.

"Was there a very brief discussion about his wife, Melania?" Hoffinger asked.

"Yes. Very brief," Daniels said. "He said, oh, don't worry about that. We actually don't even sleep in the same room."

At the defense table, Trump slowly shook his head. All his energy seemed to be going toward holding himself in check, and we in the gallery could feel it. Merchan looked stricken, but the jurors' faces gave nothing away.

At the dinner, Daniels grew tired of Trump interrupting her, waving around some magazine he'd recently been featured in.

"I said, 'Are you always this rude, arrogant and pompous? You don't even know how to have a conversation.'" Trump was taken aback, and Daniels poured it on, saying that the only interest she had in the magazine was to spank him with it. He gave her a look that dared her to do so and, she testified, she felt she had no choice. She grabbed the magazine, told him to turn around and swatted him on the butt.

In the courtroom, Trump could clearly be seen mouthing the word "bullshit." Izzy Brourman sketched a cartoon of the spanking scene.

After that, Daniels said, Trump had been more polite, and their conversation had continued. Trump said that Daniels should be a contestant on "The Apprentice" and told her she reminded him of his daughter: smart and blonde, beautiful and underestimated for it.

The dizzying feeling in the courtroom was increasing, and it was all we could do to continue to provide updates on the testimony. We knew what was coming. In the gallery, Eric Trump was slowly turning from pale to pink.

"Did he suggest that if you did get on 'The Apprentice' what might happen with other aspects of your career?" Hoffinger asked.

"Just that people might be able to take me serious—know that I wasn't just an airhead. That I could finally—he knew, and we talked essentially about what I really wanted to do, and that is—be taken seriously as a writer and director," Daniels said. "And at the time I hadn't done any mainstream writing or directing, and that's still what I wanted to do. I wanted to write and direct film and music videos, things like that. Nothing against the adult entertainment business. I have no shame. That's who I am. But I also wanted to direct other bigger things."

Trump, she said, told her an appearance on his show was an opportunity for her to realize her ambitions.

"After all of that discussion that you just described, did you sense any red flags or reason that you were concerned about being there?" Hoffinger asked.

"No," Daniels said flatly.

"At some point did you need to use the restroom?"

"Yes."

"And did you tell . . ."

Merchan cut in. "Is this a good time to take a break?" Hoffinger said it was. The courtroom exhaled as one.

The jurors filed out. Daniels left the witness stand. After she was gone, the judge asked the lawyers to the bench, where he spoke to them out of earshot of the reporters.

"I understand that your client is upset at this point, but he is cursing audibly, and he is shaking his head visually and that's contemptuous," he told Blanche. "It has the potential to intimidate the witness."

"I'll talk to him," Blanche said.

⚜   ⚜   ⚜

We didn't know what the jury was thinking, but all the reporters I talked to during the break were stunned at the decision to call Daniels. Her manner was a major distraction from Alvin Bragg's case. And if Necheles could show her to be lying, the distraction could be fatal.

Merchan wasn't done with his scolding. After the break, he told Hoffinger she was eliciting too much information. He hadn't needed the details of the room, or the conversation with Trump. He directed her to move more quickly.

Both Daniels and Trump returned to the courtroom the worse for wear. Trump's skin looked looser than normal, as if it had been drawn tight by the tension of the room, then released during the break. Daniels appeared stricken. She mounted the witness stand and resumed her testimony.

She'd left the dining room table in the Nevada hotel suite for the bathroom, walking through the master bedroom to get there.

"It was a very large, beautiful bathroom," she said, describing Trump's personal items, his Old Spice deodorant and Pert Plus hair product, his gold tweezers. She opened the door, expecting to return to the dinner table. But Trump was sitting on the bed, wearing only a t-shirt and boxer shorts.

Daniels was startled. "I wasn't expecting someone to be there, especially minus a lot of clothing," she said. "That's when I had that moment where I felt the room spin in slow motion. I felt the blood basically leave my hands and my feet and almost like if you stand up too fast, and everything kind of spins. Then I just thought, *oh, my God, what did I misread to get here*. Because the intention was pretty clear, somebody stripped down in their underwear and posing on the bed, like, waiting for you."

Daniels made to step around the bed and leave. She was furious with herself.

"He stood up between me and the door, not in a threatening manner. He didn't come at me. He didn't rush at me. He didn't put his hands on me and nothing like that. I said, 'I gotta go.' He said, 'I thought we

were getting somewhere, we were talking, and I thought you were serious about what you wanted. If you ever want to get out of that trailer
park . . .'"

She began to digress about having been offended at the remark.
Necheles objected.

"Sustained," said Merchan, looking angry. "Move along."

"You were both standing up at this time?" Hoffinger asked.

"Yes."

"And what happened next, briefly?"

"I just think I blacked out. I was not drugged. I never insinuated
that I was on drugs. I was not drunk. I never said anything of that sort.
I just don't remember. . . ."

"Did you feel threatened by him?" Hoffinger asked.

"No, not physically. Although, I did note there was a bodyguard
right outside the door. There was an imbalance of power for sure. He
was bigger and blocking the way. But, I mean, I was not threatened
verbally or physically."

"Can you briefly describe—" Hoffinger began. "At some point, did
you end up on the bed having sex?"

"Yes."

"Can you very briefly describe where you had sex with him?"

Merchan was staring at the defense table, as if pleading for them
to object. They did not.

"The next thing I know, I was on the bed, somehow on the opposite side of the bed from where we had been standing. I had my clothes
and shoes off. I believe my bra, however, was still on. We were in the
missionary position."

Necheles objected. Merchan sustained the objection.

"Without describing the position, do you remember how your
clothes got off?"

"No," said Daniels.

"Is that a memory that has not come back to you?"

Necheles objected, Merchan sustained.

"And did you end up having sex with him on the bed?" Hoffinger
asked.

"Yes."

"Do you have a recollection of feeling something unusual?"

Necheles objected and Merchan again sustained the objection.

"Do you remember anything other than the fact that you had sex on the bed?" Hoffinger asked.

"I was staring at the ceiling. I didn't know how I got there. I made note—like, I was trying to think about anything other than what was happening there," Daniels said.

Necheles again objected, and Merchan sustained, striking the answer from the record. It appeared that he would strike anything the defense asked. The jurors were watching, blank-eyed, as Daniels kept testifying, with Trump at the defense table, compelled to listen, rage still radiating through the room.

"Did you touch his skin?" Hoffinger asked.

"Yes," Daniels said.

An objection, sustained.

"Was he wearing a condom?"

"No."

"Was that concerning to you?"

"Yes."

"Did you say anything about it?"

"No."

"Why not?"

"I didn't say anything at all."

❧   ❧   ❧

She testified that they'd never, ultimately had dinner, and that it was dark out when she left the hotel. Though she felt ashamed, she told several friends what had happened. Trump called her about once a week, and continued to dangle the possibility of an appearance on "The Apprentice." He called her "honey bunch." The tension had eased, now that she'd moved on from the sex, though Merchan still looked furious.

Daniels saw Trump several more times, though she never slept with him again. She attended a party for the release of his personal vodka brand, where she met Karen McDougal of all people, and visited him at Trump Tower. Hoffinger asked her why she'd continued to reach out, and Daniels tried to explain how helpful "The Apprentice" would be to her career, but the judge cut her off. Eventually, Trump told

Daniels that he wouldn't be able to get her on the show and she stopped taking his calls.

Now, the testimony grew choppy and difficult to follow. She did an interview with InTouch about her liaison with Trump; it never ran. The story was briefly posted on the website, TheDirty.Com in 2011, but quickly taken down.

Five years later, the "Access Hollywood" tape made it easier for Daniels to sell her story. She testified that she wanted to get the story out, and added that she wasn't motivated by money. Which made very little sense: Daniels had accepted a deal to remain silent. If getting the story out was more important to her than the money, why had Cohen's payment been acceptable to her? Juror Seven stared at her, and I wondered if he was thinking the same thing.

If she continued in this vein, cross-examination would be deadly. Necheles excelled at exposing logic-confounding contradictions like the one Daniels was offering.

Daniels testified that she'd signed the NDA and that Michael Cohen slow-walked the payment. And then—to everyone's great relief but perhaps nobody so much as Eric Trump, who looked completely aghast—the trial broke for lunch.

❖   ❖   ❖

As soon as the afternoon session began, Todd Blanche stood up and moved for a mistrial, based on Daniels's testimony. If he were successful, the entire trial would be thrown out; given the logistical difficulties, it was unlikely that a new trial would take place before the election. Still, Merchan looked ready to hear Blanche out. The judge's index finger covered his upper lip, his signature gesture of close listening.

Blanche said that Daniels's testimony was so prejudicial to his client—and so irrelevant to the actual charges—that there was nothing to do but start over. He mentioned several examples of testimony that went beyond the boundaries of acceptability: Daniels having said she blacked out, that Trump hadn't worn a condom, and her description of the power dynamics generally.

"All of this has nothing to do with this case," he said. "The only reason why the government asked those questions, aside from pure embarrassment, is to inflame this jury to not look at the evidence that matters."

He went on for a bit, accusing Daniels of changing her story. Merchan did not seek to interrupt him. Once Blanche was seated, the judge asked Susan Hoffinger to respond. Hoffinger seemed shaken, but her voice was steady. Merchan took notes as she spoke. She said that Daniels's story showed Trump's intent and motive paying her off, ensuring the American public wouldn't hear of it before the 2016 election.

"It is precisely what the defendant did not want to become public," she said.

Merchan stirred in his seat. "I can rule on this," he said.

He told Blanche that Daniels had said things better left unsaid, and that she'd been a difficult witness to control. But he didn't believe that a mistrial was warranted. He had sustained almost every objection, and struck almost every part of the testimony Necheles had asked him to strike. He was surprised, he said, that there had not been more objections.

"The defense has to take some responsibility," he said. "Whether these are new stories or not new stories, the remedy is on cross-examination."

Trump looked furious, again shaking his head, but he kept control.

Hoffinger asked for the judge's permission to talk to Daniels, to warn her against any further prejudicial testimony. Merchan agreed that she could, and she left the courtroom.

＊　＊　＊

When Daniels returned, she was an entirely different person. She gave one-word answers, responding quietly, subdued and compliant. It was as if she understood that her morning performance had not been effective. She was quietly recalibrating, training herself on the courtroom environment in real time. I wondered what the jurors would make of her sudden transformation.

With sex in the rearview mirror, the room was far calmer. Trump sat quietly with his eyes closed. The pulsing feeling was gone.

Susan Hoffinger finished up with a vastly more helpful witness. Daniels talked about her initial denial of the hush money payment story once it broke in the Wall Street Journal, and the turnaround that led her to begin speaking out. Her about-face—which prefigured that of Michael Cohen—began with a bizarre appearance on Jimmy Kimmel's show in early 2018 where she refused to answer questions about whether she'd signed an NDA and continued with a cameo on "Saturday Night Live." It was the mainstream exposure Daniels had always wanted, but it had not come thanks to her own efforts as a writer and director but because of her association with Trump.

Still, Daniels met the moment gamely, hiring a new lawyer named Michael Avenatti and telling her story to Anderson Cooper on "60 Minutes" on March 25, 2018. Eventually, she was freed from the NDA and the fear of being sued. But she ended up owing Trump several hundred thousand dollars in legal fees for a failed defamation case that Avenatti brought on her behalf without consulting her.

Hoffinger concluded by showing Daniels a Trump social media post from March 15, 2023—the day that prosecutors met with her virtually as they prepared for an indictment. In the post, Trump said that he hadn't seen or spoken to Daniels since taking a picture with her on a golf course eighteen years earlier, and called her "horseface" and a "sleazebag."

"Who did you understand Mr. Trump to be referring to 'horseface' and 'sleazebag' here?" Hoffinger asked.

"Me," Daniels said.

"Is Mr. Trump's statement in this Truth Social post that he hasn't seen or spoken to you since he took a picture with you on the golf course; is that true or false?"

"False," Daniels said, and the direct examination concluded.

❖   ❖   ❖

Susan Necheles had studied the different iterations of Stormy Daniels's story for days on end—and anyone who did so would notice a curious phenomenon. When interviewed by InTouch magazine, in 2011, Daniels couched the story as a lighthearted but embarrassing exploit. (That interview didn't ultimately run until 2018). It was a far cry from the ominous tale the jurors had just heard.

A person studying the evolution of Daniels's tale could put stock in one of two distinct possibilities. Option A: Daniels, over time, had come to understand her story more deeply, and no longer saw it as a tabloid trifle but rather as the shameful, awful experience that it was. Or, Option B: Daniels had cunningly studied the narrative landscape of the post-Me-Too world, and understood that her story would be maximally effective in attracting sympathy from Trump's enemies if it had shades of intimidation and coercion baked in.

It was not in Necheles's interest to put stock in Option A. Better to lean in to Option B, portraying Daniels as a crafty liar, embarrassing her on the witness stand, and hoping that she would break under the weight of her own contradictions.

Daniels sat up straight, squaring for a fight as Necheles approached the lectern, and the two began their question and answer dance like a pair of boxers, jabbing at each other conservatively. Then, after a few questions, Necheles swung hard.

"Am I correct that you hate President Trump?"

"Yes," Daniels said, with a 'fuck-you' expression.

"And you want him to go to jail, right?"

"I want him to be held accountable."

Necheles pressed the issue. "You want him to go to jail. Am I correct?"

"If he is found guilty, absolutely." Daniels said.

It was remarkable to watch Necheles, sidelined for so much of the trial, bring the skills of an experienced defense lawyer to bear. She was loose and improvisational; she said things that she knew would garner objections, to plant ideas in the jury's head that she didn't need to follow up on. She described Avenatti's defamation lawsuit against Trump as "your frivolous litigation against President Trump."

Hoffinger interrupted with a successful objection and, Necheles changed her phrasing, as had been her plan all along.

"Because of your *cases that you brought that were dismissed* against President Trump, courts have awarded President Trump over $660,000 in attorney's fees, correct?"

"Roughly, yes," Daniels admitted.

Necheles asked that a tweet be shown in the courtroom. It was from Daniels, saying of Trump, "I don't owe him shit and I'll never give that orange turd a dime." Trump's eyes were closed again.

"That's you calling President Trump names, right?" Necheles asked.

"In retaliation for what he said to me, yes," Daniels said.

"You call him names all the time, right?"

"Yes."

"You despise him, and you made fun of how he looks, right?"

"Because he made fun of me first."

It was juvenile. But Daniels was growing comfortable with the more aggressive format of cross-examination.

"Isn't it true that you are hoping that if Donald Trump is convicted, you'll never have to pay him?" Necheles asked.

"I hope I don't have to pay him no matter what happens," Daniels said, drawing laughs from the gallery. She smiled.

"Now, while you've been refusing to pay President Trump the money that you owe him, you've also been making money by claiming that you had sex with President Trump; right?" Necheles asked, turning the corner into a new topic.

"I have been making money by telling my story about what happened to me," Daniels said.

"And that story, in essence, is that you say you had sex with President Trump; right?"

"Yes."

"And that story has made you a lot of money; right?"

"It has also cost me a lot of money." Daniels said.

Necheles took a different approach. Daniels, in her book, described a phone call with the lawyer Gloria Allred in 2011. Allred was famous for bringing claims of sexual misconduct against powerful men. But Daniels had not told Allred about the sexual encounter with Trump. Necheles saw it as an inconsistency, and moved to fluster Daniels with it.

"You said in a prior statement that you gave Gloria Allred an extremely abbreviated version of your interactions, leaving out sex, right?" Necheles asked.

"Yes. During that phone conversation," Daniels said. "When I met her in person later, I told her everything."

"Alright," said Necheles, apparently surprised by the answer. "In your book, you said that you left out sex and anything in the least bit interesting, right?"

"Yes," Daniels said. "I did not tell her all the sex details. I did not trust her." Then, out of nowhere, an accusation: "And she wanted me to accuse him of forced—basically rape, and so I did not continue that conversation."

Necheles seemed taken aback. "None of that is in your book, is it?" she mustered.

"No," Daniels said, stubbornly.

"You're making this up as you sit there, right?"

"No."

"Well, you wrote a whole book, and you specifically describe that encounter, and you didn't say anything like you just said. Right?"

"Which I said it's an abbreviated version of my interaction—leaving out the sex part," Daniels said, turning to the jury. "I'm pretty sure that backs up my story. She wanted to force me into saying things that were not true."

Necheles sprang a punchline. "You learned from that, did you not, that a story about President Trump that doesn't include sex will make you no money, right?"

But Stormy Daniels, acting as her own defense lawyer, had an alternative narrative. "It taught me that I should tell the truth and not trust people that I didn't feel like I could trust, and she was one of them," she said.

Allred sent a statement later that day asserting that under no circumstances had she ever advised a client to make false allegations—a clarification made in the news media that, if the jurors were heeding the rules, they would not have seen.

   ❖   ❖   ❖

Necheles continued nibbling around the edges of Daniels' account, focusing on the motivations that caused Daniels to tell her story, rather than the story itself. Daniels had long claimed—since 2018—that she was frightened to tell her story because a mysterious man warned her against it in a shopping center parking lot in 2011. Necheles spent some time pointing out that Daniels had not mentioned the parking lot encounter to anyone, including her own husband, until seven years after the purported encounter.

Necheles wanted the jurors, and the press, to believe that Daniels had conjured up her story for money, echoing the attack line the defense had used against Keith Davidson. "You were looking to extort money from Donald Trump, right?" Necheles asked.

"False," Daniels said sharply.

"Well that's what you did, right?"

"False!" she said again, her voice raised to a shout.

Necheles reminded her that she'd kept the story to herself based on the 2011 threat in the parking lot. But then in 2016—inexplicably, the defense lawyer suggested—Daniels decided to do exactly the opposite of what the mystery man had warned her against doing.

"Correct," Daniels said.

"So you weren't really very scared, were you?" Necheles asked.

"I was terrified," Daniels said. "I decided to change my tactic. It was a new ball game. There is a big difference between a reality TV star and someone running for office."

Necheles suggested that Daniels had seen an opportunity to make her story known, and Daniels agreed, again offering a confounding statement. "I saw my opportunity to get the story out," she said. "I didn't put a price tag on it."

It was another contradictory statement; the jurors knew that a price tag was eventually affixed to the story, and they knew the amount: $130,000. The day ended shortly thereafter, and Susan Necheles left the courtroom looking like the cat who'd swallowed the canary. Nate Schweber caught up with her outside of 100 Centre Street. She was still smiling when he asked her how the day had gone.

"You tell me," she said.

❖   ❖   ❖

It was sunny on Thursday, May 9, and the press and public lines outside 100 Centre were buzzing more than ever before. Civilians had lined up overnight to see the second episode of Stormy v. Trump. Trump himself brought an entourage, including Sen. Rick Scott of Florida. The former president couldn't attack Matthew Colangelo or the judge's daughter, Loren Merchan, for fear that Justice Merchan would make good on his promise of jail. But there were no such limits on Scott, who willingly played marionette in a television interview in Collect Pond Park. He lashed out at Colangelo and Merchan's daughter with particular fervor. The case, Scott said, consisted of "a bunch of Democrats saying we want to make sure that Donald Trump can't talk."

Trump, Scott and Boris Ephsteyn walked into the courtroom at 9 a.m. Greg Kelly, from the pro-Trump channel NewsMax, stood and gave the former president a thumbs up from the gallery. Bragg was absent again, but Merchan came in before 9:30, all business, and within a few minutes, Daniels came striding in from the entrance on the left. Her demeanor had changed yet again. Gone were the nervousness of the Tuesday morning and the combativeness of the afternoon; her demeanor on Thursday was harder to read. Merchan welcomed her. Then Susan Necheles was at the lectern, and the prizefight was back on.

Daniels began the day pushing the same, confusing contradiction: That, in 2016, she had wanted her story public, but that she had been content to accept money to stay silent. She attributed her willingness to sign the NDA to a blind trust in Keith Davidson's advice and acknowledged that when the Wall Street Journal first published its story about the hush-money payment two years later, she'd cooperated with the Trump team by signing her name to a statement that denied any "sexual and/or romantic affair." Trump listened to the testimony impassive, his eyes flicking open and closed.

"So, even though you had agreed that you would not discuss this supposed story, and you had received a lot of money for that agreement, you then decided you wanted to publicly say that you had sex with President Trump, right?" Necheles asked.

Daniels saw an opportunity, and she pounced. "No," she said. "Nobody would ever *want* to publicly say that." There were sounds of stifled laughter from the gallery. Trump's eyes were closed.

Necheles was undeterred by the punchline. She noted that, after Daniels's "60 Minutes" interview, she negotiated a book contract that netted her $800,000.

"And after you wrote the book, you capitalized even more on the story you were selling by doing a strip club tour called the Make America Horny Tour?" Necheles asked slyly.

"I did *not* name that tour and I fought it tooth and nail," Daniels said.

On the four screens in the courtroom an image appeared, of the photo of Daniels and Trump from the golf course. "HE SAW HER LIVE," the poster said. "YOU CAN TOO!"

Necheles quoted Daniels to herself, reminding her that she'd reflected in her memoir on having become an emblem of anti-Trump sentiment, as evidenced by the fact that women, gay couples, immigrants and other liberals had begun to turn up at her strip shows. Necheles accused Daniels of attaching her career to Trump at every turn, making money by selling a story designed to put him in jail. She showed the courtroom the tweets from March 2023, in which Daniels had celebrated the indictment, and promoted merchandise from her online store.

"You're celebrating the indictment by selling things from your store, right?" Necheles asked.

"Not unlike Mr. Trump," Daniels said, in another exchange that delighted the press.

There was no question in my mind that Daniels had made money off her encounter with Trump. Everyone who became defined by Trump ended up basing some part of their livelihood on him. Our gallery seats in Part 59 contributed to our livelihoods as well. Those were the dynamics of the Trump attention economy. He was the wellspring of his own industry; Daniels, merely a prominent vendor among the thousands of us inside it.

I was growing restless with the defense's reluctance to focus on Daniels's 2006 encounter with Trump. If Necheles was not going to discredit the story from which Daniels made money—which she had yet to touch in any real detail—what exactly was she doing? Who, other than Trump himself, cared how many $40 "Stormy, Saint of Indictments" candles Daniels sold?

And then, as if on cue, Necheles made the turn.

"You were an actress—a porn actress, right?" she asked.

"Yes," Daniels said. She sat up.

Necheles established that Daniels had appeared in 200 films, and written and directed 150, emphasizing the word *porn* with disgust in her tone. "Is that correct?" she asked.

"Give or take," Daniels said.

"And so, this was your career for over 20 years: Writing, acting and directing sex films, right?"

"Yes."

"So you have a lot of experience in making phony stories about sex appear to be real, right?" Necheles said witheringly.

There was a pause.

"Wow," Daniels said. "That's not how I would put it. The sex in the films is very much real—just like what happened to me in that room."

The sound of typing amplified. Daniels had gotten the better of Necheles again.

Necheles continued to pursue the theme, asking short, clipped questions to elicit quick responses. Yes, Daniels directed and wrote sex films, and yes, acted in them.

"And now you have a story you've been telling about having sex with President Trump, right?" Necheles finished, looking for a killing blow.

"And if that story was untrue, I would have written it a lot better," Daniels said, smirking. The courtroom burst out in laughter. Another win for Stormy. The momentum was on her side.

Necheles started in on the disparities between Daniels's Tuesday testimony and her book: For example, Daniels had told InTouch that Trump himself had asked for her number, neglecting to mention Keith Schiller's brief involvement, and that she'd been happy to go to dinner with him.

But the story Daniels told on the stand two days earlier sounded far more authentic than the fluff that InTouch had declined to print a decade earlier. It had the ring of truth, and the disparities that loomed so large on paper seemed silly and beside the point in the live context of the trial. In the moment, in the courtroom, Stormy's performance distracted from Necheles's lawyerly logic.

In perhaps the best example, Necheles got bogged down on the subject of whether Daniels had dinner at Trump's hotel. In 2011, she'd suggested she had. But from 2018 on, it had become a canonical part of her story that no food was served. Necheles threw herself into the contradiction with gusto, but Daniels maintained that there had been no food. The courtroom briefly became an episode of "Seinfeld," exploring the question of whether a person could have dinner without any food.

Daniels said it was obvious to her that she had not eaten, because she'd never discussed the meal in her previous interviews, a neat bit of Trumpian logic that she sold convincingly. "I would have talked about the food," she said. "I'm very food motivated."

Necheles lost her patience. "Your words don't mean what they say, do they?"

Hoffinger objected, Merchan sustained, and Necheles resumed, tiptoeing her way toward the 2006 sex itself. Trump leaned forward, frowning with his elbows planted on the defense table. "So you say you came out of the bathroom and he was on the bed in his T-shirt and boxer shorts, right?"

"Yes," Daniels said, bracing herself.

"And, according to you, when you saw him sitting on the bed, you became faint, the room started to spin and the blood left your hands and feet, yes?"

"Yes," Daniels said.

"Just so I can be clear on what you're saying, you've acted and had sex in over 200 porn movies, right? And there're are naked men and naked women having sex, including yourself, in those movies right?"

"Yes." Daniels said.

"But according to you, seeing a man sitting on a bed, in a T-shirt and boxer shorts, was so upsetting that you got light-headed, blood left your hands and feet, and you almost fainted, right?"

"Yes," Daniels said. Her voice had grown soft. "When you are not expecting a man twice your age in their underwear . . . I have seen my husband naked almost every day. If I came out of the bathroom and it was not my husband and it was Mr. Trump on the bed, I would proba-bly have the same reaction."

The jurors, typically glued to the action, were staring downward as if they were embarrassed. It was impossible to know what they were thinking but the exchange felt poisonous, dreadful.

Necheles cut to the chase. "You've made all of this up, right?"

"No," said Daniels, with effort. She was still sitting up straight and she seemed becalmed and ready for anything. I was impressed at the final phase of her courtroom evolution. She'd gone from a liability for the prosecution on direct examination to a far stronger witness on cross.

"You were saying, when you testified on Tuesday, that his actions made you feel like you had to have sex with him, right?" Necheles asked.

"My own insecurities made me feel that way," Daniels said. "I've maintained that he hasn't—that he didn't put his hands on me."

Necheles clearly felt that victory was in sight, the articles spread out in front of her mind's eye, all the minute contradictions and lack of details, the inexplicable morphing of Daniels's public story from embarrassing dalliance to sexual coercion. But she wasn't reading the room. She pointed out things that Daniels *hadn't* said in InTouch, that she *hadn't* said in Vogue. "Now, in 2024, your story has changed, hasn't it?" Necheles said triumphantly.

"No," Daniels said. "Not at all. You are trying to make me say that it changed, but it hasn't changed."

Susan Hoffinger returned to the lectern. She always seemed to prefer the re-direct portion of witness testimony, in which the prosecutors got a chance to ask their witnesses a second round of questions, in a kind of cross-examination of the cross-examination. Hoffinger began to show the jurors the way that Daniels was insulted by strangers online, called a slut and a prostitute, that she'd had to hire security, move homes and deal with a constant barrage of threats.

"Have you been telling lies about Mr. Trump, or the truth about Mr. Trump?" Hoffinger asked.

"The truth," Daniels said. She looked exhausted, as if she had no fight left in her, and we kept expecting her to cry, but she didn't.

"Ms. Daniels, on balance, has your publicly telling the truth about your experiences with Mr. Trump had a net positive or a net negative in your life?"

"Negative," Stormy Daniels said.

Ten minutes later, she stepped down from the stand, walked past Donald Trump and out of the courtroom, having told her story on the biggest stage possible—albeit one where cameras were forbidden. And in that moment, I believed that the most intense testimony of the trial was over.

But the conclusion was premature. Since February, we'd heard reports that Michael Cohen was a nervous wreck, continually threatening to back out on the prosecution. But once it became clear he *would* testify, we knew for a fact *when* it would happen. Michael Cohen was a creature of the press and there was never any doubt that his appearance date was going to leak. A few hours after Stormy Daniels left the stand on Thursday, *The New York Times* reported that Cohen would enter Part 59 first thing the following week.

CHAPTER EIGHT

SHARKSUCKER

In late October 2023, Susan Hoffinger, Susan Necheles and Todd Blanche sat quietly among rows of reporters in a large, light-filled New York courtroom, watching Michael Cohen testify against Donald J. Trump.

Cohen had been called as a witness by the New York attorney general's office in its civil trial against Trump. He was perfectly respectable when questioned by the state's lawyer, describing his involvement in inflating Trump's net worth. But his cross-examination was nothing short of calamitous.

One of Trump's lawyers, Alina Habba, got under Cohen's skin immediately. He lost his temper and shouted objections to her questions from the stand. Ultimately, he admitted to a number of lies, including several he'd told to a federal judge. Ever since, the broader Trump team had accused him of perjury, and insisted the district attorney's office should prosecute him for it.

It was a stroke of luck for the attorney general, Letitia James, that her trial was decided by a judge—who said he found Cohen credible—rather than a jury. And that Cohen's testimony, though useful, was inessential to her case.

Susan Hoffinger didn't have that luxury. Cohen was the prosecution's star witness. Only he could place the blame for the felony falsification of business records—New York penal code 175.10—squarely at the feet of Donald J. Trump. Cohen claimed that the plan to disguise the reimbursements was approved by Trump himself during a January 2017 conversation at Trump Tower. They'd had another conversation about the reimbursements at the White House the following month, he said.

All other evidence of Trump's involvement in the disguise of the reimbursements was indirect. Only by eliciting evidence of those two conversations could the prosecution truly prove its case. Stormy Daniels was a risk Alvin Bragg didn't have to take. She merely corroborated the event and its subsequent cover-up, neither of which were illegal unto themselves. But Cohen was the risk built in from the beginning—absolutely essential to the case, and absolutely volatile.

The defense knew that Cohen wasn't just volatile; he was also breakable. They'd observed the methods used to break him.

So not only did Hoffinger have to elicit case-making testimony from Cohen. She was also tasked with protecting him during the climactic cross-examination of the trial, preparing the jury for the most damaging blows the defense would land and, somehow, disrupting any momentum Trump's team was able to build.

❋   ❋   ❋

We spent the weekend preparing to cover Cohen's testimony, asking our line sitters to report to Centre Street at midnight on Monday, May 13. By this point, five weeks into the trial, the courtroom was all but impossible to reach for those without a guaranteed seat. Scores of New Yorkers eager to see the final showdown between the boss and his turncoat fixer lined up in hopes of getting in. This, after all, was the main event, the title fight which put the Stormy Daniels undercard to shame. In Collect Pond Park, Trump supporters unfurled more than a dozen flags. MAGA's presence outside the courtroom was growing.

I lined up outside the north entrance in the early morning, sheltered from the buzz of Collect Pond Park. The weather was getting warmer by the day. I was beginning to look forward to the time when I could enjoy it.

The court officers, too, were losing patience with the trial. Some took it out on the media—blocking witnesses in the courtroom, or thwarting us when we wanted to sit on the left side of the gallery, the better to see Trump at the defense table. An exception was the red-haired lieutenant, Brendan Mullaney, who'd been promoted to captain during the course of the trial; he treated us like colleagues.

At 8 am, the officers ushered us in to the building and I raced up to the 15th floor, snagging a seat directly behind the defense table. Alvin Bragg sat on the opposite side of the gallery, reviewing the contents of a large manila folder. Trump was still in the hallway, speaking to the cameras enthusiastically.

The Republican politicians were multiplying. The previous week's senator was replaced by Representative Nicole Malliotakis, Senator Tommy Tuberville and Senator J.D. Vance, all of them standing mutely behind Trump. As the former president addressed the cameras—"It's like an armed camp outside. You can't get one person within three blocks of this courthouse!"—Vance lined up a careful picture with his iPhone, looking for all the world like a dad at Disneyland.

Merchan took the bench at his usual time. Susan Hoffinger strode to the lectern and called Cohen to the stand.

By this point, the jurors knew more about him than any other witness. Per David Pecker, he was an anxiety-ridden basket case. Per Keith Davidson, a "jerk" and an "asshole." According to Hope Hicks, he was selfish and credit-seeking, a person mostly occupied with cleaning up messes of his own making. Jurors had heard recordings of Cohen's husky, affronted voice and seen his goofy posed picture. The only thing that remained was the man himself.

He emerged from the left side of the courtroom in a dark suit and pink tie, and limped to the witness stand. After he was sworn in, he turned his face toward the gallery and we saw how awful he looked: pale and gaunt, his eyes large and worried. Hoffinger had been preparing him for months, cajoling him, helping him, holding his hand, but she could do nothing to alleviate the havoc the stress was wreaking on his appearance. This was Michael Cohen's moment of truth.

"Good morning," the prosecutor said, standing at the lectern, her voice crisp. She began asking Cohen about his background.

◆   ◆   ◆

Enchanted by the power and celebrity of the mafiosi he'd been exposed to in his youth, Cohen seemed custom-built to fall under Trump's spell. He craved the swirl of power, glamour and celebrity and he had the same attraction to publicity. As he put it in his memoir, "Disloyal," "the most dangerous place in America was between me and a camera."

Cohen offered the courtroom his biography. The fixer grew up in Lawrence, on the south part of Long Island. His family was filled with doctors and lawyers, but in that era of hostile takeovers and preening businessmen, Cohen was eager to work on Wall Street. He'd been obsessed with making money since he was a kid, and he had no problem bending the rules. The business plan for his lemonade stand involved a makeshift barricade, which forced passing cars to stop. As a teenager, he opened an ice cream stand at El Caribe, a country club in the Mill Basin area of Brooklyn owned by his Uncle Morty, where mobsters fraternized with the civilian club members. He was enchanted by the entrepreneurialism and machismo, and not particularly put off by the criminality.

Ultimately, Cohen conceded to pressure from his family, and applied to law school. Still, even after he received his degree from Western Michigan's Thomas M. Cooley Law School, he considered himself a dealmaker, an entrepreneur with a law degree.

A Trump superfan, having read "The Art of the Deal" twice while still an undergraduate, it was he who made the first move toward his future boss, buying apartments in Trump World Tower and Trump Park Avenue. He also encouraged his family—his parents, in-laws and friends—to purchase apartments in Trump World Tower, building himself coalitional power within the building. Cohen eventually befriended Donald Trump Jr., whom he saw as a peer, a fellow New York real estate tough guy.

In 2006, several years into his residency, the board at Trump World Tower began to foment rebellion, pushing to have Trump's name removed from the building. Cohen, employed at a law firm, was contacted by Don Jr., and summoned to Trump Tower. There, on the 26th floor, Trump himself personally asked him to put down the uprising. Cohen leapt at the chance to work for his idol and poured energy into the fight, successfully assembling a bloc of owners on Trump's behalf. After a few other favors, the following year, Trump offered to hire

Cohen away from his "sleepy old firm."

"Are you aware that in connection with your work for him, some people described you as his 'fixer'? Hoffinger asked.

"Some have described me as that," Cohen responded.

"Is that in some ways an accurate title?"

"It's fair," Cohen said brusquely, spitting out the words, though with pride or dismissively, I couldn't tell.

Michael Cohen loved working for Donald Trump. You could see it as he testified, his face lit with an inner glow as the old memories resurfaced. At the Trump Organization he felt as if he truly belonged. He renegotiated his boss's debts, fired employees on Trump's behalf, and threatened journalists with litigation. He brought every little thing he accomplished back to Trump for his approval.

Hoffinger asked him what Trump would say, when Cohen reported his wins.

"'It's fantastic. It's great,'" Cohen said.

"How did that make you feel?" Hoffinger asked.

"Like I was on top of the world," Cohen said.

Cohen was among the supplicants who encouraged Trump to run for president, even starting a website in 2011, "ShouldTrumpRun.com." He helped plan the 2015 campaign announcement in Trump Tower and testified that Trump warned him to be prepared for negative publicity: "There's going to be a lot of women coming forward." At the defense table, Trump's eyes were again shut tight, as if he were willing the courtroom, the jury, and his former fixer to simply disappear.

Cohen's story began to dovetail directly with David Pecker's. He echoed the publisher's testimony, agreeing that Pecker had offered at the August 2015 Trump Tower meeting to promote Trump's candidacy, denigrate his opponents and keep an eye out for negative stories that he would work to suppress if possible.

Though many of the events that Cohen began to describe were familiar, he was the sole witness who connected each and every beat of the catch-and-kill negotiations to Trump himself. It was Cohen who told Trump that the doorman, Dino Sajudin, was hawking his tale in the fall of 2015. Cohen testified that the candidate had directed him to ensure the story didn't get out.

Cohen had little to do with the Sajudin deal; it was mostly handled by A.M.I. But, he testified, he updated Trump every step of the way, making sure to highlight his own contributions to the contract's details.

"Why did you do that?" Hoffinger asked.

"In order to get credit for accomplishing the task," Cohen said.

No one would deny that Cohen had an axe to grind. But his desperate need for approval was a rationale unrelated to revenge. It explained why he'd been motivated to report everything back to Trump. Cohen confirmed Hope Hicks's assessment. He was a credit-seeker.

Justice Merchan swiveled in his chair, index finger on upper lip, as he listened closely to the testimony about Karen McDougal and Cohen's diligent updates on every twist and turn, from the National Enquirer's initial meeting with McDougal in the summer of 2016 to the setup of Resolution Consultants LLC as the shell company for potential reimbursement of Pecker—before Pecker asked Cohen to rip up the papers.

Nearly every piece of the 2016 story came with corroborative evidence. Jurors saw Cohen's text to Trump's bodyguard, Keith Schiller, in the summer, asking to speak to Trump after the McDougal meeting. (Cohen often used Schiller, a constant presence at Trump's side, as a go-between.) And they saw the phone record for a seven-minute call Trump placed to Cohen on September 29, the day Cohen claimed he told Trump about the financial preparations.

"I have never seen anything more rehearsed!" Eric Trump tweeted, a sign that Cohen's testimony was going smoothly.

Eric Trump was, of course, correct. Susan Hoffinger knew what Michael Cohen was going to say before he said it; she'd met with him for hours upon hours over the course of weeks, reviewing phone records from 2016 to ensure that his story hewed to the documentary evidence. As Cohen's testimony progressed, it became clear that the prosecution's entire case sprang from his story.

Soon, it was time for the midday break, and Justice Merchan encouraged everyone emphatically to enjoy their lunch. Lunch was an objective, bipartisan good.

Cohen left the stand, holding his neck stiffly as he hobbled past the defense table, staring straight ahead as if he were trying to send a message: That he would not be paying Donald Trump any attention, either. But that was ridiculous. Beginning in 2007, Cohen had made his whole life about Trump. Nothing that transpired in the intervening years had changed that.

❖   ❖   ❖

The Republican politicians who'd flocked to support Trump left the courtroom to set up a press conference in Collect Pond Park. J.D. Vance folded his arms over his long red tie as reporters lobbed questions at him. One asked about Trump's morning remark, that his supporters couldn't get within blocks of the courthouse.

"I think they try to make him feel pretty lonely," Vance said. "Because there are lot of supporters out there and obviously, they can't get close to the courthouse . . ."

"Supporters right there, sir," the reporter said, gesturing at one of the demonstrators in the park.

"Yeah, not too close to the courthouse, right?" Vance said.

"There's the courthouse right across the street," the reporter said.

Vance began the news conference in earnest.

"I'm here for a simple reason to show support for a friend," he said, before continuing. "The thing that the president is prevented from saying—which is a disgrace—is that every single person involved in this prosecution is practically a Democratic political operative." He singled out Merchan's daughter, and Matthew Colangelo. "What's going on inside that courtroom is a threat to American democracy, ladies and gentlemen. We cannot have a country where you get to prosecute your political opponents instead of persuading voters."

❖   ❖   ❖

As the break wound down, Trump meandered back into the courtroom, accompanied by Eric Trump, both of them looking sour. The former president slammed a sheaf of positive press clippings down on the defense table. Eric Trump scrutinized Izzy Brourman's drawing-in-progress, where his father was sketched with eyes closed, projecting a Buddha-like calm.

Michael Cohen returned to the stand and described the contentious days in which he'd led Keith Davidson on. We could tell it was contentious, because, in an October 17, 2016, email to Cohen, Davidson used Latin. "Please be advised that my client deems her settlement agreement cancelled and void ab initio," he wrote.

The email led Cohen to believe he could not delay the payment any further, for fear of Daniels going public. He testified that Trump had reached the same conclusion "He stated to me that he had spoken to some friends, some individuals, very smart people, and that: *It's $130,000. You're, like, a billionaire. Just pay it. There is no reason to keep this thing out there. So do it.*"

After some hesitation, Cohen decided to front the money. Trump, in his telling, assured him he would be repaid: "'Don't worry about it.'"

For Keith Davidson, Cohen's turnaround was like magic. Long periods of delay and silence and then, all of a sudden, funds received. But on the other side, there'd been a veritable frenzy of phone calls between Cohen, Trump and the other major players.

One of the relevant records came on October 24, 2016. Cohen said he'd placed a call to Keith Schiller, Trump's bodyguard, but spoke to Trump himself, updating him on the arrangements for the Daniels payment. In fact, the records showed that Schiller called Cohen first, and left a voicemail, only for Cohen to immediately call him back. I paid no attention to the tiny discrepancy. The story was moving too fast and there were so many other records to review.

In April, Cohen had secured a $500,000 line of credit on his home, so he knew he could get the $130,000 if necessary. He made a last-ditch attempt to convince Pecker to pay Daniels ("not a chance," he recalled Pecker saying, prompting laughter in the gallery). Then, on October 26, he sought another assurance from Trump that he approved of the hush-money payment. He got it.

Cohen filled out a bank form with a false reason for opening Essential Consultants LLC, the shell company he used to make the payment to Keith Davidson. Shortly after the cash from the loan on his home was deposited in the new account, he wired it to the Beverly Hills lawyer. Davidson sent him back the signed agreement on October 27.

"Did you let Mr. Trump know once you received it?" Hoffinger asked.

"Immediately," Cohen said.

"Why did you do that?"

"For two reasons. One, so that he would know the matter, the task that he gave to me was finished, accomplished and done. But, also, to take credit for myself, so he knew that I had done and finished it. Because this was important."

The election was less than two weeks away.

❖   ❖   ❖

There it was again, the final hush money payment, this time with Trump's approval built in. The foreperson leaned forward enthusiastically. Juror Three bobbed around in his seat and Juror Seven, the skeptic, scribbled notes to himself. It was 3 pm on Monday, and we still held out hope that Cohen's direct examination might finish that day.

No such luck.

Susan Hoffinger began to lay the groundwork for a second story, the events that led from Cohen's unquestioning loyalty to his turn away from the man he'd once loved. Embedded within that story were the all-important 2017 conversations with Trump about the reimbursement plan, and the creation of the 34 false business records for which the former president had been charged.

After the 2016 election, Trump had less use for his old fixer. Cohen's days by his side were numbered. Reince Priebus, the incoming chief of staff, offered Cohen a job in the administration as assistant general counsel, but Cohen felt it was a lowball, given his loyalty to Trump. In fact, he'd hoped to be named chief of staff himself. When Hoffinger asked him about it, he insisted it was "solely for my ego" and that he knew he wouldn't have been qualified for the job.

Instead, Cohen proposed to Trump that he be named personal attorney to the president, a title he could use to drum up business as a consultant to those who wished to win favor with the new White House. It was Cohen's old shtick, repurposed for his patron's lofty position: lawyer in name, but moneymaker in deed. Kate Christobek watched on the overflow room feed as, at the defense table, Trump looked at Emil Bove pointedly and shook his head.

But at the time, the president-elect accepted Cohen's proposal. But December 2016 brought an unmistakable sign of Cohen's plummeting status. Trump cut his annual bonus by two-thirds. "I was truly insulted, personally hurt by it," Cohen testified. "I didn't understand it. It made no sense." As with the other witnesses, Cohen appeared to be reliving the events as he recounted them. Trump smirked, and passed a note to Todd Blanche. Blanche, more focused on Cohen than any previous witness, put it in his pocket and turned his gaze back toward the stand.

Cohen testified that he stormed into Allen Weisselberg's office and screamed at the Muppet-like bookkeeper, raving and cursing at the unfairness of the limited bonus, not to mention the fact that he still had yet to be reimbursed the $130,000 he was owed. Weisselberg told him to calm down. Everything would be made right after the holidays.

Apparently, word of the temper tantrum got back to the boss. Just before New Year's, Cohen said, Trump called him and told him he'd be taken care of.

The first piece of crucial testimony—the conversation in which Trump explicitly approved the scheme to disguise Cohen's reimbursements as legal payments—was coming up.

Days before the 2017 presidential inauguration—though Cohen couldn't be sure of the exact date—he stormed into the Trump Tower office, and Weisselberg told him to fetch a copy of the bank statement that showed the $130,000 transfer. In the courtroom, Susan Hoffinger displayed it on screen: It was the same document that Jeff McConney had testified about a week earlier. Cohen agreed that the scrawl on the left side of the document, indicating that he was ultimately owed $420,000, was Weisselberg's. The scrawl on the right was his own.

Hoffinger reviewed the math we'd already seen with McConney: $130,000 for the Daniels reimbursement plus $50,000 for the Red-Finch reimbursement totaled $180,000. The total was then "grossed up" to $360,000 for tax purposes, after which $60,000 was tacked on to appease Cohen's outrage about his 2016 bonus.

Hoffinger took a brief digression, the purpose of which wasn't entirely clear. She noted that, though Cohen was reimbursed $50,000 for having paid RedFinch, the tech company responsible for skewing online polls in Trump's favor, he hadn't actually paid RedFinch back in full.

It was 4 pm, and reporters were shifting in their seats. Hoffinger deliberately saved the most important testimony for the end of that grueling Monday. She wanted the jurors to go home that evening with the most important testimony ringing in their ears. She asked Cohen where he and Weisselberg had gone after they'd annotated the document with the reimbursement math.

"We went to Mr. Trump's office in order to speak to him about this," Cohen said.

Once they were with Trump, Weisselberg explained to Cohen that he would be paid in monthly installments. The payments would be marked as a retainer for legal services. Weisselberg showed Trump the document containing the math, saying that Cohen would receive $420,000 over the course of 12 months.

"And what, if anything, did Mr. Trump say at that time?" Hoffinger asked.

"He approved it," Cohen responded. "And he also said, 'This is going to be one heck of a ride in D.C.'"

The quote set off the usual clatter of typing from the gallery. But Hoffinger's next question was just as important.

"Did Mr. Weisselberg say in front of Mr. Trump that those monthly payments would be a retainer for legal services?"

"Yes," Cohen said.

Those two short lines—"he approved it" and "yes"—were the only pieces of testimony that directly linked Trump to the falsification of the reimbursements, the violation of 175.10. Hoffinger got what she needed. But if Todd Blanche could call those four words into question, the prosecution's case would be in danger.

❖   ❖   ❖

It was bright and beautiful again the following morning and the trees in Collect Pond Park were radiant with sunlight. Below them stood House Speaker Mike Johnson, third in line to the presidency. The speaker, like J.D. Vance before him, said that he had traveled to 100 Centre Street as a friend of Donald Trump's to pay firsthand witness to the travesty of justice. He attacked Michael Cohen and Merchan's daughter. "President Trump is innocent of these charges," he declared.

Inside the courthouse, Trump addressed the cameras in the 15th floor hallway, backed by his largest entourage to date. The vice-presidential hopefuls Doug Burgum, Vivek Ramaswamy and Byron

Donalds were the most prominent. They wore navy suits and long red ties, in apparent tribute to the party leader.

Trump looked delighted to have so many allies present. He addressed the cameras with unusual good cheer. "I do have a lot of surrogates and they are speaking very beautifully," he said. "They come from all over Washington, and they're highly respected and they think this is the biggest scam they've ever seen."

When he entered Part 59, they trailed behind him like vassals, along with the now daily attendees on the Trump side of the gallery. Boris Epshteyn assumed the role of usher, directing the politicians where to sit. Many had their phones out, but the court officers were in no rush to discipline them. It all felt more chaotic than usual. Only Merchan's entrance sufficed to quiet the gallery so that the day's session could begin. Susan Hoffinger summoned Cohen back to the witness stand.

The fixer limped into the courtroom, passed the defense table, and stiffly climbed the steps. We knew Hoffinger would begin with the second crucial conversation between Cohen and Trump, this one on February 8, 2017. Given the lack of detail in the first conversation, I expected this one to be far more incriminating, indicating more clearly Trump's involvement in falsifying the business records related to Cohen's reimbursements.

Instead, the testimony was threadbare. In the Oval Office, Cohen said, Trump had asked him if he needed money. Cohen said he was set, and the president told him to be sure to deal with Allen, and that he'd receive a check for the January and February installments.

That was it. After four weeks of witnesses giving ample evidence of the predicate crime, all direct evidence of Trump's involvement in the false business records came down to a few lines of testimony from Michael Cohen.

Cohen testified rotely about his submission of false invoices in 2017. That year, he profited not from work for the president, but from proximity to the presidency. He parlayed his "personal attorney" title, which required him to do very little lawyering, into approximately $4 million in fees for clients outside the White House. Even Trump seemed astonished. "Four?" we saw him mutter to Emil Bove at the defense table. Bove nodded.

Even so, all was not well for Cohen that year; clouds were gathering. Interviewed by a Senate committee about Trump's hopes to build a Moscow skyscraper, Cohen knowingly lied. There was some consolation: the lawyers who accompanied him to the interview were paid by The Trump Organization, a sign that the boss still had his back.

But in the spring of 2018, just a few weeks after Cohen told The *Times* that he'd paid Daniels of his own volition, that support began to erode. Cohen was staying at the Loews Regency Hotel that spring, his home under repair for flood damage. In the early morning hours of April 9, there was a knock on the hotel door. Cohen came to the peephole wearing Nike shorts. He saw a hallway filled with FBI agents.

Cohen was under investigation by the Southern District. He was terrified. He soon received a call from the president, who urged him to stay tough, assuring him he would be ok.

It was their last time speaking.

Justice Merchan dismissed the jurors for their morning break, and the Trump surrogates left to give the now-standard Collect Pond Park press conference, showcasing their loyalty. Minutes later, in the courtroom, Cohen resumed the story of how he lost his.

As he searched for a lawyer to help him avoid criminal charges, Cohen took a meeting at the Regency Hotel with Robert Costello, a former federal prosecutor and a new character for the jurors at this late stage. Cohen recalled Costello describing himself as a very close friend of Rudy Giuliani's. At Hoffinger's prompting, Cohen also testified that Costello had told him that, through Giuliani, he could maintain "a backchannel communication to the president."

In that first meeting, Cohen said, he lied to Costello, saying that he knew nothing incriminating about Donald Trump. Cohen testified that he'd believed any show of disloyalty would be conveyed through Costello and Giuliani back to Trump. But it was a lie that Robert Costello took to be true, and would never forget.

On April 19, Giuliani officially joined the president's legal team, and soon, Costello was emailing Cohen, carrying messages from the president's new lawyer. The messages encouraged Cohen to stay loyal. "You are 'loved,'" "Sleep well tonight, you have friends in high places."

Cohen met willingly with Costello, clearly eager for all the legal help he could get. But Cohen did not formally retain Costello. By June

2018, according to the emails that Hoffinger was showing the court-room, Costello was asking Cohen to clarify their legal relationship.

Cohen had begun to believe that Costello did not have his interests at heart. "My concern here was that all of these conversations were being relayed back to Mr. Giuliani and, of course, his client, President Trump," he testified. Fretting about his legal bills and terrified of his own criminal exposure, he began consulting with his family about what to do next.

"My wife, my daughter, my son, all said to me, 'Why are you holding onto this loyalty? What are you doing?'" he said. Cohen's voice slowed. We were poised in the gallery, waiting for him to describe the moment he flipped. He looked down, and gathered himself.

Then, suddenly, the double doors in the back opened. Trump's Republican surrogates streamed into the courtroom, interrupting the climax of Cohen's story. The journalists turned to stare, mouths agape, but Hoffinger indicated to Cohen that he should continue.

"So what decision did you make?" she asked.

Cohen said he'd decided it was time to listen to his family.

"What did you decide about where your loyalty should be going forward?"

"To my wife, my daughter, my son, and the country," Cohen said.

In August 2018, he pleaded guilty in federal court to two campaign finance violations.

"At whose direction and on whose behalf did you commit that crime?" Hoffinger asked.

"On behalf of Mr. Trump," Cohen said.

Cohen also pleaded guilty to five counts of tax evasion and one count of false financial statements. He testified that those crimes were unrelated to Trump.

"Mr. Cohen, what was that day like for you, pleading guilty to all those crimes?" Hoffinger asked.

"Worst day of my life," he said.

A few months later, Cohen pleaded guilty to a ninth count, for having lied to the Senate committee. He was sentenced to 36 months in prison, and began serving time in May 2019. Since then, he'd been disbarred and stripped of his taxi medallions. He'd sold off much of his real estate. His list of losses was similar to that of Stormy Daniels.

Like her, Cohen had turned to media work, which is to say, discussing Trump on his podcast, "Mea Culpa," writing about Trump in two books, "Disloyal," and "Revenge," and selling Trump-related merchandise. Though he'd turned on Donald Trump, his life was still wholly, obsessively concerned with his former boss.

"Mr. Cohen, do you have any regrets about your past work and your association with Donald Trump?" Hoffinger asked.

"I do," Cohen said. He understood the moment to require a measure of solemnity.

"What are they?"

"I regret doing things for him that I should not have: lying, bullying people in order to effectuate a goal. I don't regret working at the Trump Organization, 'cause, as I expressed before, some very interesting, great times. But to keep the loyalty and to do the things that he had asked me to do, I violated my moral compass. And I suffered the penalty. As has my family."

Justice Merchan excused the jurors for lunch.

❖   ❖   ❖

By the point that Todd Blanche stood to question his client's former lawyer, he had an advanced degree in Michael Cohen. He'd studied the way the former fixer thought, the way resentment for Donald Trump burned at the very core of his being, such that he continued to swim in Trump's wake like a remora, a sharksucker.

Blanche would later tell the *Financial Times* that he understood Michael Cohen's motivations, and the comment made all the sense in the world, given the way that Blanche clung to Trump at the defense table, sharing laughs during the breaks in testimony and scowls when a witness offered a damaging piece of testimony. By all appearances, Blanche enjoyed the company of his client in much the way Michael Cohen once had.

Hoffinger had gotten what she wanted out of Cohen by handling him as gently as possible. Now, it was time for Blanche to shake things up. He marched to the lectern that afternoon for the defense's last, best chance at a hung jury.

"Mr. Cohen, my name is Todd Blanche," he said. "You and I have never spoken or met before, have we?"

"We have not," Cohen said. He leaned forward, his face tense.

"But you know who I am, don't you?"

"I do."

"As a matter of fact, on April 23rd, so, after the trial started in this case, you went on TikTok and called me a "crying little shit," didn't you?"

Cohen looked surprised—and amused. "Sounds like something I would say," he said. At the defense table, Susan Necheles looked down, apparently to hide a smile.

Hoffinger objected, Merchan sustained it, and Blanche began to confront Cohen with another insult he'd lobbed on TikTok. This time, Hoffinger's objection pre-empted Blanche and Merchan asked the lawyers to approach.

"Why are you making this about yourself?" the judge asked Blanche.

"I'm not making it about myself, your honor," the defense lawyer sputtered. "I have a right to show this witness's bias, and he has expressed bias about the lawyers just because of who we represent."

"It's not admissible if it's not about the defendant," Hoffinger said.

"It doesn't matter if he has bias towards you; it doesn't matter," Merchan said. "The issue is whether he has bias towards the defendant. Don't make it about yourself."

Blanche returned to the lectern, his stride broken. He got Cohen to testify that he'd been paying close attention to the trial, then again returned to his TikToks.

"You referred to President Trump as a 'Dictator Douche Bag,' didn't you?" Blanche said.

Cohen smirked. "Sounds like something I said."

"And on that same TikTok, so again on April 23rd, you referred to President Trump when he left the courtroom, you said that 'he goes right into that little cage, which is where he belongs, in a fucking cage, like an animal.' Do you recall saying that?"

"I recall saying that," Cohen said.

Trump sat at the defense table, eyes closed. Juror 5's eyes sparkled; she looked like she was having fun, waiting patiently to see where the cross-examination was headed.

Having just been accused of attention-seeking himself, it seemed that Blanche wanted the jury to understand it was Cohen who was desperate for attention. He asked the witness if he had gone on television several dozen times in the course of the district attorney's investigation.

"I have gone on television," Cohen acknowledged.

Blanche asked him if it was more than 20 times.

"Could be," Cohen said.

"Well, do you have any doubt in your mind that it's more than 20, sir?"

"No," Cohen said.

"So when you say it 'could be,' you mean, yes, it is more than 20?"

"Yes," Cohen said. "Could be."

Blanche was taking his task seriously, but the topics about which he was questioning Cohen were absurd, leading to a mismatch between the inquisitor's tone and the content of his inquiry. It was indisputable that Michael Cohen spent much of his time criticizing, baiting and otherwise discussing Donald Trump. But Cohen leaned into it; he understood himself as Trump's foremost antagonist. It would undermine his brand to deny that role.

"Do you want President Trump to get convicted in this case?" Blanche asked.

"Sure," Cohen said.

Blanche pivoted to Cohen's monetization of his antagonism. He established that, like Stormy Daniels, Cohen sold merch, including a coffee mug that said, "Send him to the Big House, not the White House" and a t-shirt picturing Trump behind bars.

"You actually wore that T-shirt last week on your TikTok, didn't you, on Wednesday night?" Blanche asked.

"I did," Cohen said.

"And you were offering—encouraging people to go buy it, correct?"

"Yes," said Cohen, adding, as any salesman would, "It's part of the merch store."

The overflow room erupted in laughter. Even the jurors were beginning to look as if they were holding back their smiles.

Blanche rubbed his head with the back of his palm. He started anew, quoting Cohen, in 2015, saying that all Trump wanted was to make the country great again.

"At the time, you weren't lying, right?"

"At that time, I was knee-deep into the cult of Donald Trump, yes." Cohen said.

Nothing worked for Todd Blanche that afternoon. This was the most important cross examination of the entire trial. But there was no friction between Blanche and Cohen and no momentum to the questioning. It was warm in the courtroom, and the jurors kept yawning. Blanche would have to be a lot better for the defense to stand a chance.

✳   ✳   ✳

There was a time when I was the opposite of Michael Cohen; I would do anything to avoid a camera. So it took weeks for me to acknowledge that I enjoyed the recognition that came with The *Times* videos. But by the point Cohen was being cross-examined, I had to admit there was upside. It was flattering. I was asked out by strangers on LinkedIn, recognized in the park on the weekend. Immediately, I became 10 percent more paranoid and at least 40 percent more insufferable. Anytime someone looked at me sideways, I wondered if it was because they recognized me.

The videos were just capsule summaries of what happened in court each day. Their scant runtime made it impossible to capture the breadth and nuance of the reporting we did throughout the day, or the longer stories that Ben Protess and I worked on during evenings and weekends. So much was lost in translation.

So even as I enjoyed the experience, I found it disquieting, a reflection of the way that sound and image continually trumped the word. And it made me feel, in a way news stories never had, that in a very minor way I, like Michael Cohen, was becoming better-known because of Donald Trump.

✳   ✳   ✳

On Wednesday, May 15, the House Judiciary Committee, chaired by Representative Jim Jordan, took advantage of the mid-week trial break to hold a hearing on the "Weaponization of the Federal Government" in the Rayburn Office Building in Washington. Seated in front of yellow curtains in the grand, wood-paneled room, Jordan used his opening statement to accuse every prosecutor who'd indicted Trump of election interference. They were working as one to hinder the 2024 Republican campaign, he said.

The most prominent witness at the hearing was one Robert Costello. Costello was silver-haired and pugnacious, and immediately began to testify about his relationship with Michael Cohen. Cohen's testimony about him in Manhattan the previous day, Costello said, had been nothing but lies. He'd provided honest legal advice to Cohen, and suggested that he could cooperate with the Southern District if he had damaging information about Trump. But Cohen had assured him that he had nothing on Donald Trump.

An hour into the hearing, Costello was questioned by Representative Elise Stefanik, who asked him about "lawfare." The word had become the right's shorthand for Trump's legal troubles, reframed as the work of an out-of-control partisan justice system.

Stefanik, seated next to Rep. Matt Gaetz, asked Costello a number of questions about Bragg's trial. Costello eagerly agreed with her premises: Yes, Bragg had run for district attorney on a platform of pursuing Trump. Yes, the trial was a sham, Cohen was a perjurer, and Matthew Colangelo was "transferred" to Bragg's office to "run this weaponized prosecution of President Trump."

"It's unheard of," Costello said, in response to the last question.

"Un-*heard* of. It's a disgrace," Stefanik said. "Do you agree that this weaponization of lawfare goes straight to the top for the purposes of helping Joe Biden's failing presidential campaign?"

"The circumstantial evidence definitely supports that," Costello said.

❖   ❖   ❖

After the hearing, Matt Gaetz traveled from Washington to New York and on Thursday, May 16, he and Lauren Boebert ranked as the most high-profile members of the 11-Republican-strong congressional delegation that formed Trump's courtroom coterie. The gallery couldn't hold them all, though Boris Epshteyn did his best to wrangle seats. Anderson Cooper was in the gallery that morning, ignoring Boebert and Gaetz as they smirked at him. The trial was more popular than ever.

Michael Cohen walked to the witness stand and straight into the jaws of Todd Blanche, who was ready with multimedia. Blanche cued up the clip of Cohen celebrating Trump's indictment on his podcast. Cohen's bizarre, affected broadcast voice streamed into Part 59, playing far louder than was necessary.

> "... HE IS ABOUT TO GET A TASTE OF WHAT I WENT THROUGH AND I PROMISE YOU IT'S NOT FUN! PICTURING DONALD TRUMP BEING LED THROUGH THE BOOKING PROCESS, GETTING FINGERPRINTED, HAVING HIS MUG SHOT TAKEN, FILLS ME WITH DELIGHT! AND SADNESS ALL AT THE SAME TIME ..."

Cohen's face sank. Blanche played another clip, and the voice was back.

> "... I TRULY FUCKING HOPE THIS MAN ENDS UP IN PRISON! ... YOU BETTER BELIEVE I WANT THIS MAN TO GO DOWN AND ROT INSIDE FOR WHAT HE DID TO MY FAMILY!. ..."

The difference between the tamed, hangdog Cohen on the stand, and the feral, revenge-obsessed voice from the podcasts was striking. Even Trump, who'd successfully ignored Cohen's testimony, was paying attention.

Blanche started a new line of questioning and immediately established a rhythm. He noted that Cohen had testified many times over the years, and had sworn the same oath each time.

"You were asked to do the same thing every single time you put your right hand up correct?" Blanche asked.

"Correct," Cohen said, warily.

"You swear to tell the truth?"

"Correct."

"Exactly like what you did in this courtroom?"

"Correct."

But, as Blanche proceeded to point out, Cohen had lied numerous times under oath. He'd lied to the Senate committee in 2017. He'd lied to the Special Counsel's office the following year. He'd lied when he told a federal judge that he felt no pressure to plead guilty in August 2018, and when he'd told Congress he'd never be willing to accept a presidential pardon. The word "lie" became a refrain in every question Blanche asked. Cohen appeared to be slowly breaking down. His voice grew hoarse and he looked relieved when Merchan interrupted Blanche to call for the morning break.

The break didn't do Cohen much good. Soon, he was back on the stand, hammered by Blanche, who insinuated that he was still telling lies under oath. Cohen insisted he hadn't *really* wanted to be chief of staff, only to be confronted by Blanche with evidence of the multiple people he'd told, at the time, that he did.

With thirty minutes to go until the lunch break, Blanche pivoted to the evening of October 24, 2016, and the unusual call Cohen placed to Trump through Keith Schiller. The significance of that date hadn't initially been clear to me. It was just one of the innumerable calls in the mad sequence before Cohen finally wired the hush money to Keith Davidson on October 27.

Blanche asked Cohen to repeat his Monday testimony about the call that evening. Cohen, nonplussed, obliged. He'd called Keith Schiller, spoken to Trump and moved closer toward making the payment.

"Do you remember at that time," Blanche asked, "you were receiving a bunch of ongoing and continuing harassment phone calls?"

Cohen said he did. He didn't know where this was going either.

Reporters began whispering to each other, trying to figure it out. On the defense side of the gallery, Trump's supporters were paying close attention. Blanche remained focused.

"And do you remember that on the 24th, at around 7 o'clock at night, the person who was harassing you forgot to block the number and you got the number, do you remember that?"

Cohen did not remember. Blanche pulled up some old texts. The person who'd been prank calling had indeed revealed his number, and Cohen reacted with characteristic hyperbole.

"This number has been sent to Secret Service for your ongoing and continuous harassment," he texted.

"It wasn't me," the prankster responded. "My friend told me to call,

I am sorry for this, I won't do it again."

"They're going to have to explain that to the Secret Service," Cohen insisted. He told the prankster that if he was a minor, he might want to alert his parent or guardian.

"I am 14," the prankster said. "Please don't do this."

The courtroom burst into laughter, this time at Cohen's expense.

Susan Hoffinger sought to disrupt the defense momentum with a couple of successful objections, noting the document Blanche was using as a reference point was not in evidence. But Blanche quickly laid the foundation to introduce it into evidence, then got right back to his questioning.

After having threatened the prankster, Cohen texted Keith Schiller to ask who he should speak to about the harassment. Schiller said "call me," then, apparently impatient, called Cohen himself. The call went to voicemail, but Cohen called Schiller back and was on the phone for 96 seconds. After getting off the phone, he texted Schiller the 14-year-old's number.

Blanche raised his voice as he prepared to lower the hammer.

"You had a specific recollection that that 1 minute and 36 second phone call on October 24th was not with Keith Schiller. That you called Keith Schiller and he passed the phone to President Trump. You finalized the deal with Stormy Daniels and you said, 'We're going to move forward,' and he said, 'Yes.'"

"That's correct," Cohen said.

"That was a LIE," Blanche shouted, his voice oddly high-pitched. "You were actually talking to Mr. Schiller about the fact that you were getting harassing phone calls from a 14 year old, correct?"

Cohen sputtered. "Part of it was the 14 year old, but I know that Keith was with Mr. Trump at the time and there was more than potentially just this. That's what I recall based upon the documents that I reviewed."

Blanche noted that five minutes earlier, Cohen hadn't remembered the prankster at all. Now he was changing his testimony to say that in 96 seconds, he both updated Schiller about having been bullied by a teenager and also updated Trump on the Daniels situation. "That's your testimony?!" he asked.

"I always ran everything by the boss immediately," Cohen said.

Blanche pushed Cohen—it almost seemed as if he was hoping the witness would lose it on the stand and confess. "You did not talk to President Trump on that night. You talked to Keith Schiller about what we just went through. You can admit it!"

"No sir, I can't," Cohen said, in his most polite tone. "I am not certain that is accurate."

"You were certain it was accurate when you were under oath and testifying," Blanche roared. "You were certain it was accurate you had a phone call to President Trump. But now you are saying you are not certain it was accurate?"

"Based upon the records that I was able to review, in light of everything that was going on, I believe I also spoke to Mr. President Trump and told him everything regarding the Stormy Daniels matter was being worked on and it's going to be resolved."

"We are not asking for your belief!" Blanche shouted. "This jury doesn't want to hear what you *think* happened."

Blanche was practically glowing when Merchan dismissed the jury for lunch a few minutes later. Anderson Cooper hurried out of the courtroom.

❖ ❖ ❖

During the break, as I was seeking to muster enthusiasm for an ancient bagel from the cafe on the courthouse's ground floor, Cooper was on CNN, exclaiming over the prankster revelation.

"It was *incredible*," he said, breathless. "Michael Cohen was cornered in what appeared to be a lie, I think, to many in the room, and had to adjust, suddenly, his memory that he had just testified to on Tuesday."

Another commentator asked Cooper what the jury had made of it. Cooper noted that the jurors were not, generally, reactive.

"But you could tell the import of the moment and everybody in the courtroom could tell. And if you were unaware of it, the clicking of every reporter in the room's typewriters, it was like a crescendo."

Certainly, the press reacted strongly. The clip of Cooper's comments circulated broadly. As we re-entered the courtroom for the afternoon session, the momentum had definitively swung toward the defense. You could see it in everything Todd Blanche did, in the way he asked his questions and the way he stood. No more rubbing of his head now. He seemed eager, always on to the next question.

Again, he reviewed Cohen's testimony about the prankster, just to wring every last drop from his big win. Then, he moved on to Cohen's interactions with the press, hoping to coax him into admitting that he did not *always* check in with Trump when providing a statement to a journalist.

But Cohen stayed firm on this point, too. Always, when an original statement was on the line, he had checked in with the boss.

It remained true for the rest of the afternoon. Cohen stuck to his story. At one point, Blanche did the math and ended up estimating that Cohen was conducting 350 phone calls a week, 1,400 a month and more than 14,000 a year.

"And so, when you testified on Monday and Tuesday, about specific conversations that you had with different folks, Mr. Pecker, Mr. Howard, and President Trump, you were not testifying from a specific recollection of that phone call, were you?" Blanche asked, his tone drowning in disbelief.

"I was," Cohen said, staring at him.

"You were?"

"I was. Because these phone calls are things that I have been talking about for the last six years. They were extremely important, and they were all-consuming."

The day ended early, due to a juror appointment, and the trial was off on Friday, so that Trump could attend his youngest son's high school graduation. The prosecutors filed out of the courtroom. They had three days to think about how they could reverse Blanche's win.

❖   ❖   ❖

Monday, May 20, was the first day of the final week of testimony. By that point, the television cameras on the west side of Centre Street were a permanent fixture of the sidewalk. The line north of Collect Pond Park was like a tent city and line-sitter prices had spiked. A spot in the front went for nearly $2,000. The Trump attention economy was roaring.

It could be the day everything came together for the defense. Blanche could introduce an alternative theory that would establish reasonable doubt as to Cohen's testimony about the January 2017 conversation, exonerating Trump. Short of that, he might simply break Cohen, causing him to lose control and either admit to lies or otherwise impeach his credibility to the point that the jury could no longer put stock in any of his testimony.

Cohen entered the courtroom just after 9:30, and Todd Blanche stalked to the lectern. He was confrontational from the get-go.

"How many reporters have you talked to about what happened last week?" he spat at Cohen.

"I didn't speak to reporters about what happened last week," Cohen said, subdued.

Having re-established the proper, antagonistic atmosphere, Blanche began to wind up for an extended attack. The defense team had noticed something hiding in plain sight in Michael Cohen's direct testimony: The issue of Cohen failing to pay his contact at RedFinch Solutions—the digital poll hacker—the full $50,000 he was owed.

"You only paid the RedFinch owner $20,000, right?" he asked Cohen.

"Yes, sir," Cohen said. He testified that he'd visited a bank across from his house over the course of several days, placing the money in a brown paper bag, long before his January 2017 conversation with Allen Weisselberg about the Trump Organization's debts.

Blanche reminded the jury that Cohen had been paid $50,000 by the company for this transaction; $100,000 once the money was doubled for tax purposes.

"You stole from The Trump Organization, right?" Blanche asked, raising his voice as he sought to corner Cohen again.

But Cohen was amenable to Blanche's interpretation, and he didn't put up a fight: "Yes, sir."

Blanche asserted that, because the money was doubled—"grossed up"—Cohen had pocketed $60,000. He asked Cohen if he'd shared the story with the prosecution. Cohen said he had.

"Did you ever have to plead guilty to larceny?" Blanche asked

"No, sir," Cohen said, looking downcast.

"Have you paid back The Trump Organization the money that you stole from them?"

"No, sir."

Another triumph for Blanche. He'd successfully portrayed Cohen first as a liar and then as a thief. It could be a prelude to discrediting his most important testimony.

＊　＊　＊

In Collect Pond Park, Angela, she of the shofar and the Burger King crown, was back. She'd determined a way to evade the prohibition on her bullhorn; rather than using it to broadcast her own speech, she instead used it to amplify an old Trump address, lip-syncing the remarks to the assembled crowd. Melding herself with Trump paid dividends; the anti-Trump protesters in the park were furious.

＊　＊　＊

Back in the courtroom, Blanche zeroed in on Cohen's conversation with Weisselberg in January 2017. Going by the prosecution's timeline, Cohen and Weisselberg would soon move to Trump's office, where, in Cohen's telling, the president-elect had signed off on the reimbursement scheme.

I sat in the gallery, waiting for a killing blow, in which Todd Blanche would show the jurors the hole in that story. His line of inquiry would follow Michael Cohen into Trump's office. He would ask question after question, putting Cohen on edge until the former fixer contradicted himself. Then, Blanche would pounce.

He began.

"Except for that one conversation with Mr. Weisselberg about that, and then you guys go in and talk to President Trump about it, supposedly, right—do you remember that, except for those two conversations, did you have other conversations before that with Mr. Weisselberg about your role as President Trump's personal attorney?" Blanche asked.

"No, sir," Cohen said.

"The conversations that you had with Mr. Weisselberg about the retainer agreement—and the fact that there would not be one—all took place in the meeting you had with him alone and the meeting you had with President Trump, is that your testimony?"

"Yes, sir."

This was the time to ask about the meeting with Trump. But instead, Blanche began to ask dutiful questions about retainer agreements. He left the content of Michael Cohen's damning testimony behind. I kept waiting for him to return to it. Blanche's questions occasionally came in loops. But he never did.

Even in retrospect, it's hard to say why. Maybe Blanche felt it'd be implausible to argue that Donald Trump did not have final authority over how his money was spent. Maybe he was concerned that, if Cohen disclosed more details and Trump didn't testify in response, the jury would wonder why. Or maybe he simply believed that the prankster revelation had been enough to thoroughly discredit Cohen as a witness. But whatever the justification, he left the most damning testimony of the trial undisputed. It was an unexpected win for the prosecution.

❖   ❖   ❖

The jurors were beginning to look bored. Maybe Blanche had reached the highs of his cross too early, because now he was floundering. Juror Nine shot him a glance, her head resting on her palm, then turned doggedly back to her notepad.

The sun shone through the tall windows as Blanche drifted toward his grand finale. He reminded the jurors that Cohen made $4 million from his consulting agreements, and another $420,00 from the hush-money reimbursements. Thanks to his books and his podcasts, Cohen had made another $4 million since 2017. There was also a television show being pitched about his life, with the working title "Fixer," as well as a potential third book. And he was considering a run for Congress, too, given that he believed he had "the best name recognition out there."

"Because of your work and what you have been doing over the past several years, going after President Trump, that's your name recognition?" Blanche said.

"I wouldn't characterize it that way," Cohen said, leaning forward, gathering residual energy. "My name recognition is because of the journey that I've been on. Is it affiliated to Mr. Trump? Yes. Not because of

Mr. Trump."

"Well the *journey* you have been on," Blanche said, scoffing at the therapy-speak, "at least for the past few years has included daily attacks on President Trump. That's part of your journey, right sir?"

"My journey is to tell my story, yes sir," Cohen said.

Blanche turned away from the subject for a few minutes, then pounced.

"Do you have a financial interest in the outcome of this case?" he asked.

"Yes, sir," Cohen said.

"Because if President Trump is convicted that would benefit you personally, financially, right?"

"No, sir," Cohen said.

Blanche looked surprised. "Well then what is your financial interest in this case?"

"I may talk about it on my podcasts. I talk about it on TikTok, and they make money," Cohen said. "That's how I was viewing your question. Whether Mr. Trump is ultimately determined innocent or guilty is not going to affect whether I speak about it or not."

"Well, I didn't ask whether it would prevent you from speaking about it," Blanche said, his frustration growing. "The question to you today is, whether a conviction benefits you financially?"

Susan Hoffinger objected, saying Cohen had already answered the question. But Merchan overruled her. "You can answer it," he said.

"The answer is . . . no," Cohen said, with that little bit of showmanship.

"It doesn't?" Blanche asked, in disbelief.

"It's better if he is not, for me," Cohen said. "Because it gives me more to talk about in the future."

The jurors, so sleepy moments before, were all paying attention now. Cohen looked pleased with himself. His answer revealed the dynamics of the anti-Trump marketplace, where demand never waned. In a world where the president's story had ended—a world where a conviction was the first domino in Trump's downfall—there would be no use for Michael Cohen.

"Notwithstanding everything that you have said over the years, you have specific recollections of having conversations on the phone with then-candidate Donald J. Trump about the Stormy Daniels matter, correct?"

"Yes, sir," Cohen said.

"No doubt in your mind?"

"It's no doubt."

Cohen was bent, but unbroken. His insistence on the truth of his story, after all the embarrassing things he'd conceded, strengthened his testimony. The Michael Cohen who left the stand on Monday afternoon was stronger and more believable than the version who'd entered the courtroom that morning. As he walked out, ignoring the leering gang in the gallery, the prosecution rested its case.

CHAPTER NINE

CONTEMPT

The entourage assembled behind Trump on the final day of Michael Cohen's testimony was filled with ominous-looking figures whose knowing entry into Part 59 spoke of a familiarity with courtrooms. The standout was an older man with an enormous head of slicked black hair, and a pinstripe suit. He resembled an Elvis impersonator who'd been put through a wood-chipper. It turned out to be Chuck Zito, the former head of the New York chapter of the Hells Angels, one of the few non-mafia attendees at John Gotti's wake.

Zito, who had served years in prison on drug charges, was in good company. Bernie Kerik, another of Trump's guests, was a former New York City police commissioner who'd been sent to prison for tax crimes and lying to federal officials, only to be pardoned by Trump. And Boris Epshteyn, the legal adviser indicted in Arizona, was again serving in his role as usher, having by then become a staple of Part 59, someone we greeted each day. Emily Saul of the Law Journal even began tracking his cuff links, so often was his beefy arm draped over the second row on the left side of the gallery. Kash Patel, a former federal prosecutor and well-known Trump loyalist was there too, as were Alan Dershowitz and another full complement of congressmen.

If the previous week, Trump's guests had demonstrated his control of the Republican party, this new crew sent a harsher message: That the power Donald Trump wielded was more seductive than the rule of law—and that the former president could associate with anyone he wanted and still come out on top. Fucking with him was a dangerous choice. Standing at the front of the courtroom, Trump looked thoroughly satisfied, surveying his posse with his lips pursed and his thumbs looped through his belt like the head of some white-collar outlaw gang.

❖   ❖   ❖

Blanche and the rest of the defense team could have called any number of witnesses. They could have called campaign loyalists, to downplay the importance of the "Access Hollywood" tape. They could have called Trump's employees, either at his company or the White House, to emphasize all the paperwork that was processed without the boss's knowledge. They could have called members of Trump's family, who could pay lip service to the amount of work Michael Cohen had done for them in 2017.

They could also have called Allen Weisselberg, though the prosecution had certainly made it difficult. Weisselberg, the only other participant in the all-important conversation in January 2017, was in jail for perjury; in March, he'd pled guilty to the district attorney's charges of lying in a separate case. The defense was concerned that Weisselberg might plead the fifth for fear of further self-incrimination. If he declined to answer questions, it would not reflect well on their case, particularly if it were explained to the jury why he was in a jail in the first place.

So the defense did not call Weisselberg. Instead, Trump's lawyers, who'd aggressively cross-examined the prosecution witnesses, barely put on a case. They called one substantive witness: A man who so despised Michael Cohen that he effectively embodied their attack on the former fixer.

Robert Costello's a brief, passing relationship with Cohen in the spring and summer of 2018 had been covered by Hoffinger the previous week. As the walls of Cohen's life began to crash down around him and he weighed his diminishing options, Costello had arrived in Cohen's life, offering some measure of support and the ability to maintain his ties to Trump from a distance. But the arrangement was unacceptable to Cohen, who soon cut ties altogether, pleaded guilty and pointed the finger at his former boss.

Ever since, Costello had told the same story: That in their initial meeting, he'd advised Cohen to go to the feds with any incriminating information he had on Trump, only for Cohen to insist he knew nothing incriminating. Given Cohen's distress in that moment, Costello never doubted he was telling the truth then, and lying later, a perfect inversion of the prosecution's explanation of the sequence.

It was Trump's idea to call Costello, after his Congressional testimony the previous week and related television appearances. In front of a friendly, Republican-led committee and on Fox News, Costello seemed unimpeachable. He didn't engage with the possibility that Cohen may have been lying to him in 2018 and had no rebuttal to the prosecution's explanation of Cohen's eventual turn. Costello simply stuck to his own story, refusing to countenance anything that conflicted. His reluctance to engage made him a perfect fit as Donald Trump's single substantive defense witness.

Though Susan Hoffinger was aware that Costello had tried and failed to convince the grand jury not to trust Cohen, she couldn't know in advance the gift she was being given. In a bench conference before Justice Merchan, she expressed fierce opposition to Costello testifying. She argued that state law barred him from appearing as a witness only to impeach the former fixer's credibility.

But Emil Bove said that Costello would challenge the prosecution's argument that he had been the front for a Trump-directed pressure campaign to keep Cohen from flipping in the summer of 2018. It was a reasonable aim. Cohen had testified that Costello was like a bird of prey who'd swooped down on him at the behest of the president, in order to ensure that he was sticking to the party line. But there was little evidence that Costello was dispatched by Trump. And Cohen had used Costello, as he sought to evade the federal investigation that was wrecking his life.

Merchan did little to hide his frustration at being asked to set limits on a witness's testimony on the spot; it was a decision he'd usually make ahead of time. He excused the jury, asked the lawyers to repeat their arguments, then stood up abruptly and excused himself, saying he wanted to think the matter over in his chambers for five minutes.

"Don't leave the courtroom," he barked at the lawyers as he left, his robes sweeping behind him.

He returned soon afterward, and informed Emil Bove that he'd give him some freedom, not only to explore potentially inconsistent statements by Cohen, but to elicit testimony about what prosecutors had characterized as a Trump-backed pressure campaign.

But, Merchan warned, "I'm not going to allow this to become a trial within a trial as to whether or not there was, in fact, this pressure campaign and how it affected Cohen. That's not the purpose of this trial."

As a result, Bob Costello's testimony was severely restricted. But no one took the time to tell the witness. He had no idea.

❖ ❖ ❖

Within an hour of Cohen leaving the stand on Monday afternoon, Costello walked into the courtroom, his spine stiff, his shoulders thrown back. A student assistant to Rudy Giuliani, he was a self-made lawyer from Forest Hills, Queens. He'd worked for seven years as a prosecutor at the Southern District, overlapping with Walter Mack. Unlike Mack, Costello had no issue with the press.

In fact, after his time at Southern, Costello represented tabloid stars of the glossy era, among them George Steinbrenner and Leona Helmsley. More recently, he'd represented Giuliani himself, and Steve Bannon. A man of the law who believed the law as practiced by Alvin Bragg was giving Donald Trump short shrift, Costello mirrored several of the former president's guests in the gallery.

Once at the lectern, Emil Bove didn't dwell on Costello's background, or seek to repair his credibility with the jury, who knew him as the lawyer who'd sought to keep Cohen on a leash. Instead, Bove immediately began asking him about Michael Cohen.

Costello told the jury that he and Cohen first met on April 17, 2018, at the Regency, about a week after the F.B.I. raid on Cohen's. The fixer, he testified, was "absolutely manic," unable to sit still, "pacing back and forth, left and right." Cohen asked Costello for an "escape route," some way out of his legal dilemma.

Costello's testimony was cut short by Susan Hoffinger, who began to lodge objections anytime the witness came close to digressing.

"What was your view that day about whether or not Michael Cohen should cooperate?" Bove asked.

Hoffinger objected. Merchan sustained the objection. Bove posed another question. Costello began to digress, and Hoffinger objected.

Bove was irritated and Costello, ignorant of the limitations on his testimony, shook his head in disbelief. He could barely get a word out. Neither he nor the jury knew why but the jurors trusted Merchan's authority. Costello, as would soon become obvious, did not.

Finally, Bove managed to an answer from the witness.

"I explained to Michael Cohen that this entire legal problem that he was facing would be resolved by the end of the week if he had truthful information on Donald Trump and cooperated with the Southern District of New York," Costello testified. But, he added, Cohen had told him, "'I swear to God, Bob. I don't have anything on Donald Trump.'"

Hoffinger swamped Bove's next few questions with objections, prompting Costello to glance at Merchan questioningly several times. Trump shook his head.

After a brief sidebar, Bove again tried to tailor his questions to fit within Merchan's strict guidelines. "I want to focus very narrowly on whether Cohen said anything about whether President Trump knew about the payment to Stormy Daniels," he told Costello.

"Michael Cohen said, numerous times, that President Trump knew nothing about those payments," Costello replied, projecting his contempt for Cohen toward the jury box as if it were a ball one of the jurors might catch. "He did this on his own."

Bove made his way toward the subject of whether Cohen had formally retained Costello as his lawyer. Hoffinger lodged an objection and Merchan sustained it. This time, Costello ignored the judge's ruling and kept talking, so eager was he to complain about Cohen's perfidy.

Merchan halted him. "When I sustain an objection, you don't need to answer it," he said. Costello nodded.

Bove managed to get two more questions out before another successful objection. Costello ran roughshod over this one as well.

Costello told the jury that Cohen had asked him to probe Giuliani for more information about the origin of the F.B.I. inquiry. Costello had obliged, reporting his findings in an email with the subject line "Assignment."

When Bove began to ask questions about the email, Hoffinger lobbed her tenth objection. Justice Merchan sustained it.

"Jeez," said Costello, as if he were at home, watching the trial on television.

"I'm sorry??" Merchan said, staring down at the witness sitting just below him.

Costello's face reddened. As Bove asked another question, prompting yet another objection, Costello said "strike it," directing the court reporter to strike his testimony.

Justice Merchan, angrier than I'd ever seen him, asked Bove to pause and the jury to step out. They filed out of the well. Costello, his face still red, made to stand up, too, and Justice Merchan directed him to remain seated.

"Mr. Costello," he said, "I would like to discuss proper decorum in my courtroom." Costello began to speak, but the judge spoke over him. "If you don't like my ruling, you don't say 'jeez.' Ok? And then you don't say 'strike it,' because I'm the only one that can strike testimony in the courtroom. Do you understand that?"

"I understand," Costello said, staring up at the bench.

"Okay. And then, if you don't like my ruling, you don't give me side eye and you don't roll your eyes. Do you understand that?"

Costello continued to stare at Merchan mutely, apparently furious.

"Do you understand that??"

"I understand that. I understand what you're saying," he said.

Merchan briefly looked away, telling a court officer to bring the jury back. But when he turned back toward the witness, he saw Costello's expression. "Are you staring me down right now?" he asked, his face mottled in anger.

"No," Costello said. "I'm just wondering . . ."

"Clear the courtroom!" Merchan yelled to the court officers. "Clear the courtroom right now."

Led by Captain Mullaney, the court officers sprang into action, yelling at us to leave.

It made no sense; there was no justification for us to go. While some reporters left, others near the front—Emily Saul, Frank Runyeon, and I—started bellowing back at Mullaney and the others.

Emily yelled an objection on behalf of the press, while Frank tried to use a halfway reasonable voice. But I'd lost my temper; after passively observing the trial for so long, I was in the middle of everything. "This is an open courtroom!" I yelled, pushing for the press lawyer, Robert Balin, to be heard.

Balin tried to make his way forward, but he was dwarfed by Mullaney, his voice overpowered by the shouting of the court officers. One of them took his arm and led him forcibly from the room. Once I saw our lawyer escorted out, I gave up. I joined the others and left the courtroom. Even in Part 59, in that moment, persuasion would not work. After six weeks, in the midst of the defense case, Merchan had lost control.

❖   ❖   ❖

There was no valid justification for our ejection, not then and not since. We were simply the most vulnerable targets. Merchan couldn't completely lose his temper with Costello, or the defense. A judicial outburst could be grounds for a mistrial, or an appeal. The prosecution had the legal means to fight back. So Merchan took his anger out on us, the press.

"Alright," Merchan said, once we were gone. "Let the record reflect that it's now five after four. Let the record also reflect that the court officers had great difficulty clearing the courtroom, because the courtroom is made up, primarily, of the press. And I can appreciate that the press wants to be present for every part of these proceedings. Therefore, this record is not sealed. The press will have access to this record.

"The fact that I had to clear the courtroom and that the court officers, including the captain, had great difficulty clearing the courtroom, and that there was argument back and forth between the press and including counsel for the press, goes to why I had to clear the courtroom in the first place. And that is, sir, your conduct is contemptuous right now." This was clearly directed toward Costello.

"I'm putting you on notice that your conduct is contemptuous. If you try to stare me down one more time, I will remove you from the stand.

"I will strike his entire testimony. do you understand me?" he said to the defense.

"Yes, judge," Bove responded. "I understand."

"Listen to the question and answer the question," Merchan told Costello.

"Can I say something please?" Costello asked.

"No," Merchan said. "No. This is not a conversation."

Reading the transcript that evening, I imagined him finally sitting back, working to get himself under control now that the outburst was over. We were brought back into the room, as was the jury.

❖   ❖   ❖

Costello managed to illustrate several more times that Cohen had not objected to the backchannel he provided, and had, in fact, made use of it. There was no question that the two men had a more complicated relationship than the prosecution's story suggested. But the restrictions on Costello's testimony, enforced strictly by Merchan, didn't allow for much progress.

Soon, Bove gave up and it was Susan Hoffinger's turn. She appeared eager to get started, speaking at a quick clip, unbound by the strict rules of a direct examination. As a longtime defense lawyer, Hoffinger was a cross-examination specialist, and Robert Costello was an easy witness to cross, particularly given that he seemed to dislike the prosecutor from the very start. She asked him several questions about an email sent by his law partner to Michael Cohen, asking if Cohen would be interested in meeting with Costello.

The witness was reluctant to answer the questions, and kept insisting that the email "speaks for itself."

Hoffinger moved on. "You were hoping that Michael Cohen would hire you as his lawyer, correct?"

"I wasn't hoping anything," Costello said, noting that it was his law partner who'd reached out to Cohen. "I didn't know Michael Cohen from a hole in the wall," he added.

"So you weren't interested in having him as your client?" Hoffinger asked. This was hard to believe.

"No, I wasn't," Costello said.

Hoffinger asked several more questions and Costello insisted he'd been indifferent to Cohen. She then pulled up an email from Costello to his son, informing him excitedly that he would be representing Michael Cohen. The younger Costello had responded warmly, congratulating his father on the win. "Wow. That's big news. Congrats, Dad. I hope this leads to a lot of good things coming your way."

❖ ❖ ❖

The cross-examination of Robert Costello lasted into Tuesday, May 21 Trump brought a fresh crop of Republican supporters to court including, finally, Donald Trump Jr. Costello entered the courtroom in a light grey suit and a light pink shirt, perhaps hoping to contribute to a lighter mood. Justice Merchan welcomed him back, then sat making notes, ignoring the witness until the jurors filed in and Susan Hoffinger began the day's questioning. She started by suggesting to Costello that he'd mentioned his longstanding relationship with Rudy Giuliani to Cohen at their very first meeting in April 2018.

"That's not true," Costello said.

Hoffinger then showed the witness two emails—both of them sent two days after the first meeting, one to Cohen and the other to Costello's law partner. In both emails, Costello acknowledged having mentioned to Cohen how useful his relationship with Giuliani could be.

Then, Hoffinger displayed an email in which Costello told Cohen that Giuliani had thanked him for opening a back channel of communication. "The email speaks for itself, right sir?" she said, teasingly.

"I'm sorry?" Costello said.

"The email speaks for itself?"

"No, not quite, because there are surrounding circumstances . . ."

"Mhm."

". . . about that email, which I'd be delighted to tell you about."

Hoffinger, clearly convinced of the jury's support, said "That's alright."

Her next question involved an email in which Costello wrote, "Our issue is to get Cohen on the right page without giving him the appearance that we are following instructions from Giuliani or the president."

"Now, you sent this email to your partner, about your goal of getting Cohen to follow instructions from Rudy Giuliani and the president without it appearing so, correct?" she asked.

Costello sputtered. "No, not to follow instructions, but to get everybody on the same page because Michael Cohen had been complaining incessantly, frankly, that Rudy Giuliani was making statements in the press . . ."

"Thank you," Hoffinger said. "And, as you said yesterday, the email speaks for itself, correct?"

"Sometimes," Costello muttered.

Hoffinger had a last email, this one from June 2018. "What should I say to this asshole?" Costello had said of Cohen, in an email to his law partner. "He is playing with the most powerful man on the planet."

"You had lost control of Michael Cohen for President Trump, didn't you?" Hoffinger asked.

"Absolutely not," Costello said. He stayed his ground as Hoffinger pressed the point. She moved on, satisfied.

"And you still have a lot of animosity against Michael Cohen, don't you?" she said, asking a question whose answer had been clear from the first two minutes Costello was on the stand.

"I don't have any animosity," Costello said. "I just don't think Michael Cohen is telling the truth . . ."

"Yes or no. Yes or no. Do you have animosity toward Michael Cohen?"

"No."

Hoffinger brought up Costello's congressional appearance. "You went there to publicly vilify Michael Cohen while he was in the middle of his testimony, isn't that correct?" she asked.

"I went there to testify," he said.

"And it was an effort by you, wasn't it, to try to intimidate Michael Cohen while he was testifying here, isn't that correct?" Hoffinger said.

"I was intimidating him?" Costello said, in disbelief.

"Yes, that's my question," Hoffinger said.

"That's ridiculous. No."

"Nothing further," Hoffinger said. She seemed satisfied and we could see why. Her highest profile examinations of the trial had been less than perfect. Stormy Daniels had gone astray, threatening the case, and Michael Cohen had been made to look like a clown and a thief. Now, finally, she had the chance to cross-examine a witness like a defense lawyer. It was impossible for Costello to recover.

❖   ❖   ❖

In the hallway, Trump announced that his lawyers would rest their case in short order. "We'll be resting pretty quickly," he said. "Resting meaning resting the case. I won't be resting. I don't rest. I'd like to rest sometimes but I don't get to rest."

The defense rested, and Justice Merchan explained to the jurors that it was unlikely that there would be time for the lawyers to deliver closing arguments and the jurors to deliberate before the Memorial Day holiday. He excused them for a full week, which passed far, far more quickly than we wished.

❖   ❖   ❖

The following Tuesday, May 28, we were back in line, readying ourselves for closing statements.

On Google, people wondered why Trump was on trial. In Collect Pond Park, the lines were the longest they'd ever been. Under New York law, the defense delivers its closing first, followed by the prosecution, a massive structural advantage for the government that Trump seized upon as a new line in attack on the case's general fairness.

The trail of black SUVs that comprised his motorcade arrived at 100 Centre Street by 9 am on Tuesday, and Trump strolled into the courtroom, accompanied by three of his children—Eric, Don Jr. and Tiffany—his campaign manager, Susie Wiles, and the rest of his regular entourage. Alvin Bragg was already seated in the courtroom, staring forward, shoulder to shoulder with some of the other senior leaders of the district attorney's office. Few would pass up a chance to watch the most significant closings ever delivered in Manhattan state court. The trial of the president was coming to an end.

Merchan entered the courtroom at 9:30 and asked the lawyers how long they expected to take. Todd Blanche said he would be two and a half hours; Steinglass, four and a half hours. The judge said he would ask the jurors if they would stay late in order to finish both arguments, and summoned them in for the final day of proceedings.

Todd Blanche began. He thanked the jury for their service and reminded them of what he'd said on April 22: That his client was innocent and had not committed any crimes.

Blanche sought to narrow the aperture of the prosecution's case. He told the jurors that their verdict was not about Stormy Daniels's story, or even the hush money payment.

"The reason why you all are here, is whether and to what extent President Trump, while he was living in the White House, as the leader of the free world, whether he had anything to do with how payments to Michael Cohen, his personal attorney at the time, were booked on his personal account and ledger at Trump Tower," he said.

I looked up. That was exactly right. Was Todd Blanche about to finally tell the story I'd been waiting for, the story of two 2017 conversations—the only evidence that tying Donald Trump to 175.10—that couldn't be trusted? Would he combine his more general discrediting of Cohen—the prankster revelation and all those lies under oath—with an emphasis on the limited testimony that pointed toward Trump's knowledge of the reimbursement scheme?

He would not. Blanche lived in a world in which the prosecution's case was so patently ridiculous that it did not require a direct rebuttal.

He began his closing with a reasonably organized set of ideas. The first was that Bragg's case was purely about the paperwork. The second was that Trump, the leader of the free world, had nothing to do with the way documents were organized at the Trump Organization. And the third was that Michael Cohen, the prosecution's star witness, could not be trusted. But his argument quickly seemed to lose its structural integrity, and the first two ideas were soon swallowed by repeated attacks on Michael Cohen and the case itself.

Blanche attacked Cohen on issues big and small. He said that Cohen had not, in fact, sought credit from Trump while working for him, but rather had borrowed the idea of credit-seeking from Hope Hicks's testimony, to make his story more believable. He argued that there was no way to believe that Trump had been involved with every step of the hush money payment to Daniels in 2016, without believing the words of Michael Cohen.

"Period," he said. "And you cannot. You cannot believe his words."

And, of course, he celebrated his greatest success of the trial, the prankster revelation.

"It was a LIE," Blanche shouted to the courtroom again. "He told you he talked to President Trump on October 24th at 8:02 p.m., updating him about the Daniels' situation. That was a lie, and he got caught red-handed. We all know that he called Keith Schiller to talk about the fact that a 14-year-old had been harassing him for several days.

"That," he added, "is PER-JUR-Y."

Then, he pointed his finger at the prosecutors. "They are perfectly happy to have a witness come in here and commit perjury, to lie to you."

His denigrated the prosecutors and their case throughout. He said it was "preposterous" to think that Trump and Pecker believed that positive stories in The National Enquirer could make a difference to voters; "absurd" to suggest that categorizing payments to Cohen as a legal expense was a criminal act. The idea that a 2015 meeting at Trump Tower could influence the election, he said, "makes no sense."

Blanche clearly did not trust in the jury's ability to focus on the key points of the state's argument. He didn't think they would understand that it was not simply positive stories that were meant to influence the election but also the suppression of negative stories. He didn't think they would believe that the "Access Hollywood" tape had prompted a seismic reaction within the 2016 Trump campaign. And he didn't seem worried that they would trust what they'd heard about the January 2017 conversation between Cohen, Weisselberg and Trump—unless he explicitly gave them a reason not to.

Blanche's closing gave me a new appreciation for the breadth of the people's case. There were too many facts to address, too much to deal with, and the defense's general dismissiveness of the case prevented more thorough engagement with it. Blanche was unable escape the gravity of the prosecution's narrative. Rather than constructing an alternative, he merely tried to poke holes in the superstructure wherever possible. Some of those holes were bigger than others: Blanche accused Keith Davidson of extortion, and reminded the jury that Hope Hicks had testified about Trump's concern for his family. But he did not weave those useful elements into a believable alternative story. He rejected so many of the prosecution's assertions that he was left with very little material to work with. Certainly nothing that could help him sell the idea that Cohen had been a rogue actor who, coincidentally, had been reimbursed by the Trump Organization in amounts that directly matched the arithmetic of Allen Weisselberg's scrawl.

Instead, Blanche simply attacked Cohen.

Blanche told the jurors that Cohen was obsessed with Trump. He replayed for them the recording in which the former fixer maniacally celebrated his former boss's indictment. Cohen, Blanche said, was the "human embodiment of reasonable doubt." He asked the jurors whether they'd heard the acronym G.O.A.T., as in Michael Jordan is the G.O.A.T., or Tiger Woods is the G.O.A.T.

Well, Blanche said, "Michael Cohen is the G.L.O.A.T. He's literally the greatest liar of all time." He smiled winningly. The jurors did not react.

"You cannot send somebody to prison—you cannot convict somebody, based on the words of Michael Cohen," he said.

He began to wrap up, thanking the jurors again for paying attention and imploring them not to let their politics decide his client's fate.

"The verdict that you are going to reach has to do with the evidence you heard here in this courtroom and nothing else, he said. "If you focus just on the evidence you heard in this courtroom, this is a very, very, very quick and easy not guilty verdict."

The Biden-Harris campaign, having mostly ignored their rival's trial, finally decided that the free publicity outside the courthouse was too beneficial to pass up. The campaign dispatched a surrogate, Robert DeNiro, to speak to the cameras directly on Centre Street directly south of Collect Pond Park. Standing in front of two former U.S. Capitol Police officers who'd protected the building on Jan. 6, he was immediately surrounded by newscasters, pulling them briefly away from the courthouse.

DeNiro, in his famous accent, warned the cameras that were Trump to be elected, democracy would "perish from the earth," and that if he were to return to the White House, elections would be a thing of the past. "If he gets in, I can tell you right now—he will never leave," he insisted.

The actor was repeatedly interrupted by Trump supporters who flocked toward the cameras. Once he concluded his official remarks DeNiro began yelling at them, jabbing his finger for effect: "We're trying to be gentlemen, the Democrats. You are gangsters. You are *gangsters!*"

He walked away, followed by the crowd, and an increasingly agitated police escort, which strove to drive the hecklers back as they made to swarm DeNiro's getaway SUV.

"You're a fucking mook, M-O-O-K," a MAGA-hatted heckler shouted at the departing vehicle, as if he were spelling the insult for a court reporter. "You're a traitor to Italians and Jews. Bobby DeNiro, you're a fucking cunt!"

❖ ❖ ❖

The courtroom was sweltering as Josh Steinglass rose to give the prosecution's closing. He began with a review of some of Blanche's arguments. He told the jurors they could think what they wanted of Keith Davidson's business. It didn't really matter: Being the victim of an extortion attempt was not a defense of falsifying business records.

And where Blanche had tried to lay most of the case at the feet of Michael Cohen, Steinglass reminded the jurors of all the witnesses whose testimony aided the prosecution's case. David Pecker alone, he said, established that Trump had entered a conspiracy to influence the 2016 election. The testimonies of Rhona Graff, Hope Hicks, and Jeff McConney, all of whom had great affection for Trump, provided critical pieces of the puzzle.

Stormy Daniels, he acknowledged, was an enemy of Trump's, and her story was messy and uncomfortable. "That's kind of the point," he said. "That's the display the defendant didn't want the American voter to see. In the simplest terms, Stormy Daniels is the *motive.*"

When his review reached Michael Cohen, Steinglass reminded the jurors that he'd warned them from the beginning that Cohen had baggage, as a convicted felon, a liar, and one of Trump's number one enemies. Several of the jurors smiled, seemingly nostalgic at the thought of their first encounter with the prosecutor seven weeks earlier.

Steinglass reiterated the story about Michael Cohen's arc—his loyalty to Trump, the fraying of that loyalty, and ultimately, Cohen's turn on his boss in the summer of 2018. He said it didn't matter to the case that Cohen had stolen from the Trump Organization . . .

And then, switching his tone abruptly, Steinglass leaned in, as if something had occurred to him and he was eager to tell it to his closest friends.

"I'll tell you something kind of funny," he said. "I don't know if somebody caught this. Mr. Blanche said, well, he stole $60,000, because it was grossed up. That means the defense is trying to have it both ways, right?" They were denying the $420,000 was a reimbursement at all, yet still claiming that the reimbursement math to which Cohen testified was accurate.

"They can call him a thief or claim this wasn't really a reimbursement but not both," Steinglass said. He assumed an expression of bemused empathy. "Their arguments are not necessarily consistent, but they *are* passionate."

Then, Steinglass raised the 96-second phone call to Keith Schiller on Oct. 24, 2016—the basis of Blanche's assertion that Michael Cohen had committed perjury. Steinglass asked the jurors to forgive him for a moment as he tried an experiment.

"I will be Cohen," he said, prompting puzzled expressions from the gallery. He indicated that he was setting a timer on his phone, the purpose of which was unclear.

Steinglass hunched his shoulders and shuffled, enacting a B-movie transformation. He began an on-the-spot recreation of the infamous October 24 phone call, complete with an unmistakable impression of Michael Cohen.

"Hey Keith, how's it going," he said in a New York accented voice, an octave lower than his own. "It seems uh . . . like this prankster might be a 14-year-old kid. If I text you the number, can you call and talk to his family? See if you can let them know how serious this is. It's not a joke!"

Laughter in the courtroom as Steinglass took a long pause, still in character as Cohen. "Uh huh," he said, responding to an imaginary Schiller on the other end of the line. "Yeah. Alright. Thanks pal. Hey, is the boss near you?" Another pause. "Can you pass him the phone for a minute?"

Here, Steinglass took another, excruciating pause. Then: "Hey, Boss. I know you're busy, but I just wanted to let you know that that other thing is moving forward with my friend Keith and the other party that we discussed. It's back on track. I'm going to try one last time to get our friend David to pay, but if not, it's going to be on us to take care of."

A final pause as Steinglass-as-Cohen listened to imaginary Trump. "Aha. Yeah. Alright. Good luck in Tampa, bye."

With his piece of impromptu theater concluded, Steinglass picked up his phone timer. Even with all the pauses, and stumbles, the scene had only taken him 49 seconds; about half as long as the actual Oct. 24 phone call.

"These guys know each other well," Steinglass said, returning to his own voice. "They speak in coded language. And they speak fast."

The jurors, of course, might still believe the defense. But Steinglass's act cut into Blanche's confidence. The defense had believed that Cohen's failure to remember the prankster would speak for itself. But, like the defendant, Steinglass knew that even the most effective argument could be undercut by an entertaining performance.

❖   ❖   ❖

Having dispensed with the defense arguments, Steinglass began to make the case against Donald Trump and the force he exerted on those around him.

"We didn't choose Michael Cohen to be our witness. We didn't pick him up at the witness store," he said. "The defendant chose Michael Cohen to be his fixer, because he was willing to lie and cheat on Mr. Trump's behalf." He argued that Cohen and David Pecker were drawn to the president like moths to a flame, only for Trump to take what he wanted from them. "Mr. Trump not only corrupted those around him, but he got them to lie to cover it up," he said.

On the monitors appeared a visualization of the way that Bragg and his team envisioned the case when they'd first conceived of it two summers earlier. First came the August 2015 meeting, "three rich and powerful men, high up in Trump Tower, trying to become even more powerful by controlling the flow of information that might reach the voters."

Steinglass reminded the jurors of Blanche's line in openings, that seeking to influence an election was simply another way to describe democracy.

"In reality, this agreement at Trump Tower was the exact oppo-site," Steinglass said. "It was the subversion of democracy. Democracy gives the people the right to elect their leaders, but that rests on the fundamental premise that the voters have access to accurate informa-tion about the candidates. The entire purpose of this meeting at Trump Tower was to deny that access, to manipulate and defraud the voters, to pull the wool over their eyes in a coordinated fashion."

"This scheme cooked up by these men at this time could very well be what got President Trump elected," he said.

With that, he embarked on a marathon run through the evidence relating to the first two hush-money deals—to Dino Sajudin and Karen McDougal—the "Access Hollywood" tape, and the final payoff to Stormy Daniels. Astoundingly, there was documentary evidence of almost every single phone call, particularly in October 2016. Steinglass proceeded methodically through phone records and text messages for each individual day ranging from October 7, the day the "Access Holly-wood" tape was released through October, 28 2016, the day after Cohen made the final hush money payment.

Even if, as Blanche argued, Cohen was lying about the subject of a single call, it seemed an unbelievable coincidence that a frenzy of calls between the major players accompanied every key date that October. As the witnesses testified, the prosecution had spared the jury the full force of their corroborating evidence about the fall 2016 event sequence. But this was a brute strength presentation of those facts.

If Blanche, in his closing argument, had drawn the jurors' atten-tion more emphatically to the January and February 2017 conversa-tions between Cohen and Trump, he could have forcefully condemned the paucity of evidence related to those conversations. The top charge relied heavily on Michael Cohen's testimony. In the wake of such a closing by the defense, Steinglass's endless collection of 2016 evidence about the predicate crime 17–152 might have come across as gratu-itous, even deceitful, as if he were directing the jurors' attention away from what truly mattered.

But Blanche had not focused on the 2017 conversations. Instead, he'd echoed Trump's insistence on denying *everything* damning, even if it wasn't criminal. And the Trump team's strategy of "deny, deny deny" possessed a fatal flaw: if everything the prosecutors were asserting was wholly false, then no one set of facts could be *more* false than any other. Blanche couldn't deny the truth of the 2017 conversations more strongly than he had denied the truth of the 2006 sex with Daniels, or 2015 and 2016 meetings and payments as explained by the prosecution. Blanche's denial of the entire conspiracy was a de facto acceptance of Bragg's novel legal theory, with the state election law violation, 17–152 and falsifying business records, 175.10 ranked equally rather than as predicate and top charge.

Having the last word, Steinglass could aim the firehouse of evidence at the defense's denial of all events in chronological order. The same disposition that allowed Trump to foster a nationwide epistemological crisis was a massive drag on his lawyers' ability to do their jobs.

About two hours in, Merchan asked Steinglass how much longer he expected to speak. Steinglass smiled and said he was about a third of the way through.

Steinglass soon reached the point of his narrative in which Trump won the 2016 election. "Of course, we'll never know if this effort to hoodwink the American voter made the difference in the 2016 election," he said. "But that's not something we have to prove."

❖   ❖   ❖

At 5 pm, Merchan thanked the jurors for their flexibility and, when they left the courtroom, told the lawyers he thought they still seemed attentive. He decided that Steinglass would be allowed to continue into the early evening.

For the gallery, the prosecution's closing became an endurance game. Every so often, a groan would arise from the hard-backed seats, as an anonymous reporter realized just how much work was left. The jurors, however, looked perfectly satisfied; they'd agreed to stay late and, of course, they weren't live-blogging, trying to capture each and every word in real time. "FILIBUSTER!" Trump posted on Truth Social. "BORING!"

After a 20 minute break, Steinglass resumed, reviewing the prosecutor's post-election narrative, when Cohen and Weisselberg had received Trump's signoff to falsify the records. Steinglass breezed over the 2017 meetings between Cohen and Trump, devoting considerably more attention to Jeff McConney's testimony about Allen Weisselberg informing him that Cohen needed to be reimbursed. Steinglass called Weisselberg's scrawl on Cohen's bank statement a smoking gun.

It was a clever move, if misleading. While the Weisselberg document showed beyond any doubt that Cohen had been reimbursed for the hush money payment, Trump's fingerprints were nowhere near it.

But Steinglass asserted that the defense's argument that Trump had inattentively signed $35,000 checks without demanding to know what they were for beggared belief. There was a better explanation, Steinglass said: "Despite his frugality and his attention to detail, the defendant didn't ask any questions, because he already knew the answers."

Shortly after 6:30, Merchan gave the jurors a final break and, while they were still out of the room, told Steinglass that he needed to wrap up by 8 pm. Then—to the great frustration of many reporters but with the apparent consent of the jury—Steinglass returned to the very beginning of the timeline in an attempt, it seemed, to punctuate Trump's connection to each portion of the run-up to the final hush-money payment.

"The defendant's intent to defraud in this case cannot be any clearer," he said. "How easy would it have been for the defendant to just pay Stormy Daniels directly? Why not just do that? One single transaction. Instead, the defendant, Weisselberg and Cohen devised this elaborate scheme, requiring the involvement of at least ten other people, a series of monthly transactions. That's a whole lot of time, thought and energy to conceal the truth."

People were beginning to stream out of the overflow room, and the sky outside the courtroom was dark. Steinglass was still going and we began to wonder whether he'd make his deadline. Even Trump was in disbelief. "More??" he mouthed from the defense table, when Steinglass kept talking after thanking the jury.

"You, the jury, have the ability to hold the defendant accountable," he said. "And, like in any other case, he can be judged by a jury of his peers, based on the evidence and nothing else. Very soon there will be time to go deliberate and to review any testimony or exhibits that you need to and to come back in here and say 'guilty.' 'Guilty' of 34 counts of falsifying business records in the first degree to cover up a conspiracy to corrupt the 2016 election.

"In the interest of justice, and in the name of the people of the state of New York, I ask you to find the defendant guilty."

Finally, he was done. The length of his closing would become a running joke in the district attorney's office. Some reporters, exhausted, questioned whether he had been effective. We left the courthouse shortly after 8 pm and I walked toward the Brooklyn Bridge, grateful to be walking through the fresh evening air after so many hours stuck in Part 59.

CHAPTER TEN

VERDICTS

The backdrop of Rachel Maddow's MSNBC set is an inviting image of the East River waterfront, the Manhattan skyline offering a peaceful backdrop as Maddow delivers her monologues and greets her guests. On July 2, in the first television appearance since her testimony, Stormy Daniels sat in front of a luminescent image of the 59th Street bridge, looking pensive, dressed all in black. Maddow welcomed her warmly and began the interview by expressing surprise that Daniels had agreed to come on the show.

"I guess I mostly just want to know how the last few weeks have been," Maddow said, smiling at her guest. "This has been a many-year saga for you, but this is a qualitatively different time. Since the conviction."

The camera cut to Daniels. "It's been a lot," she said. "It's been intense. Part of that comes from my mistake of, in my mind, thinking that this would be an ending. That this would be a light at the end of the tunnel. This was what I was working towards. That it would be like a movie when the judge hits the gavel,"—she did the gesture—"the credits roll and it would be tied up in a nice little gift bow and it would be done.

"But that's not how real life works."

❖   ❖   ❖

A few weeks earlier, on Wednesday, May 29, the day after the marathon closing arguments, the jurors began their deliberations. The court officers, seeking to do the reporters a favor, asked us to move to an adjoining room on the 15th floor where we could talk as loudly as we pleased and use our cell phones to our heart's content.

This created a massive fight between the reporters—many of whom preferred to stay in the courtroom for fear of somehow missing the verdict—and the court officers, who saw us, correctly, as a bunch of neurotic ingrates. Everyone blew off some steam; Mike Sisak, an AP reporter, did some nice yelling at red-headed Captain Mullaney and Mullaney yelled right back. The feud ended in a compromise, with reporters allowed to stay in the courtroom, but only if we maintained quiet, as if the testimony were still ongoing. The court officers had to stay on their feet, patrolling to ensure we didn't break any rules. They were displeased.

Trump wasn't happy either. There was nothing he could do about the twelve New Yorkers deliberating over his fate. Instead, in a half-hearted news conference in the hallway, he attacked Robert DeNiro as a "broken down fool."

"He got MAGA'd yesterday," Trump said, smiling to himself. "He got a big dose of it."

Around 3 pm, the phone in the well buzzed. It was the jurors. They'd sent a note, asking whether they could hear the judge's instructions on the law and four readbacks of testimony: Three of them from David Pecker and one from Michael Cohen. They specifically asked for both men's testimony about the August 2015 meeting at Trump Tower, suggesting they wanted to compare Pecker's testimony about the August 2015 meeting with Cohen's. The notes augured poorly for the defense. Focus on anyone except Michael Cohen augured poorly for the defense. An hour later the judge dismissed the jury for the day; no verdict.

※   ※   ※

With a conclusion close at hand, Trump's fans in Collect Pond Park were becoming more numerous—and boisterous. They arrived late, by our standards, but once there, they were far more dominant than their counterparts.

Rise and Resist protesters Julie DeLaurier and Kathleen Zea were surrounded by a group of them and a rival protester stabbed Zea in the arm with a pro-Trump flag, leaving an ugly yellow bruise. As the president's motorcade passed behind the courthouse, his supporters chanted "we love Trump," tooting their air horns and waving their flags.

❖   ❖   ❖

We lined up the following morning, Thursday May 30, outside the north entrance to 100 Centre. There was a lot of speculation as to the verdict's timing, and reporters took bets and exchanged opinions. Some explained at length why they believed the juror's notes were a bad sign for Trump. Others were circumspect. After we filed into the courthouse, around 8 am, Collect Pond Park was calm.

But as the hours passed, it grew more crowded and more contentious. The police divided the park into partisan sections, placing a makeshift boundary between the pro- and anti-Trump camps. A Rise and Resist protester made the mistake of wandering into the wrong side with a sign. A Trump supporter seized her sign and ripped it, and the scuffle devolved into shoving until the police, some amused, some irritated, wandered over to break it up. Helicopters circled overhead.

Inside 100 Centre Street, the hours passed without incident and at 4 pm, the prosecutors re-entered the courtroom. Their expressions were muted; it didn't seem as if there had been any developments. There'd been no more notes from the jury. Trump returned, too, patting the bar behind the defense table as he passed. Merchan emerged from his door in the back of the courtroom and ascended the bench.

"At this time, I'm going to excuse the jury about 4:30," he told the room. "We'll give them a few more minutes, and then we'll excuse them."

Tweets began to go up: "No verdict today." But I held off on reporting the same on our liveblog. It wasn't clear that Merchan had actually excused the jurors. There was no harm in waiting a little longer.

At 4:30, neither the judge nor the jury was in the courtroom. The minutes began to crawl by. We could hear the noise of the protesters outside through the tall windows behind the jury box. 4:35, then 4:36.

Trump and Todd Blanche were joking around at the defense table, the president smiling broadly.

"This is so painful waiting," I said, reminding Kate Christobek what she'd said just minutes before we'd broken the news of the indictment.

Then, Merchan strode quickly back into the courtroom. He told us that at 4:20, the jurors had sent a note: They had reached a verdict. They requested 30 minutes to fill out the necessary forms.

The smile disappeared from Trump's face. Alvin Bragg walked expressionless into the courtroom and sat behind the trial team.

Outside, the noise ceased; it was as if we could hear the news that the jury had reached a verdict ripple out from the courthouse in real time. The internet flickered in and out, and we spent a good portion of the half-hour wait for the jurors just trying to get back online, to ensure we'd be able to report the verdict when it arrived.

Shortly after 5 pm, the jurors filed by Trump and into the jury box. All but one proceeded without looking at him, but Juror Nine looked directly at him. She knew what was about to happen.

Justice Merchan addressed Juror One. "Mr. Foreperson," he said. "Has the jury in fact, reached a verdict?"

"Yes, they have," the man said, his accent barely audible in the silent thrumming intensity of Part 59. Eric Trump shook his head.

The clerk of the court asked the foreperson to rise and Trump's gaze followed him as he rose. "Have the members of the jury agreed to the verdict?"

"Yes, we have," the foreperson confirmed, again.

"How say you to the first count of the indictment, charging Donald J. Trump with the crime of falsifying business records in the first degree, guilty or not guilty?"

"Guilty," the foreperson said and Trump shut his eyes and shook his head, willing the truth away. The clerk began to ask about the other counts and the foreperson rained down guilty after guilty at remarkable speed, as we struggled to keep pace. The president's eyes remained closed. Izzy Brourman painted the words in watercolor. Jane Rosenberg began a new drawing: The felon-president. Todd Blanche furrowed his brow, then rested his face in his hands. There was a gasp in the overflow room, as the news reached the reporters seated there, then traveled outward to Collect Pond Park and beyond.

Trump was guilty on all 34 counts. He slumped back in his seat at the defense table, all the air gone out of him. The jurors unanimously confirmed the verdict and the clerk asked if either of the parties wanted the jury polled. "Yes, please," Blanche said, and the clerk went down the line, confirming with each juror that he or she had reached the verdict of guilty on all 34 counts. Trump's eyes were open again, and he stared at each juror as he or she agreed. Bragg did not react visibly. He just kept listening.

Justice Merchan thanked the jurors for their service, telling them he admired their dedication and hard work. He told them they were now free to discuss the case with anyone, if they liked, and asked to meet with them in the jury room in a few minutes, to thank them personally. For the final time, they filed out of the courtroom.

Merchan asked the lawyers if they had any motions or anything else. Blanche immediately called for the judge to set aside the verdict and acquit Trump, saying that it was impossible for the jury to have reached its decision without relying on the word of Michael Cohen, who'd definitively perjured himself. He said that Merchan couldn't allow the verdict while knowing that Cohen had committed that crime, which had been used to convict the president.

"I'm sure you misspoke when you said 'knowing,'" Merchan said cooly. "You're not suggesting that I *know* anybody committed perjury, right?"

"Correct," Blanche said.

Merchan asked the prosecutors to weigh in, and Steinglass, of course, disagreed. "There's more than enough evidence in this case for a reasonable jury to have reached the verdict that it did," he said, urging the judge to deny the motion.

"Your motion is denied," Merchan said. He set sentencing for mid-July.

Trump rose slowly and turned to face the gallery, stopping to shake Eric's hand as he left. I could see the effort in his face as he jutted his jaw forward and strode out of the courtroom. The prosecutors packed up their bags, their expressions carefully neutral.

In the hallway, Trump looked defeated, old and tired as he addressed the cameras. "This was a disgrace," he said, his voice listless. "This was a rigged trial by a conflicted judge who is corrupt." He repeated the words "rigged" and "disgraced" several times. "The real verdict is going to be November 5, by the people," he said. "And they know what happened here and everybody knows what happened here."

"We didn't do a thing wrong," he added. "I'm a very innocent man." He walked away from the cameras without taking any questions.

By 5:30, his fundraising website had crashed. It was later reported that he collected $100 million in the next 24 hours.

❖   ❖   ❖

Bragg called a news conference for 6:30 on the 8th floor of 80 Centre Street, the same place he'd held his ill-fated post-arraignment presser. Outside the courthouse, all was chaos. Trump supporters far outnumbered their counterparts, and I ducked around the flag-bearing, hat-wearing masses, seeking to find a feasible entrance into the building. Finally, I found a press line, on the corner of Centre Street and Leonard, where DeNiro had delivered his remarks. After an excruciating wait, the police let us into the building and I scrambled through the body scanners and up to the 8th floor, failing even to refasten my belt in my haste to land a reasonable seat, which led to an embarrassing scene when I ran smack into prosecutors Becky Mangold and KC Ellis.

The inside of 80 Centre sometimes seemed as if it were all corridor, but we found the shabby room where the news conference was to begin. As we waited for Bragg to emerge, I scanned social media. Eric Trump announced that May 30 might be remembered as the day Donald Trump won the 2024 election. R.F.K. Jr., the third-party candidate, denounced his former employer's work, calling it "bad for our country and bad for Democracy."

Alvin Bragg walked onto the stage with a serious expression, and it was only because I was so close to the front that I could see his eyes were red, as if he'd shed tears of relief—or gratitude, or validation or some unknown mix of emotions—behind closed doors. The trial team filed in behind him, Steinglass behind his right shoulder with a barely suppressed expression of pride, Colangelo over his left, betraying nothing.

The moment had not sparked in Bragg any eagerness to chest-thump or even celebrate the vindication of the jury.

"This type of white collar prosecution is core to what we do at the

Manhattan district attorney's office," Bragg insisted, harkening back to the tenure of Frank Hogan to illustrate his point. He said that the trial team *embodied* the finest traditions of the office. "Donald J. Trump is guilty of 34 counts of falsifying business records in the first degree to conceal a scheme to corrupt the 2016 election. And while this defendant may be unlike any other in American history, we arrived at this trial and ultimately today at this verdict in the same manner as every other case that comes through the courtroom doors: By following the facts and the law and doing so without fear or favor."

He was asked if he planned to ask the judge for a jail sentence. He said that would be public at the sentencing hearing in mid-July. He was asked if he had a response to Trump's constant attacks on him, and his trial team. "I do not," he said.

Then his communications director, Danielle, called on me. I reminded him of the criticism that had come in February 2022, when he'd declined to bring the first Trump case and in April 2023, when he'd gone forward with his own, drawing the derision of so many. "How do you think of all that now, seeing the result today?"

He paused for a moment. "I did my job," he said. "We did our job. Many voices out there. The only voice that matters is the voice of the jury and the jury has spoken."

The news conference marked the last time that he would agree to answer a question from me, or any other journalist who wanted to talk to him about the most important event of his public life. After the presser, the Manhattan D.A., Alvin Bragg, rarely mentioned Donald Trump in public.

❖   ❖   ❖

The work did not speak for itself and the voice of the jury, which rang out so strongly in the courtroom, was soon drowned out. In place of the massive, life-consuming, news-dominating event of the trial were left only a few phrases, inadequate metonyms for all that had been.

For Donald Trump's foes, the words were "convicted felon." The gravity of Steinglass's closing, the jury's finding that Trump had worked illegally to corrupt the first election he won—those ideas were never metabolized by the commentariat, let alone the public. Alvin Bragg's suggestion that the trial was about election interference, a first fraud-ulent effort to win a presidential election that foreshadowed the more intensive, 2020 effort to hold onto the office after losing, were never taken seriously. Donald Trump owned the phrase "election interfer-ence." It was part of his brand. Pundits continued to refer to the "hush money trial."

For the former president's allies, the term for the trial—grouped indistinctly among Trump's other legal troubles—was "lawfare." They continued to argue that the trial and its conviction had been the result of a politicized war on their man.

If this were true of the Manhattan prosecution, it was not in any simple sense. Though there were clear professional and political incen-tives for Bragg to bring a case against Trump, I never found any evi-dence to suggest that Bragg acted in bad faith or that he did not believe in his case.

Alvin Bragg, the elected district attorney of Manhattan, had inherited an investigation into Trump. He had evaluated an initial case, found it wanting and abandoned it. He was intrigued by a second case, found that the facts matched a workable legal theory and brought an indictment. It was what prosecutors did.

Insofar as the prosecution was political, those politics were not the lowest-common-denominator dichotomy of Democrat vs. Republican, but rather the untold power granted to prosecutors to pursue any target they chose. Alvin Bragg was the face of a faceless institution in which many Americans had lost faith. His insistence on the facts and the law was inadequate. He was never equipped to fight Donald Trump on his own turf, the domain of politics and media to which the focus now shifted.

The 2024 election quickly overtook the attention that had been swallowed by the trial. I stopped making videos, left The *Times* for parental leave, and began working on this book.

But the trial didn't disappear. Better, maybe, to say that it slipped below the first layer of the country's consciousness, like an unsuccessful foreign invasion or a deadly pandemic. It was buried somewhere in our collective psyche, and you knew that if you watched closely. After a month of quiet, the characters of Trump's world and those of the trial appeared in the news every week that summer, as the election ramped up. Donald Trump's singular abilities reasserted themselves, no longer suppressed by the defendant's chair, the judge's authority.

It was only then that I realized just how much the trial had done to control not only the president himself, but the narrative around him. Unbound by the four walls of the courtroom, his story—the story of the presidential race and the future of the country—lost all sense of order. One could only track it by noting prominent developments as they ticked by, month by chaotic month.

✦   ✦   ✦

On June 27, President Biden's disastrous performance in the first presidential debate made Trump the clear favorite to win the presidency, setting off furious intraparty fighting among Democrats as many sought to push the incumbent out of the race.

Five days later, on July 1st, the Supreme Court finally released the ruling on the presidential immunity issue that had so effectively delayed Jack Smith's Washington prosecution. The court found that presidents were "absolutely immune from criminal prosecution" for acts they took as president. "The relationship between the president and the people he serves has shifted irrevocably," wrote Justice Sonia Sotomayor in a dissent. "In every use of official power, the president is now a king above the law."

The ruling made it highly unlikely that Jack Smith's charges against Trump—those that accused the former president of seeking to illegally overturn the results of the 2020 election—would result in a trial before Election Day. And it had potential implications in New York.

Todd Blanche and Emil Bove wasted no time. That day, they sent a letter to Justice Merchan asking that the verdict be set aside—the pending presidential immunity ruling had been one of the many reasons they'd offered as they sought fruitlessly to delay the trial. They noted that the prosecution had made use of evidence that was arguably inadmissible under the new ruling, most importantly, the testimony of Hope Hicks while she was White House communications director. Steinglass himself had called her testimony "devastating."

Blanche and Bove also suggested a delay of the July 11 sentencing. The D.A.'s office did not object. Merchan rescheduled the sentencing for September 18.

✦   ✦   ✦

On July 13, two days after the sentencing had been scheduled to take place, Donald Trump held a campaign rally in Butler, Pennsylvania. A MAGA hat pulled low atop his head, he ascended a stage festooned with flags and held his fist upright, connecting individually with supporters in the crowd.

Less than ten minutes into his speech, several pops rang out. Trump clutched at his ear, then quickly lowered himself behind the lectern where the Secret Service piled atop him, knocking the hat off his head. Supporters began to scream. But Trump was down for less than a minute. As the security officials sought to bundle him into a van, he ordered them to wait. He reared up, again visible to the crowd, and struck the air with his fist, baring his teeth. He mouthed the word "Fight!" then twice again: "Fight! Fight!" He understood immediately the power of the image, indelibly freezing his pose of defiant courage.

Two days later, the Republican National Convention began. The Collect Pond Park phenomenon of Republicans talking and dressing like Trump was taken even further on the floor of the Milwaukee convention arena. Trump's ear was wrapped in gauze, and so delegates from all over the country bandaged their own ears in imitative tribute to the party leader. Some paired the bandages with t-shirts that said, "I'm voting for the convicted felon."

The party was the most united it had ever been under Trump. The candidate announced his running mate: J.D. Vance, the first of the contenders to visit the trial and speak on the boss's behalf.

That week, the fundraising numbers for Alvin Bragg's 2025 reelection campaign were released publicly. The trial had done little to galvanize support; his numbers were lower in the period between January and July 2024 than they had been the previous six months. Bragg continued to omit the conviction of Donald J. Trump in his fundraising emails. As of this writing, he has yet to campaign on it.

✦   ✦   ✦

The week after the Republican convention, President Biden finally caved to the pressure. He announced his decision to drop out of the presidential race and threw his support behind his vice president, Kamala Harris, who immediately put her history as a "smart on crime" prosecutor to use. On July 22nd, the day after Biden's withdrawal, she addressed staff at her new campaign headquarters in Delaware. She reminded the audience of her previous jobs as California's attorney general and San Francisco district attorney.

"In those roles, I took on perpetrators of all kinds," she said, suppressing a grin as the crowd whooped, then slowly letting it free. She waited for the applause to subside, before continuing. "Predators, who abused women. Fraudsters, who ripped off consumers. Cheaters, who broke the rules for their own gain. So hear me when I say: I know Donald Trump's type!"

The crowd of campaign staffers went wild.

❖   ❖   ❖

On August 6, Olivia Nuzzi and Izzy Brourman traveled to Mar-a-Lago to see Donald Trump's wounded ear up close. The plan was that Nuzzi would interview the candidate, while Brourman painted him, but the portrait ultimately took two days to complete. Trump was unhappy with her initial effort, which depicted him with a frown. Izzy instead gave him a Joker-esque upturned mouth. She painted his eyes grey, then black. When he asked why, she paraphrased Modigliani to him: "Show me your soul and I'll paint your eyes." Trump nodded, knowingly.

❖   ❖   ❖

Briefly, Kamala Harris coasted on vibes, social media clips and memes, like a Democratic version of Donald J. Trump without the nativism. She flew around the country hosting packed rallies, refining a stump speech that was heavy on concepts like "aspiration" and "democracy" and short on specific policy proposals. She was embraced by celebrities and celebrated online in goofy TikTok mashups that blended the music of Charli XCX with Harris's past statements, gifting her a persona that worked in the media overlay, that made people excited about her, that came with its own iconography, coconut emojis, the Beyonce song "Freedom" and even its own emotion: joy. Joy was the watchword of the Harris campaign.

Meanwhile, Trump, responding to criticism of his frequent digressions during campaign rallies, introduced a concept he called "the weave." "You know what the weave is?" he asked. "I'll talk about nine different things, and they all come back brilliantly together and it's like, friends of mine that are, like, English professors, they say, 'It's the most brilliant thing I've ever seen.'"

On August 14, Todd Blanche and Emil Bove argued that Merchan should delay Trump's sentencing until after the election. "There is no basis for continuing to rush," they wrote, other than "naked election interference objectives." Two days later, the prosecutors told the judge that they had no position on whether the sentence should be delayed again, or not. "We defer to the court," they wrote, adding that they were willing to appear for sentencing "on any future date the court sets."

In early September, Merchan responded to the defense's request. His patience, apparently, was gone, though this time there were no reporters present on whom he could exercise his ire. Instead, he took aim at the prosecution, writing that despite their stated stance of neutrality, they too wanted him to delay the sentencing. His frustration was understandable: Without the support of his fellow institutionalists, Merchan would have been out on a limb were he to demand that things go forward as scheduled.

"The public's confidence in the integrity of our judicial system demands a sentencing hearing that is entirely focused on the verdict of the jury," Merchan wrote. "The members of this jury served diligently on this case, and their verdict must be respected and addressed in a manner that is not diluted by the enormity of the upcoming presidential election."

And so, he concluded, the sentencing would be delayed until November 26, "to avoid any appearance—however unwarranted—that the proceeding has been affected by or seeks to affect the approaching presidential election in which the defendant is a candidate."

Then, for anyone who might doubt it, he added: "The court is a fair, impartial and apolitical institution."

* * *

On September 10, Kamala Harris and Donald Trump competed in their first and only presidential debate. Both declared themselves victors. Most mainstream pundits sided with Harris. Trump, however, created the most successful meme of the night when he insisted that Haitian migrants in Springfield, Ohio, were stealing and consuming the pets of the local populace.

"They're eating the dogs," he said angrily. "They're eating the cats. They're eating the pets of the people that live there."

Soon, this sentence was everywhere; quoted in memes, set to music. I couldn't pass a dog on the street without it ringing in my head.

* * *

Trump's cultural influence continued to expand. Every major news event was at most a few degrees removed from him.

Toward the end of September, the Southern District indicted two minor players in the grand Trump saga. Sean "Puffy" Combs, Trump's hip-hop acquaintance of the 1990s, was indicted and charged with racketeering and sex trafficking. And Mayor Eric Adams, who'd declared the question of whether Trump could receive a fair trial to be "above his pay grade," was charged with conspiracy, bribery and campaign finance crimes. Both men pleaded not guilty.

Olivia Nuzzi, a prominent trial attendee, made news when it was reported that she'd engaged in an "inappropriate relationship" with R.F.K. Jr. whom she'd profiled back in November 2023, during her brief pretrial attempt to escape Donald Trump's energy field. Nuzzi quickly released a statement that the relationship was "never physical," a disclosure that CNN quasi-clarified when it reported that the tryst was, instead, "emotional and digital in nature." In a Page Six follow-up, an unnamed source made a reference to "incredible" FaceTime sex. A spokesman for Kennedy, in a statement, said that the two had only met once and that her profile of him had been a "hit piece." Trump trial veterans did not need Keith Davidson to identify a non-denial denial when they saw one.

✦   ✦   ✦

Over time, Harris's joy fell like so many autumn leaves. On October 23, amplifying comments made by Trump's former chief of staff, John F. Kelly, Harris said that Trump wanted a military like Adolf Hitler's. The news cycle reminded me of Godwin's Law, an axiom conceived in 1990 by web forum pioneer Mike Godwin: The longer an online debate continued, the more likely it was that someone would invoke Hitler or the Nazis. The law had a less often cited corollary: Whoever reached for the Hitler comparison typically lost the argument.

Four days later, Trump and the left side of the courtroom gallery returned to New York City for a rally at Madison Square Garden. It was a show of force in the heart of the city, the rafters packed to the brim with the former president's fans. His allies from the trial were there in force: Matt Gaetz and Vivek Ramaswamy, Donald Trump Jr. and J.D. Vance, Todd Blanche and Emil Bove and Hope Hicks.

"The king of New York is back to reclaim the city that he built," Don Jr. told the sold-out crowd.

After a warm-up comedian, Tony Hinchcliffe, referred to Puerto Rico as a "floating island of garbage," the lowlight of a barrage of 90s-era insults attacking various ethnic groups, the event was widely billed as a catastrophe for the Trump campaign. On the other hand, it was all that anyone seemed to be talking about less than two weeks before the election.

The social internet popularized the concept of the attention economy; the idea that the surplus of information available to Americans made attention more scarce and thus, more valuable. What differentiates Trump from other politicians is his remarkable ability to attract positive and negative attention in equal measure, from which stems his dominance of the social media age, where even negative attention is so often an asset.

✦   ✦   ✦

By October 29, exactly a week before Election Day, Harris's attention was fully given over to her opponent. Speaking from the Capitol ellipse, she reminded her audience of the Jan. 6 attack on the Capitol. "America, this is not a candidate for president who is thinking about how to make your life better," she said. "This is someone who is unstable, obsessed with revenge, consumed with grievance and out for unchecked power. Donald Trump has spent a decade trying to keep the American people divided and afraid of each other. That is who he is. But America, I am here tonight to say that is not who we are."

I was reminded, in retrospect, of Todd Blanche's closing. Of the way he seemed to have no choice but to hew so closely to the prosecution's case, because he had no alternative narrative of his own. Harris's campaign was entranced by Trump, in thrall to the power of his story.

◆   ◆   ◆

November 4, the day before Election Day, Hope Hicks wrote an op-ed for the New York Post: *"I Was At Trump's Side in 2016—Here's Why He'll Win Again."*

It was striking how her article mirrored her testimony. She reflected not on Trump's turbulent first term but rather, her fond memories of his first campaign, the ones that had brought her to tears on the witness stand.

She was right, of course. On Nov. 5, Donald J. Trump won the 2024 presidential election.

◆   ◆   ◆

Donald Trump's ubiquity, his shamelessness, his talking points and his near-constant clashes with his adversaries added up to a mesmerizing discord—identified by his colleague, Kanye West, as "dragon energy." These were the keys to Trump's political success. His criminal trial briefly interrupted his power. But the institutionalists who sought to bring him to heel were undone by the 21st century politics that came so naturally to the defendant.

The election extinguished his most pressing legal troubles. The law would not allow Jack Smith's cases to continue into Trump's second term and on November 13, it was reported that Smith would resign. Nine days later, Justice Merchan again delayed the New York sentencing at the request of Todd Blanche and Emil Bove.

Other trial attendees were quickly drafted into Trump's administration. Susie Wiles was named his chief of staff. Doug Burgum was to be the Secretary of the Interior and Kash Patel, the F.B.I. director. Matt Gaetz was chosen as attorney general, though he withdrew his name after reports began to emerge about his having had sex with an underage girl. Boris Epshteyn, the self-appointed courtroom usher, was accused of charging would-be cabinet officials to "promote" them to Trump, for tens of thousands of dollars apiece. He denied the allegations.

Blanche and Bove—named as Trump's choices for the second and third highest-ranking officials in the Justice Department—made it clear that they would do everything they could to erase the conviction before the inauguration. In early December, they filed an 80-page motion calling on Merchan to dismiss the conviction once and for all. It was a victory lap, posing as a legal brief.

"This case would never have been brought were it not for President Trump's political views, the transformative national movement established under his leadership, and the political threat that he poses to entrenched, corrupt politicians in Washington, D.C. and beyond," the lawyers wrote.

As before the trial, Merchan was buried in paper, but this time, Trump's lawyers were insisting that he dismiss the case outright. When, on Monday, December 16, Merchan ruled that the Supreme Court's presidential immunity opinion did not bear on the verdict, Trump went berserk on Truth Social, calling the ruling "psychotic" and declaring the judge a "radical partisan" whose ruling if allowed to stand would be "the end of the presidency as we know it."

On January 3, 2025, Merchan denied a second motion to throw out the conviction. "To vacate this verdict on the grounds that the charges are insufficiently serious given the position defendant once held, and is about to assume again," he wrote, would "cause immeasurable damage to the citizenry's confidence in the rule of law." In an act of surprising judicial optimism, he scheduled a fourth and final date for a sentencing, for 9:30 am on January 10.

Merchan wrote that he was not inclined to try to send the former and future president to jail, or impose any punishment whatsoever. He expected to sentence him with an unconditional discharge. The outcome comes with no consequence. It merely ends a case.

But if Merchan's preemptive announcement of leniency was meant to persuade Trump's lawyers not to fight the sentencing again, it failed. Blanche and Bove mounted a final, furious effort to stop it. They went to New York's mid-level appeals court, and after being denied there, to both New York's highest court and the Supreme Court of the United States, simultaneously. On Thursday, January 9, the state's Court of Appeals denied them. But the Supreme Court continued to weigh the matter as the light died in New York City that day.

❖   ❖   ❖

The evening was frigid and wind whipped the banners and metal awnings of Chinatown as I hurried to a gallery on Pike Street where Izzy Brourman was mounting a modest show of her trial art. Inside the brightly lit gallery, Izzy held court in a blue fur coat as denizens of the art world mixed with trial reporters and the occasional government lawyer, admiring paintings of an event that was beginning to fade in memory for all those who hadn't covered it.

I ran into Katrina Kaufman, a reporter from CBS News, who I hadn't seen since the trial. We huddled in the back room, discussing the Supreme Court decision we were still awaiting. At about 7:15, our phones buzzed. The Court had narrowly declined to stop the sentencing, in a 5–4 decision. After months away, there was to be one last showdown on Centre Street, just ten days before Trump took office again. It would be the last time that Merchan would address Trump as a defendant in his courtroom, the last time in the foreseeable future that anyone would hold that kind of sway over the future president. And Merchan had decided to allow an audio recording of the proceedings, to be disseminated to the public once the hearing was over. When I saw that, I figured that Merchan's ruling would be scathing—that he would emphasize the seriousness of the prosecution, as he had in writing a week before, and take Trump to task for the damage he'd done to the system. I left the gallery to get some sleep.

The sky was a deep blue the following morning. The north

entrance of 100 Centre Street was all but unrecognizable; the scaffold-ing had come down, and the courthouse looked naked in the winter light. Despite the cold, the journalists began to congregate well before 7 am and the feeling on the line was of a long-awaited reunion. Emily Saul and Frank Runyeon held positions toward the front, as did Insid-er's Laura Italiano, right in front of me. Collect Pond Park was all but empty, according to Nate Schweber, in part because Al Baker, the court spokesman, allowed all the journalists—not just those of us with reserved seats—to congregate right outside the courthouse. Trump wasn't expected to attend in person, and without the Secret Service, security concerns were lessened. Maggie stood next to us in a second line, worrying over whether she could get a seat in the courtroom. I had little doubt that she would make it in.

We were allowed inside around 8 am, narrowly missing a demon-stration by 14 protesters from Rise and Resist, who held a banner that proclaimed "TRUMP IS GUILTY" and a handmade sign: "Orange is the new Orange."

Part 59 had changed. The tiles on the floor were scrubbed clean, off-white with blue flecks; they looked brand-new. The light streamed in from the high windows behind the jury box, reflecting off the floor. The room was clean, comfortable and pleasant but of course, very cold. The sketch artists were seated in the jury box and as there was no crowd on the left side of the gallery to support Trump, we sat closer to the front than ever as we waited for the proceedings to start. The future president sent out a fundraising email. "It's truly unbelievable that they're bring-ing this case today," it said. "All designed to bring chaos and disrupt the peaceful transfer of power during this crucial time."

The prosecutors entered the courtroom first, unburdened by the boxes of evidence that weighed them down during the trial. They were followed by Alvin Bragg, whom I hadn't seen in person since May. He took his usual seat in the second row on the right, and sat impassively, waiting. Just before 9:30, Trump beamed in from Mar-a-Lago, appear-ing on computer screens at the prosecution and defense tables, sitting shoulder to shoulder with Todd Blanche in front of a pair of American flags. Onscreen, Trump wore his trademark camera-ready scowl.

Merchan walked into the courtroom shortly thereafter. His grey hair had silvered and the lines in his face grown harder but his voice was calm as he asked the lawyers to introduce themselves for the record. The prosecution and the defense would weigh in before he delivered his final ruling. And at a sentencing, the defendant is able to speak for as long as he likes.

Joshua Steinglass went first. He didn't seem particularly cowed by the president-elect. Though he agreed that Trump's win necessitated an unconditional discharge, he said that the future president's behavior before during and after the trial should not be overlooked. "Far from expressing any kind of remorse for his criminal conduct the defendant has purposefully bred disdain for our judicial institutions and the rule of law," he said. "And he's done this to serve his own ends and to encourage others to reject the jury verdict that he finds so distasteful."

Trump, on screen, crossed his arms and shook his head, mirroring a pose we'd seen in person many times. Steinglass continued. "Put simply, this defendant has caused enduring damage to public perception of the criminal justice system."

Merchan thanked him, and asked Blanche to speak. I halfway expected the rhetoric of recent legal filings, in which Blanche had referred to the case as an "abomination." But the lawyer—soon to face a Senate confirmation hearing—was restrained. He simply reiterated a point on which he was as unshakable as his client. "What the government just said presupposes something that we disagree with very much, which was that this was an appropriate case to be brought," he said. "It was not." He asserted that the election result had definitively reflected the American people's opinion of Bragg's prosecution.

Merchan asked if Trump would like to be heard. The answer from the computer screen was yes.

"This has been a very terrible experience," the president-elect said in his slow drawl, speaking at length for the first time in the courtroom where he'd sat mutely for seven weeks. He asserted that Bragg had not wanted to bring the case—causing the district attorney to blink rapidly in the gallery—and implied that unnamed others had steered it, referring, it seemed, to Mark Pomerantz, Matthew Colangelo, or some amalgamation of the two.

"The fact is that, I'm totally innocent," Trump said, his face looming over the gallery, multiplied by the screens above the bench and those on the lawyer's tables. "I did nothing wrong. They talk about business records and the business records were extremely accurately counted. I had nothing to do with them." He defended himself for several more minutes.

"This has been a weaponization of government," he said. "They call it lawfare. Never happened to any extent like this but never happened in our country before and I'd just like to explain that I was treated very, very, unfairly—and I thank you very much."

It was Merchan's turn. Like any good institutionalist, the judge began with a series of understatements. "Never before has this court been presented with such a unique and remarkable set of circumstances," he said. "Indeed, it can be viewed fairly that this has been a truly extraordinary case." Still, he said, once the courtroom doors were closed, the trial had been no more "special, unique, or extraordinary" than any other.

It was in Justice Merchan's interest to say so, as he defended the legitimacy of the jury verdict. But it was untrue. A trial attended by senators and congressmen, a Hell's Angel and a future Vice President. A trial in which the legitimacy of the former president's first election win was questioned by a group of state prosecutors. A trial whose witnesses included, in two consecutive weeks, a White House spokeswoman and a porn star. It was Trump's trial; not only because he was the defendant, but because every aspect of his character had informed the proceedings, transforming Part 59 into a private spectacle, the greatest, most exclusive, show on earth.

Merchan continued. "While one can argue that the trial itself was in many respects somewhat ordinary, the same cannot be said about the circumstances surrounding this sentencing," he said. And that was because Trump had been elected president. Merchan said that while the protections of the office did not reduce the gravity of Trump's crime, or justify its commission, they amounted to a "legal mandate" that Merchan must respect and follow. "Donald Trump, the ordinary citizen—Donald Trump, the criminal defendant—would not be entitled to such considerable protections," he said.

And so, Merchan concluded, Trump would be, as expected, sentenced to an unconditional discharge. "I impose that sentence to cover all 34 counts," he said. "Sir, I wish you godspeed as you assume your second term in office." The judge got up from the bench, having wrapped up so quickly that I barely had time to look up from my laptop. He rushed out, as if any room in the building would be preferable to the courtroom in which he'd adjudicated the trial of Donald J. Trump.

It was hard to blame him. For Trump's enemies, the spotlight was increasingly dangerous.

The president-elect signed off with a digital bloop. It was over. The press corps took the elevators downstairs and left the building. Across the street, Collect Pond Park was filled with victorious Trump supporters, their banners raised against the January wind. They ignored the anonymous reporters descending the steps of the courthouse. In ten days, their candidate would return to the White House for a second term, leaving Centre Street, and all it represented, behind for good.

ABOUT THE AUTHOR

JONAH E. BROMWICH, a reporter for *The New York Times*, has covered Manhattan's criminal justice system for years. He was a lead reporter on Trump's criminal trial, reporting live from the courtroom for more than a month.

Jonah has covered a number of major legal stories for the Metro desk, including multiple trials involving President Trump, the downfall of Governor Andrew Cuomo, and the chaos on Rikers Island. Previously, Jonah worked for the Style section, reporting on cultural change brought about by social media and celebrity culture. A native of Washington, DC, he studied at the University of Wisconsin–Madison and joined *The Times* in 2012.